The Meeting of the Ways

The Meeting of the Ways Explorations in East/ West Psychology

edited by
John Welwood

Schocken Books • New York

*This book is dedicated to my parents,
and to all my teachers and friends
who have helped me appreciate
this precious human life.*

First published by Schocken Books 1979
10 9 8 7 6 5 4 3 2 1   79 80 81 82
Copyright © 1979 by Schocken Books Inc.
First Edition

Library of Congress Cataloging in Publication Data

Main entry under title:

The Meeting of the ways.

   Bibliography: p.
   Includes index.
   1. Consciousness—Addresses, essays, lectures.
2. Meditation—Addresses, essays, lectures.
3. Identity (Psychology)—Addresses, essays, lectures.
4. Psychology—Asia—Addresses, essays, lectures.
I. Welwood, John, 1943–
BF311.M437   158   78-26509

Acknowledgments

I would like to extend my appreciation to the authors and publishers who granted permission to reprint copyrighted material in this volume. I would also like to thank Shambhala Publications for allowing me to quote liberally from several of their works.

Chapter 1 is excerpted by permission from *The Journal of Transpersonal Psychology* (Box 4437, Stanford, California, 94305), Volume 7, 1975, pp. 105–30.

Chapter 2 is reprinted by permission of *The Journal of Transpersonal Psychology*, Volume 8, 1976, pp. 89–99.

Chapter 3 is reprinted by permission of *The Journal of Transpersonal Psychology*, Volume 8, 1976, pp. 41–44.

Chapter 4 is reprinted by permission of the author, Arthur Deikman.

Chapter 5 originally appeared as "The Mystery of Ordinary Experiencing" (pp. 9–17) from *The Natural Depth in Man* by Wilson Van Dusen. Copyright © 1972 by Wilson Van Dusen. By permission of Harper & Row, Publishers, Inc.

Chapter 6 is excerpted by permission from *Psychologia*, Volume 5, 1962, pp. 84–87.

Chapter 7 is a revised and condensed version of an article which appeared in *Philosophy East and West*, Volume 27, 1977, pp. 265–82. Reprinted by permission of the authors and The University Press of Hawaii.

Chapter 8 is reprinted by permission of *The Journal of Transpersonal Psychology*, Volume 6, 1974, pp. 175–80.

Chapter 9 is printed by permission of the authors.

Chapter 10 is excerpted by permission from *The Journal of Transpersonal Psychology*, Volume 5, 1973, pp. 62–74.

Chapters 11 and 12 are excerpted from *On the Psychology of Meditation* by Claudio Naranjo and Robert Ornstein, an Esalen Book. Copyright © 1971 by Claudio Naranjo and Robert Ornstein. Reprinted by permission of the Viking Press. British rights granted by George Allen & Unwin (Publishers) Ltd., London.

Chapter 13 is excerpted in a modified form by permission from *The Journal of Transpersonal Psychology*, Volume 9, 1977, pp. 1–24.

Chapter 14 is reprinted from Medard Boss, *A Psychiatrist Discovers India*, translated by Henry A. Frey. (Copyright 1965 by Oswald Wolff), pp. 184–92, by permission of Oswald Wolff (Publishers) Ltd., London.

Chapter 15 is "From a Workshop on Psychotherapy" by Chögyam Trungpa, Rinpoche from *Loka 2: A Journal from Naropa Institute*, edited by Rick Fields. Copyright © 1976 by Nalanda Foundation/Naropa Institute. Reprinted by permission of Doubleday & Company, Inc.

Chapter 16 is reprinted by permission of the author. Copyright 1974 by Marvin Casper. This material originally appeared in *The Journal of Transpersonal Psychology*, Volume 6, 1974, pp. 57–67.

Chapter 17 is excerpted by permission from *The Journal of Transpersonal Psychology*, Volume 7, 1975, pp. 133–42.

Chapter 18 is excerpted by permission from *Psychologia*, Volume 1, 1958, pp. 253–56.

Contents

Preface

Anthropologist-philosopher Gregory Bateson, in commenting on the contemporary interaction of Eastern and Western cultures, noted that "what is striking is the power of this particular mix to inspire American young people." While it is true that young people and students provide one of the most receptive audiences for ideas from the East, the influence of the Eastern traditions and disciplines is also having a broad impact on our culture at large. This book has been inspired by the current ferment and the rich possibilities being generated by the rooting of Eastern wisdom in contemporary American culture. This situation is not a one-way affair, in which the West is simply assimilating the East, or the East is simply transplanting itself to the West. Rather, it is a meeting of the ways, and a very fertile one; for the Eastern teachings are renewing themselves as they address a widely felt hunger in America for a more meaningful vision of human life. At the same time, contemporary Eastern teachers seem to be deeply appreciative of America's inquisitive mind, its generosity, and its fresh, unpretentious outlook. It is a true cross-fertilization, one that promises to have important, wide-ranging consequences.

The field of psychology is a particularly dynamic arena in which to appreciate the implications of this cultural change. The Eastern psychologies are currently having a large impact on Western psychology. Most major texts on personality, for instance, now include a chapter on "Asian psychology." Courses, programs, and institutes for the study of consciousness and meditation are springing up all over the country. The time seems ripe for bringing together many of the insights and discoveries developing out of the experience of Western psychologists with the Eastern disciplines. Thus the present volume presents what Western psychologists are learning from the Eastern traditions, and demonstrates the wide range of interest in this area. The writings chosen for this book are primarily based on a blend of personal experience and intellectual understanding, rather than on highly technical theories or experimental research. This focus was chosen because it is the *meaning* of Eastern psychology that has proved to be most elusive to the Western mind thus far. These essays should appeal both to readers who want to explore the meaning of Eastern teachings for contemporary life in the West, and to students of consciousness who want to explore the interfaces of the two psychologies.

The first generation of serious East-West study in America primarily reflected an aesthetic and intellectual appreciation of the East by Westerners who did not actually engage themselves seriously in the self-knowledge disciplines arising out of the Eastern teachings. This book is more of a second-generation work, which brings together the insights of Western psychologists, most of whom have themselves studied or practiced one or another self-knowledge discipline. The backgrounds of the contributors span most of the major psychological currents of our time, including the schools of Freud, Jung, Rogers, Gestalt, existentialism, and phenomenology. Also included are contributions by two Tibetan teachers, Chögyam Trungpa and Tarthang Tulku, whose uniqueness partially lies in their mastery of, and willingness to use, ordinary psychological language in communicating their understanding.

The book is designed to offer new perspectives on such perennial questions as the nature of consciousness, personal identity, sanity, and psychotherapy. The first section asks fundamental questions about the nature of the human mind. The exploration of different levels of consciousness soon leads to questions about the nature of one's personal identity or ego, the subject matter of the second section. In order to avoid purely speculative theories, the questions raised by the exploration of mind and self need to be grounded in a more empirical and disciplined approach. Thus the third section of the book deals with meditation, or how one might relate to these life questions in a direct, personal way. Finally, the fourth section attempts to apply the insights of the first three sections to psychotherapy, and suggests new directions for therapy that may help people to live in a more wakeful way.

I must admit to being somewhat surprised at how well the writings in this book, gathered from many different sources, reflect one another and fit together as an integrated whole. Special thanks are due Alice Primrose, without whose generosity this book would not have been possible. And finally, I would like to acknowledge my great debt to my teachers, both Western and Eastern, whose work this truly is.

Introduction

Several summers ago, while a guest student at Tassajara Zen Mountain Center in California, I was powerfully struck by a new cultural development that seemed quite significant. During the course of two weeks there I met no less than six professional psychologists and psychotherapists who had come to study Zen out of a strong sense of dissatisfaction with the limitations of traditional Western psychology and therapy. One of those I met was an ex-psychotherapist from New York who had given up his practice to become a full-time Zen student, had been doing meditation for several years, and was now on his way to Japan for further study. As a therapist he had become increasingly confused about what was most important in his life, and had felt that he could not truly help others without a better sense of what his life was all about.

This experience brought home to me how Western psychology has so far failed to provide us with a satisfactory understanding of the full range of human experience. Its concern with establishing itself as a reputable scientific endeavor has led it to concentrate primarily on collecting data about human behavior, which is organized into broad statistical patterns. Yet we lack an understanding of the import of such data, particularly its relevance for the concrete lives of individuals. It appears that we have largely overlooked the central fact of human psychology—our everyday mind, our very real, immediate awareness of being, with all its felt complexity and sensitive attunement to a vast network of connectedness with the world around us.

Western psychology's neglect of the living mind—both its everyday dynamics and its larger possibilities—has led to a tremendous upsurge of interest in the ancient wisdom of the East, which never divorced the study of psychology from the concern with wisdom and human liberation. For the East, to study consciousness is to change consciousness. Eastern psychology shuns any impersonal attempt to objectify human life from the viewpoint of an external observer, instead studying consciousness as a living reality which shapes individual perception and action.

The encounter between Eastern and Western psychology promises to have important ramifications for the human sciences of the future, potentially leading to new perspectives on the whole range of human experience and life concerns. What, specifically, do the Eastern psychologies contribute to an expanded understanding of human potentials? What is their unique perspective which complements the approach of Western psychology?

1. *They are primarily rooted in direct experience.*

The East generally does not value speculative philosophizing or purely theoretical discussions. Intellectual understanding is not devalued in itself, but is seen as important only in conjunction with the process of self-knowledge. Even where intellectual traditions have been highly refined, as in certain Indian and Tibetan traditions, the concepts are meant to develop sensitivity to the subtle complexities of lived experience. As F. S. C. Northrop points out,[1] Eastern thought is based on what he calls "concepts by intuition," which refer to actual experience rather than to other concepts in a theoretical system. Thus the many Hindu and Buddhist words for "mind" or "consciousness" refer primarily to the immediate experience of our own awareness as we live it. For instance, the continual stream of "inner chatter," consisting of ongoing thoughts, emotions, fantasies, is a very immediate, real fact of consciousness that the Eastern psychologies have examined in detail. Oddly enough, this central aspect of everyday consciousness has rarely been observed, much less studied, in Western psychology, which has chosen instead to analyze mind as though it were an object independent of the analyzer, consisting of postulated structures and mechanisms that are not directly experienced. The Eastern approach to mind sets out to examine different aspects of immediate awareness, how we relate to things, and to understand mind in a very direct, personally relevant way.

The primary tool for directly exploring mind in Eastern traditions has been meditation, an experiential process in which one becomes an attentive participant-observer in the unfolding of moment-to-moment consciousness. Meditation seems to reveal concretely that which most psychologies and philosophies speak about only in theoretical terms. The Eastern approach does not deal in theories that do not help people live fuller lives. A practitioner of meditation might well question the value of a psychology that did not directly clarify and further the deepest human needs.

2. *Eastern psychologies always view human beings holistically.*
They are concerned with human experience as a *whole process*
which is studied in relation to the whole of nature. Thus
consciousness is not seen as some kind of separate mental system
"inside" the body, split off from an "unconscious mind," or separate
from the world. The question becomes: How does human awareness
both manifest and illuminate the processes of birth, growth, change,
and death, which are also present in the rest of the universe? This
perspective recognizes the interconnectedness of all things, human
and natural, neither isolating any one phenomenon from the whole,
nor excluding experiences just because they cannot be objectively
measured.

3. *Eastern psychologies are primarily concerned with understanding human experience in light of an awakened state of mind.*
Awakening, enlightenment, or liberation is said to be a process
in which one becomes oneself most fully by realizing, in the depths of
one's being, the process of things as they are, as well as one's
interconnectedness with the world around one.

This interconnectedness should not be understood in any
primitive sense of a regression to an infantile state of oneness. The
nonduality experienced in awakened perception seems to be quite
different from any kind of underdeveloped individuality or the
confusion of self and world found in schizophrenia. The nonduality
of enlightenment comes from a clear and complete realization of
one's deepest nature, where one is *most oneself* when one is no longer
trying to maintain oneself as a separate entity of some kind. From the
Eastern perspective, the idea of a separate self is a distortion of our
natural connectedness with all things. At the same time, transcending
the idea of a separate self presupposes, for its realization, a highly
developed sense of individual self-worth and personal dignity. (For a
further discussion of this issue, see chapter 9.)

The awake mind is said to be completely clear and open, attuned
to the life process as it is happening in, through, and around oneself.
Confusion, ignorance, and defensiveness are also important experiences to understand, but usually as distortions of the awake mind,
which is seen as the fullest expression of being human. In fact, it is
said that the confusion of one's normal ego-centered life can become
the starting point or basis for the process of awakening. Awakening
arises from the state of sleep, liberation is a transformation of

enslavement, enlightenment is a dispelling of darkness and obscuration. Therefore, the study of ego-centered confusion can be part of the process of awakening itself.

The notion of awakened mind suggests the possibility of an "inspired sanity" that goes beyond the conventional notion of sanity, which too often is no more than conformity to a socially conditioned version of "normal" behavior. Inspired sanity arises from living in accord with the natural process and freshly relating to the dynamic unpredictability of every moment.

Thus the Eastern approach does not separate psychology from the search for enlightenment, but sees them as interconnected. Seeing into the nature and process of consciousness becomes a vehicle to actualizing an intuitive attunement with reality.

When I was a student in graduate school, anything not verifiable through the "hard data" of quantitative measurement and statistical analysis was called "mystical." The term *mystical* in this sense became the classic professional put-down of someone who was deemed naive for trusting the immediacy of his or her own experience. However, mysticism proper should not be confused with any kind of mystification. The word *mysticism* has been used in a limited sense to describe religious visions, ecstatic trances, or other intense illuminative experiences. But the term has also been used more broadly to denote a simpler, more ordinary kind of awareness in which mind and world are fully attuned, beyond words and concepts, if only for a brief moment.

This mystical nature of ordinary experience may be glimpsed when we are fully aware of what is actually happening at any given moment, rather than being fixated on our usual ego-centered preoccupations. Anything may become the occasion for an intense glimpse of reality on the other side of our normally clouded and distracted perception. In such moments, we may become aware of a sharpness or luminosity in our experience of the world—a leaf stands out as bright, green, "leafy" in a new way which is, at the same time, "nothing new," completely ordinary. Obviously a leaf is still a leaf, as it always has been, but the depth of our openness to experience has changed. In these "little awakenings" we catch a fleeting glimpse of how we are fundamentally not separate from the whole of life. We discover the world in ourselves, and ourselves in the world.

I often wonder if there is anyone who has *not* experienced such little flashes of his or her world opening up, though they may often be quickly passed over or forgotten. Awakened perception alerts us to how things are always much more than we think they are, how the moment is always richer than our scattered attention allows us to realize. When we become aware of this richness that is in every moment, which is usually submerged by daily preoccupations or excluded by narrow belief-systems, a glimpse of everyday enlightened reality may occur. There is nothing particularly esoteric or occult about it.

The attitude of Western psychology toward such experiences should be one that neither mystifies them nor psychologizes them. To mystify them would be to make them seem "other," exotic, cloaked in some esoteric mystery that is far from the ordinary person's experience. On the other hand, to psychologize them would be to reduce and distort their experiential import by trying to grasp or encompass them through preconceived categories of thought.

A few final clarifications are in order here. First of all, for the purposes of this book, the term *Eastern* refers to the Taoist, Hindu, Buddhist, and Sufi traditions as a whole. It is not within the scope of this book to study these traditions separately, even though there are important differences of approach and perspective among them. Although the Taoist, Hindu, and Sufi traditions have been most important for some of the contributors to this volume, most of the articles reflect a Buddhist influence.

Secondly, it seems valuable to consider the Eastern psychologies as having something to say about the mind that is of general relevance for humanity, rather than to view them as purely the product of particular and geographical circumstances. Thus the term *Eastern* may be used as a tag for designating an alternative approach to human nature from that which has developed in mainstream Western culture and psychology. The point is not to pit East against West, nor to assert the superiority of either side over the other, but to see how both approaches to psychology and human nature may be complementary. Since the Eastern approaches are still new to Western ways of thinking, they deserve a book such as this which seeks to explore their relevance for our life and thought.

The present encounter of the experiential, holistic, and enlightenment-oriented traditions of the East with the precision, clarity, skepticism, and independence of Western methods could lead to a new kind of psychology that transcends cultural limitations and opens up what Abraham Maslow referred to as "the farther reaches of human nature."[2] Such a new form of East/West psychology, as represented embryonically in the articles assembled here, is only in its infancy, but it does not appear to be just a passing cultural fancy. May this book contribute to its further growth.

NOTES

1. Northrop (1959).
2. Maslow (1971).

I
New Perspectives on Mind and Consciousness

Introduction

The father of American psychology, William James, defined psychology as "the science of mental life,"[1] the study of the process and states of consciousness. More recently, Robert Ornstein has boldly reasserted a similar position:

> Psychology is, primarily, the science of consciousness.... It is time once again to open up the scope of psychology to areas of thought that have not been fully represented in contemporary research, and to return to its primary source, to the analysis of consciousness.[2]

The psychology of consciousness is an area of major interest both to the present generation of psychology students and to laypeople in general, although it is still not widely accepted among traditional psychologists as a fruitful or legitimate area of study. Indeed, if one pursues this interest very far in Western psychology, one finds oneself in the dark as soon as one passes beyond certain mechanisms of mental habit to inquire about what actually goes on in consciousness or what the nature of consciousness is. The fear of falling into unscientific subjectivism has kept psychologists from studying consciousness as it is actually experienced. Thus it is no wonder that Western psychologists of consciousness are turning increasingly to the Eastern traditions for guidance, insight, and inspiration in their efforts to understand more fully the human mind. For thousands of years the study of mind has been pursued in great depth within certain spiritual traditions of the East. However, although the Eastern study of mind has developed within spiritual traditions, it seems to have a wide applicability and meaning for contemporary Westerners beyond its traditional religious contexts.

At the same time, one of the pitfalls of many Western interpretations of Eastern notions has been the attempt to fit these new ideas into unexamined Western preconceptions and traditional intellectual categories. It seems that one cannot truly understand the Eastern notions of mind and consciousness through Western concepts without a direct and personal experience of what they are referring to. Given this experiential basis, it does seem possible to use a psychological language to explain the Eastern teachings and make them more understandable to the average Westerner who is seeking clues and directions for studying the nature of his or her own mind.

The Eastern study of mind suggests that the nature of consciousness is fundamentally open and unconditioned. This open, receptive awareness is essentially free from habitual fixations and narrow self-limiting concerns. It fully reflects and resonates the world, the process of *what is* at every moment. Mind is thus part of the universal patterns and processes of life that also operate in the natural world around us. Mind represents an open space or unconditional presence in the world, a unique source of new meaning, creativity, spontaneity, freedom, peace, and compassion.

Such a description of mind's basic nature may seem like some kind of purely metaphysical belief to the ordinary Westerner, since this is not usually the way that one experiences one's mind. How does one verify such claims? The practice of meditation is the Eastern method *par excellence* for discovering the workings and nature of one's own mind. (Its relevance for understanding mind and self will be explored in Section III.) Each person is considered to be his or her own best laboratory for understanding human nature and the nature of mind itself. Attention to one's ongoing moment-to-moment experiencing is the major tool to be developed in this laboratory. Normally one does not pay that much attention to one's experiencing process as a whole. Our normal states of mind are dominated by fixations on certain objects (or "contents") of consciousness, either external (perceptions of the physical world; objects of hope, fear, desire, interest) or internal (thoughts, emotions, inner chatter). Developing inner attention may allow one to see these fixations for what they are and to discover the wider awareness which the articles in this section talk about in their different but related ways.

In the opening chapter, Ken Wilber provides a comprehensive overview of what he calls the "spectrum of consciousness," the full range of human experience as it has been studied in both Western and Eastern traditions. He identifies three major levels or types of consciousness, which he calls: (1) the egoic level, where one identifies with a particular personal identity; (2) the existential level, where one identifies with the mind/body organism as a whole; and (3) the level of Mind beyond all identifications with a separate ego or mind/body organism. Perhaps the most intriguing part of this chapter is Wilber's demonstration of how different Western therapies and Eastern spiritual disciplines, which seemingly contradict each other's aims and goals, actually address problems on different levels of the spectrum of consciousness. This is a major integrative paper with broad implications for human growth and development.

In the next chapter I explore three similar levels of awareness in a more experientially-oriented way. Even at the everyday level of the stream of thought (Wilber's egoic level), we can discover gaps and openings that indicate a deeper and wider way in which the mind works. Examining more closely these fleeting spaces in the fabric of thought, we may discover a more global way in which the body-mind relates to life situations, in terms of "felt meaning" (Wilber's 'existential level'). And finally, looking even more deeply into our thoughts, emotions, and felt meanings, we find that they are not solid, but open and nonfixated in their very nature (reflecting the level Wilber calls Mind).

The third chapter, by Tarthang Tulku, is a very simple, experiential exposition of different qualities of mind, which are traditionally known in Buddhism as the "eight kinds of consciousness": (1) unconditioned, primordial awareness (Sanskrit: *alayavijnana*; Tibetan: *kun-gzhi*), which is not "owned" by an ego or personality; (2) a more limited consciousness (*manas*) in which experience is always centered around oneself as a separate individual; (3) the organizing of sense data into familiar categories and patterns (*manovijnana*); and (4) the five kinds of sensory awareness. The primary significance of this breakdown, according to Buddhist scholar Herbert Guenther, lies in describing the process by which consciousness "emerges from its primordial, unqualified, and unconditioned state and glides into our ordinary way of thinking. . . . If we understood this process thoroughly, we would be able to . . . let our minds remain in the primordial state,"[3] i.e., the awakened state of mind.

Finally, Arthur Deikman describes the structure of mind by distinguishing *pure* awareness from the *contents* of awareness, which he sees as the activity of awareness. It is one's normally exclusive identification with the activity or contents of awareness that creates and reinforces the sense of "I," the separate ego. Deikman's discussion of the relationship between awareness and ego forms a bridge to Section II, which considers the question of personal identity.

NOTES

1. James (1950).
2. Ornstein (1973), pp. xi, 3.
3. Guenther & Trungpa (1975), p. 14.

1
Psychologia Perennis:
The Spectrum of Consciousness

Ken Wilber

In the past few decades the West has witnessed an explosion of interest among psychologists, theologians, scientists, and philosophers alike in what Aldous Huxley has called *philosophia perennis*, the "perennial philosophy,"[1] a universal doctrine as to the nature of man and reality lying at the very heart of every major metaphysical tradition. In all essential aspects, this doctrine has remained unchanged in over 3,000 years, for it purports to represent a reality untouched by time or place, true everywhere and everywhen.

What is frequently overlooked, however, is that corresponding to the perennial philosophy there exists what I would like to call a *psychologia perennis*, a "perennial psychology"—a universal view as to the nature of human consciousness, which expresses the very same insights as the perennial philosophy but in more decidedly psychological language. As at one time most Western philosophers had only the flimsiest notion as to what constituted the *philosophia perennis*, so today many Western psychologists appear to possess little or no knowledge about the *psychologia perennis*. Therefore, the purpose of this chapter—besides describing the fundamentals of the perennial psychology—is to outline a model of consciousness which remains faithful to the spirit of this universal doctrine yet at the same time gives ample consideration to the insights of such typically Western disciplines as ego-psychology, psychoanalysis, humanistic psychology, Jungian analysis, interpersonal psychology, and the like. At the heart of this model, the "spectrum of consciousness," lies the

7

insight that human personality is a multileveled manifestation or expression of a single consciousness, just as in physics the electromagnetic spectrum is viewed as a multibanded expression of a single, characteristic electromagnetic wave. More specifically, the spectrum of consciousness is a pluridimensional approach to man's identity; that is to say, each level of the spectrum is marked by a different and easily recognized sense of individual identity, which ranges from the supreme identity of cosmic consciousness through several gradations or bands to the drastically narrowed sense of identity associated with egoic consciousness. Out of these numerous levels or bands of consciousness, I have selected five major levels to discuss in connection with the *psychologia perennis* (see Fig. 1).

LEVELS OF THE SPECTRUM

THE LEVEL OF MIND

The core insight of the *psychologia perennis* is that man's "innermost" consciousness is identical to the absolute and ultimate

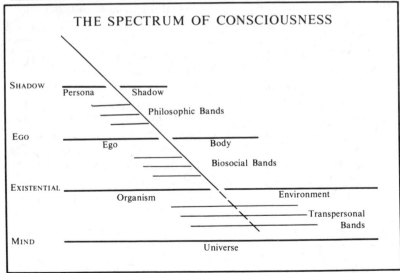

Figure 1. Some prominent nodes in the spectrum of consciousness. The major levels of identity are indicated by broad lines, while I have arbitrarily chosen three-line groupings to represent the auxiliary bands. The diagonal slash line is representative of the self/not-self boundary, so that, for example, to an individual identified with his persona, the shadow, the body, and the environment all appear as outside of self, as foreign, external, alien, and hence potentially threatening. The self/not-self boundary breaks at the transpersonal bands and vanishes at the level of mind.

reality of the universe, which, for the sake of convenience, I will simply call "Mind" (with a capital *M* to distinguish it from the apparent plurality of "minds"). According to this universal traditional, Mind is what there is and all there is, spaceless and therefore infinite, timeless and therefore eternal, outside of which nothing exists. On this level, man is identified with the universe, the All—or rather, he *is* the All. According to the *psychologia perennis*, this level is not an abnormal state of consciousness, nor even an altered state of consciousness, but rather the *only real* state of consciousness, all others being essentially illusions. In short, man's innermost consciousness is identical to the ultimate reality of the universe. Thus, to quote the founder of quantum mechanics, Erwin Schroedinger:

> Inconceivable as it seems to ordinary reason, you—and all other conscious beings as such—are all in all. Hence this life of yours you are living is not merely a piece of the entire existence, but is in a certain sense the *whole*.... Thus you can throw yourself flat on the ground, stretched out upon Mother Earth, with the certain conviction that you are one with her and she with you. You are as firmly established, as invulnerable as she, indeed a thousand times firmer and more invulnerable.[2]

This, then, is the level of Mind, of cosmic consciousness, of man's supreme identity.

THE TRANSPERSONAL BANDS

These bands represent the area of the spectrum that is supraindividual, where man is not conscious of his identity with the All and yet neither is his identity confined to the boundaries of the individual organism. In Mahayana Buddhism these bands are known collectively as the *alayavijnana*, or "supraindividual repository consciousness"; while in Hinduism they are referred to as the *karanasarira* or "causal body." Also, if "paranormal" phenomena do indeed exist, then many of them might be expected to occur on these bands, as, for instance, astral travel, out-of-the-body experiences, traveling clairaudience, and certain mystical states.

THE EXISTENTIAL LEVEL

Here man is identified solely with his total psychophysical organism as it exists in space and time, for this is the first level where the line between self and other, organism and environment, is firmly drawn. This is also the level where man's rational thought processes, as well as his personal will, first begin to develop and exfoliate, and is, in Hinduism, referred to as the *suksmasarira*, the "subtle body." Similarly, the Buddhist terms this level the *manas*,* and defines it as the persistent source of existential, rational, volitional awareness.

It should be mentioned that the "upper limits" of the existential level contain the biosocial bands, the internalized matrix of cultural premises, familial relationships, and social glosses, as well as the all-pervading social institutions of language, logic, ethics, and law. Speaking rather loosely, the biosocial bands represent those aspects of the organism's social environment that it has introjected. It is precisely because this "internalized society" is mapped or transferred from society onto the biological organism that they are called the "biosocial bands." In effect, they act so as to profoundly color and mold the organism's basic sense of existence.**

THE EGO LEVEL

On this level, man does not feel directly identified with his psychosomatic organism. Rather, for a variety of reasons, he identifies solely with a more-or-less accurate mental representation or picture of his total organism. In other words, he is identified with his ego, his self-image. His total organism is thus split into a disembodied "psyche," the ghost in the machine, and a "soma," "poor brother ass"—a fact which he betrays by saying not "I *am* a body," but "I *have* a body." He feels that he exists *in* his body and not *as* his body. This level is identified almost exclusively with a mental picture of man's total psychophysical organism, and therefore his intellectual and symbolical processes predominate. Hence the Buddhists call this level the *manovijnana*, the "intellect," while the Hindus refer to it as the *sthulasarira*, the level of the ego split from and therefore trapped in the gross body.

Manas could be defined as the separate self sense, which maintains itself through sets of personal associations, meanings, thought-patterns (Ed.).

**For a further analysis of the biosocial bands, see Ornstein, chapter 12 below (Ed.).

THE SHADOW LEVEL

Under certain circumstances, man can alienate various aspects of his own psyche, dis-identify with them, and thus narrow his sphere of identity to only *parts* of the ego, which we may refer to as the persona. This level is that of the shadow: man identified with an impoverished and inaccurate self-image (i.e., the persona), while the rest of his psychic tendencies, those deemed too painful, "evil," or undesirable, are alienated as the contents of the shadow.

The above model is an extremely abbreviated description of the spectrum. As such, it does not fully represent the flow and interaction between the various bands. Nevertheless, it should be obvious that each level of the spectrum represents an increasingly narrowed sphere of identity, from the universe to a facet of the universe called organism, from the organism to a facet of the organism called psyche, and from the psyche to a facet of the psyche called persona. (Each major level of the spectrum is also marked by a different mode of knowing, a different dualism or set of dualisms, a different class of unconscious processes, and so on. For a more detailed elaboration, see Wilber, 1977.)

EVOLUTION OF THE SPECTRUM

If it is true that the level of Mind is the only reality, we might wonder just how it is that the other levels seem to exist at all. The answer is supplied by the *psychologia perennis* in the form of the doctrine of *maya*. Maya is any experience constituted by or stemming from dualism (specifically, the primary dualism of subject vs. object). According to Deutsch, "*maya* is all experience that is constituted by, and follows from, the distinction between subject and object, between self and non-self."[3] The perennial psychology declares all dualism to be not so much unreal as *illusory*, for reasons that are described by G. Spencer Brown in his mathematical treatise, *Laws of Form:*

> Thus we cannot escape the fact that the world we know is constructed in order (and thus in such a way as to be able) to see itself. This is indeed amazing. Not so much in view of what it sees, although this may appear fantastic enough, but in respect of the fact that it *can* see *at* all.

> But *in order* to do so, evidently it must first cut itself up into at
> least one state which sees, and at least one other state which is
> seen. In this severed and mutilated condition, whatever it sees is
> *only partially* itself. We may take it that the world undoubtedly is
> itself (i.e., is indistinct from itself), but, in any attempt to see itself
> as an object, it must, equally undoubtedly, act so as to make itself
> distinct from, and therefore false to, itself.[4]

However, this act of severance, this cutting of the world into seer and
seen, only *apparently* and not actually divides the world, for the
world always remains indistinct from itself. Dualism, in other words,
is illusory: it appears to exist but remains devoid of reality. Thus the
Lankavatara Sutra proclaims that "All dualism is falsely imagined."
In the same vein, the *psychologia perennis* declares that since the
various levels of consciousness (except that of Mind itself) are the
products of *maya* or dualism—as we will shortly explain—then they
must exist only in an illusory fashion, with the *reality* of each level
remaining always as Mind.

The *original* dualism or act of severance is mythologically
referred to by the perennial philosophy as the separation of heaven
and earth, male and female, sun and moon; epistemologically, it is the
separation of subject and object, knower and known, observer and
observed; ontologically, it is the separation of self and other,
organism and environment. For our purposes, the most convenient
labels for the two halves of this original dualism are subject and
object, self and other, or simply organism and environment, for with
its occurrence, man's identity apparently (not actually) shifts from the
nondual All to his organism. Man's supreme identity becomes not
lost but obscured, and thus is created "out of the oneness of Mind"
the next major level of the spectrum, the existential level—man
identified with his organism as against his environment. We might
also mention that since this primary dualism separates the seer from
the seen, the subject from the object, it simultaneously creates *space*.

As soon as man identifies exclusively with his organism, the
problem of his being vs. his nullity—the problem of life vs. death—is
created. As soon as man separates himself from his environment,
then, in the words of Hubert Benoit: "Suddenly he becomes
conscious that *his* principle is not the principle of the universe, that
there are things that exist independently of him; he becomes
conscious of it in suffering from contact with the world obstacle. At

this moment appears conscious fear of death."[5] The creation of the dualism of life vs. death is simultaneously the creation of *time*. And Norman O. Brown concludes, "Thus we arrive at the idea that life and death are in some sort of unity at the organic level, that at the human level they are separated into conflicting opposites.... The consequence of the disruption of the unity of Life and Death in man is to make man the historical animal."[6] In separating birth from death man necessarily separates past from future, and so consequently is thrown out of the timeless Now and into historical time. And that is the existential level: man identified exclusively with his organism as it exists in *space* and *time*.

But the disruption of the unity of life and death—the creation of time itself—has yet another consequence. At the existential level, man is now in panicked flight from death, and this very flight from death results in the creation of an idealized image of himself called his "ego," for the ego, being essentially composed of fixed and stable symbols, *seems* to promise man something that his mere flesh will not: the everlasting escape from death embodied in static images. "The truth of the matter, according to Freud's later theory, is that the peculiar structure of the human ego results from its incapacity to accept reality, specifically the supreme reality of death."[7] Man, in fleeing death, flees his mutable body and identifies with the seemingly undying idea of himself. Hence his identity shifts from his *total* psychophysical organism to his mental representation of that organism which thus creates the next major level of the spectrum: the ego level, man identified with a symbolic picture of himself as against his mortal body.

Finally, in the ultimate act of dualism, man severs the unity of his egoic tendencies and identifies with only a fraction of the psychic processes that are his. He disowns, alienates, casts off the unwanted aspects of his ego (which, through the process of egoic repression, nevertheless remain his). In an attempt to make his self-image acceptable, he renders it inaccurate, thus creating the final level of the spectrum: the shadow level, man identified with an inaccurate and greatly impoverished image of himself called the persona, while the unwanted aspects of himself are projected as the shadow.

Thus through successive dualisms (e.g., organism vs. environment, life vs. death, mind vs. body, persona vs. shadow) the various levels of the spectrum of consciousness evolve. The "level" of Mind is not actually one level among many but one without a second, and so we speak of the "level of Mind" only as a convenience. The levels of the spectrum of consciousness are thus not at all discrete but, like any spectrum, infinitely shade into one another. According to the *psychologia perennis*, these levels of the spectrum exist, but only in an illusory fashion, much as the images seen on a television screen are unreal as actual events but exist as mere pictures. Thus the reality of each level is always nothing but Mind, and the actual levels themselves appear independently real only to those who are too enchanted to see through the illusion.

THERAPIES ADDRESSING THE VARIOUS LEVELS

Such, then, is an extremely brief description of the *psychologia perennis* and its interpretation according to the spectrum of consciousness. Since there exists today a plethora of psychotherapeutic techniques, methods, schools, philosophies, and disciplines, the problem—and it is a very real one, for the therapist and layman alike—is to discover a semblance of order, an inner logic, a thread of continuity in this vast complexity of different and frequently contradictory psychological systems. Using the spectrum of consciousness as a model, this hidden semblance of order may in fact be demonstrated. By means of this model, it becomes possible to integrate, in a fairly comprehensive fashion, not only most of the major schools of Western psychotherapy, but also what are generally called "Eastern" and "Western" approaches to consciousness. The very existence of a great diversity of psychological fields and disciplines suggests not so much an internal difference in methodology as a real difference in the levels of consciousness to which the various schools have adapted themselves. If there be any truth at all to the spectrum of consciousness and to the great metaphysical traditions that subscribe to its major theme, then it immediately becomes obvious that *each of the differing schools of psychotherapy*—East and West—*is primarily addressing different levels of the spectrum*. We may therefore say that, in a general fashion, the major fields of Western psychotherapy are each concerned with a different level of the spectrum; that these schools need not overly concern themselves as to which is the "correct" approach to human consciousness because each is more-or-less correct when addressing its own level; and that a truly integrated and encompassing psychology can and should make use of the complementary insights offered by each school of psychology.

Thus we may start to discern some method in this madness of innumerable and apparently contradictory psychological systems. If it is agreed that consciousness is pluridimensional (i.e., apparently composed of numerous levels), and that pathology can and does occur on *any* of these levels (except Mind), it can be concluded that the various schools of psychotherapy, East and West, fall naturally into an order that spans the entire spectrum of consciousness. By briefly outlining the complementarity of the major Eastern traditions and Western psychotherapies, we may usefully discover a truly encompassing and integrative guide to the vast number of psychotherapies available today. For this outline, let us select—besides such Eastern traditions as Vedantic Hinduism and Mahayana Buddhism—such fields as ego psychology, humanistic psychology, existential psychology, Jungian analysis, social therapies, psychoanalysis, psychosynthesis, bioenergetics, structural integration, and Gestalt therapy.

EGO-LEVEL THERAPIES

Common to this group of therapies is the belief that pathology results from some sort of breakdown in communication between the conscious and the unconscious processes of the psyche, from a split between the persona and the shadow. Pathology, according to a popular text on ego psychotherapy,[8] results when a person's *self-image is distorted* and rendered inaccurate, and "cure" consists in the establishment of an accurate and therefore acceptable self-image.

If an individual alienates certain facets of himself, he will render his self-image fraudulent. The alienated facets (i.e., the now "unconscious" shadow) will nevertheless remain his, but will be projected so as to appear to exist "outside" of himself, in the environment or in others. Therapy consists in contacting the shadow and eventually re-owning it, so that one's sense of identity expands, so to speak, to include all of the aspects of oneself which were once alienated. In this fashion, the split between the persona and shadow is healed, and the individual consequently evolves an acceptable self-image. And that is precisely the aim of ego-level therapies. Thus, although the techniques certainly vary from school to school, they all share the common goal of healing the split between the egoic conscious and unconscious, or of "making the unconscious conscious," or of integrating projections and creating a whole and healthy psyche. This group would include psychoanalytical ego psychology, along with the numerous psychotherapies that define man as *ego*.

EXISTENTIAL-LEVEL THERAPIES

Since the existential level is the level of the total organism not marked by the dualism of psyche vs. soma, these therapies deal primarily with actualizing the concrete, full human being, not cut asunder into an ego vs. a body. Their aim is not so much to develop an accurate image of the total organism as to *be* that total organism. Just as the ego-level therapies aim at "expanding identity" to all facets of the psyche, existential-level therapies aim at extending identity to *all facets of the total organism*. This is clearly stated by Fritz Perls et al.: "The aim is to extend the boundary of what you accept as yourself to include *all organic activities*."[9] Or, as Perls later put it, "Lose your mind and come to your senses!" That is, come to the total organism. As Alexander Lowen expresses it, "As long as the body remains as object to the ego, it may fulfill the ego's pride, but it will never provide the joy and satisfaction that the 'alive' body offers."[10]

It is the heretofore untapped potential of the total organism that is the driving force behind the Human Potential Movement. Thus, the aim of existential-level therapies is to show an individual that his awareness "is a living integral part of a somatic, organic whole...; a self-aware, self-controlling organism, an organic unity of many functions which have traditionally been thought of as 'bodily' and 'mental.'"[11]

Overall, then, the existential-level therapies are concerned with the total psychophysical organism and the crises it may face as well as the great potentials it may display. This group of therapies would include approaches such as existential psychology, Gestalt therapy, Logotherapy, humanistic psychology in general, bioenergetics, as well as the more somatic approaches such as Hatha Yoga, structural integration, polarity therapy, and sensory awareness. Despite their many real differences, they all seek to authenticate the full and concrete human organism.

BIOSOCIAL-BAND THERAPIES

Recall that we named the upper limits of the existential level "the biosocial bands." These bands represent the massive mappings of cultural patterns onto the organism itself, and they thus exert a profound and pervasive influence upon the entire organism's orientation and behavior. Among other things, they mold the structure of an individual's ego[12] and the pattern of his thought processes.[13] More importantly, as far as pathology is concerned, these bands act as a screen or filter of reality. In the words of Erich Fromm:

> The effect of society is not only to funnel fictions into our consciousness, but also to prevent awareness of reality.... Every society, by its own practice of living and by the mode of relatedness, of feeling and perceiving, develops a system of categories which determines the forms of awareness. This system works, as it were, like a *socially conditioned filter*; experience cannot enter awareness unless it can penetrate this filter.... *I am aware* of all my feelings and thoughts which are permitted to penetrate the threefold filter of (socially conditioned) language, logic, and taboos (social character). Experiences which cannot be filtered through remain outside of awareness; that is, they remain unconscious.[14]

Now this filtering effect is common to nearly all men by virtue of their shared membership in a particular society, and hence this "biosocial unconscious" is not to be confused with the purely personal "unconscious" of any particular member of that society.

The biosocial-band therapies are thus concerned with the very fundamental ways in which such social patterns as language and logic alter and distort awareness, and are obviously working on a "deeper" level than that of purely individual distortions, repressions, and so on. Hence the social context of pathology most concerns these therapies, but not all so-called interpersonal therapies can be classed as biosocial-band therapies, for many of them are more truly involved in "the games egos play." But some forms of very fundamental social psychology, social phenomenology, basic family therapies, and semantic therapies are directly addressing themselves to this most important band of the spectrum.

Can the screen be "lifted"?

In passing, it should be noted that the biosocial band is the last main "barrier" to the felt identity with the *total* organism. For this reason, many existential-level therapies definitely take into account the screening power of the biosocial band. This battle to undercut the biosocial band can be clearly seen in the work of Fritz Perls, who fought constantly against the bewitchment of the total organism by the powers of language and logic. "It language" must be turned into "I language"; "thing language" into "process language"; either/or logic into both/and logic. All were direct attempts to lift the screen of the biosocial band and plunge into the immediateness of existential awareness. Of course, once the screen is lifted, one is still free to use it—one is no longer, however, *forced* to use it.

TRANSPERSONAL-BAND THERAPIES

The transpersonal bands represent those aspects or levels of consciousness that by their very nature are supraindividual. At this level the "individual" is not yet completely identified with the All, and yet neither is his identity confined to the conventional boundaries of his organism. Among other things, the transpersonal bands are the home of the *bijas, vasanas,** or archetypes. To quote Jung on the archetypes (the "primordial images") of the "collective unconscious":

> The other part of the unconscious [besides the personal] is what I call the impersonal or collective unconscious. As the name indicates, its contents are not personal but collective; that is, they do not belong to one individual alone but...to the whole of mankind.[15]

And so, Jung would ask, by what myth do you live? For mythological imagery springs from the collective unconscious, the transpersonal bands, and, among other things, it is not contaminated or perverted by merely social conventions, language, logic, or the illusions of any particular cult or individual. Furthermore, the language of mythology is associative and integrative, and not dissociative and analytical, and hence it more clearly and truly reflects the actual physical reality of what Whitehead called "the seamless coat of the universe," of the mutual interdependence of all things and events. Myth, as Coomaraswamy stated,[16] embodies the

---

Bijas and *vasanas* are Buddhist terms for inherent tendencies that shape experience in conventional patterns (Ed.).

nearest approach to absolute truth that can be stated in words. For these reasons, it confers upon the individual an intimation of his universality, a direct pointer to his fundamentally joyous unity with all of creation, a wholeness that takes him far beyond the petty affairs of day-to-day routine and plunges him into the vast and magical world of the transpersonal.

Now these archetypes, or *bijas*, or *vasanas*, exert a profound effect upon every level of the spectrum existing "above" the transpersonal bands. It is entirely possible that this is a general phenomenon seen throughout the spectrum: the vicissitudes of *any* level can dramatically affect all of the levels above it. But the point to be emphasized here is that the transpersonal bands can themselves be *directly* experienced. Carl Jung himself realized this, for he stated that "Mystics are people who have a particularly vivid experience of the processes of the collective unconscious. Mystical experience is *experience of archetypes*."[17]

Now it might be said, from another angle, that the transpersonal bands represent that point where the individual touches Mind. He does not yet directly realize that what he is, *is* Mind, but through insight and experience he understands indeed that there is within him that which goes beyond him.

In recognizing a depth of one's identity that goes beyond one's individual and separate being, a person can more easily go beyond his individual and separate neuroses. For he is no longer *exclusively* identified with just his separate-self sense and hence is no longer exclusively tied to his purely personal problems. In a sense he can start to let go of his fears and anxieties, depressions and obsessions, and begin to view them with the same clarity and impartiality with which one might view clouds floating through the sky or waters rushing in a stream. The transpersonal band therapy discloses— probably for the first time—a transposition from which he can comprehensively *look at* his individual emotional and ideational complexes. But the fact that he can comprehensively *look at* them means that he has ceased using them as something *with which to look* at, and thus distort, reality. Further, the fact that he can look at them means that he is no longer exclusively identified with them. His identity begins to touch that within which is beyond.

As such, the transpersonal bands are sometimes experienced as the supraindividual witness: that which is capable of observing the flow of what is—without interfering with it, commenting on it, or in any way manipulating it. The witness simply observes the stream of events both inside and outside the mind-body in a creatively detached fashion, since, in fact, the witness is not exclusively identified with either. In other words, *when the individual realizes that his mind and his body can be perceived objectively, he spontaneously realizes that they cannot constitute a real subjective self.* This position of the witness, or we might say, this state of witnessing, is the foundation of all beginning Buddhist practice ("mindfulness"), of psychosynthesis ("disidentification and the transpersonal Self") and of Hindu Jnana Yoga (*"neti, neti"*). Further, it seems to resemble very closely what Abraham Maslow called plateau experiences, which "represent a witnessing of the world. The plateau experience is a witnessing of reality. . . . It's the transcending of time and space which becomes quite normal, so to speak."[18] It is expressly through these types of experiences that one is fully initiated into the world of meta-motivations, B-values, transcendent values, mythological and supra-individual awareness—in short, the spiritual dimension of trans-personal bands.

Given that the transpersonal bands represent, by definition, those portions of the spectrum where the individual's identity is not exclusively and rigidly confined to the conventional boundaries of his organism, and yet neither is it one with the All, we might also expect to find on these bands such phenomena as ESP and psychokinesis. This is not to say that psychic phenomena necessarily follow upon entrance into the transpersonal bands, only that their emergence is perfectly understandable in the context of the spectrum of consciousness. Thus, even a person who aspires directly to Mind might temporarily develop psychic powers for the simple reason that he has to cross the transpersonal bands.

From the above discussion on the transpersonal bands, we might get the mistaken impression that in these bands the individual simply explodes into some sort of transpersonally uniform mush. On the contrary, he begins to see himself as profoundly unique by virtue of being profoundly universal. Thus, for example, the position of the supraindividual witness is not at all to be equated with certain forms of schizophrenia. Some individuals diagnosed as schizophrenic may indeed be psychologically lost in some of the transpersonal bands for want of an adequate guide.[19] But there remains an essential difference between various transpersonal experiences and schizophrenia. Although the schizophrenic may strongly experience a partial fusion of opposites (such as self and other, past and future, inside and outside), this fusion generally produces feelings of pervasive disorientation and confusion, while in the mystic it produces feelings of profound simplicity and clarity. Mysticism is fusion without confusion; schizophrenia is fusion with confusion.

Not all therapies aimed at the transpersonal bands seek to experience these bands directly. But they do seek to contact, befriend and utilize the powerful forces residing here. In short, they all recognize a depth in man that is transpersonal. This group of therapies would include Jungian analysis, psychosynthesis, Bijamantra techniques (such as Transcendental Meditation), Progoff Dialogue, and others.

LEVEL-OF-MIND THERAPIES (Spiritual Practices)

At this point we must amend the last-quoted statement of Jung by saying certain "lesser" mystical states are the direct experience of the archetypes. "True" mysticism is beyond even the archetypes, the *vasanas*; it is of the level of Mind, wherein all *vasanas* are destroyed. That is why, to realize the supreme identity with Mind, "the yogin is striving to...'burn up' the *vasanas*."[20] In this sense, the archetypes or *vasanas* are the ultimate pointers as well as the final barrier.

This distinction between what I am calling—for lack of better terms—"lesser" and "true" mysticism is the distinction between the transpersonal witness and Mind. The transpersonal witness is a "position" of witnessing reality. But notice that this state of the transpersonal witness still contains a subtle form of the primary dualism, namely, the witness vs. what is witnessed. It is when this last trace of dualism is finally and completely shattered that one awakens to Mind, for at that moment (which is *this* moment) the witness and the witnessed are one and the same.

This is not at all to denigrate the position of the transpersonal self or witness, for it can not only be highly therapeutic in itself, but it can frequently act as a type of springboard to Mind. Nevertheless it is not to be confused with Mind itself. This is why, in Zen, a student who remains in the peaceful bliss of the transpersonal self is called a "dead-void heretic," and the Tibetan Buddhists refer to it as being "stuck in the *kun-gzhi*."

In short, for one seeking an understanding of Mind, the transpersonal bands are to be contacted, befriended, and then passed through. This is also why the enlightened masters universally shun, as an end in itself, the development of psychic powers characteristic of the transpersonal bands. In these bands one may in fact be able to develop the power to, let us say, manipulate the environment psychically, but when one *is* the environment, what possible meaning could manipulating it have? This would still imply a subtle duality.

Such, then, is the major difference between the lesser mystical states of the transpersonal self, and the true mystical state which is Mind. In one, a person may witness reality; in the other he is reality. While one invariably retains some subtle form of the primary dualism, the other does not. It is this final dissolution of any form of the primary dualism that Zen refers to by the phrase, "the bottom of the bucket breaks," for there remains in one's awareness no bottom— that is to say, no sense of any inner subjectivity confronting any world of outer objectivity. The two worlds have radically coalesced, or rather, are understood to have never been separate. The individual goes right to the very bottom of his being to find who or what is doing the seeing, and he *ultimately* finds—instead of a transpersonal self— nothing other than what is seen, which Blyth called, "the experience by the universe of the universe." The bottom of the bucket has broken.

With this, Vedanta is in perfect agreement. In the words of Sri Ramana Maharshi, "The notion that the Seer is different from the seen abides in the mind. For those that ever abide in the Heart [i.e., Mind], the Seer is the same as the seen."

Therapies aimed at this level—like those of any level—are trying to heal a particular dualism, in this case, the primary dualism of subject vs. object. In essence, they can all be summed up in the words of Huang Po, the great Ch'an master: "A perception, sudden as blinking, that subject and object are one, will lead to a deeply mysterious, wordless understanding; and by this understanding will you awake to the truth." The truth that is revealed is the truth of the real world not split into "one state which sees, and one state which is seen." And the collapse of the dualism between subject and object is simultaneously the collapse of the dualism between past and future, life and death, so that one awakens, as if from a dream, to the spaceless and timeless world of cosmic consciousness. Therapies—

and at this level we use the term "therapies" only as a concession to language—addressing this level include Mahayana Buddhism, Taoism, Vedanta Hinduism, Sufism, and certain forms of Christian mysticism.

CONCLUDING REMARKS

Having thus finished the above very abstract outline, a few points must at least be touched upon. First, the levels of the spectrum of consciousness, like any spectrum, infinitely shade and grade into one another, and in no way can they be finally separated from one another. We have merely picked out a few prominent "nodes" in the spectrum for discussion, so it immediately follows that the assignment of different schools of psychotherapy to one level or band is only a rough approximation. Second, when we assign a particular school to one major level of the spectrum, this is done on the basis of a somewhat arbitrary "deepest" level which that school recognizes. Generally speaking, the therapies of any one level recognize and even utilize the psychotherapeutic disciplines of the levels "above" it. Thus, to place Jungian psychology on the transpersonal bands is not to imply that Jung had nothing to say about the shadow level, or the biosocial bands. Indeed he did have much to offer regarding those levels. Likewise, to place Gestalt therapy on the existential level is not to imply that it ignores the integration of the shadow, and so on. Third, it *is*, however, generally the case that the therapies of any one level tend to view experience of *any* level "beneath" theirs as being pathological, and are hence quick to explain away all lower levels with a diagnostic fury, as witness the stance of orthodox psychoanalysis on mysticism. Fourth, since the descent of the spectrum of consciousness is, in one sense or another, an expanding of identity from the persona to the ego to the organism to the cosmos, we could just as well speak of a progressive dis-identification or a progressive *detachment* from all *exclusive* identifications. When it comes to the level of Mind, it does not matter whether we say the individual is identified with *everything* or whether the individual is identified with *nothing*—both are logically meaningless anyway. To elucidate the former only makes the complex story of the spectrum of consciousness a little easier to tell. Fifth, since each level of the spectrum is marked by a different sense of identity, each level will have more-or-less characteristic features associated with it. For instance, the different levels seem to produce different dreams, different needs, and different symptoms—to mention a few. For example, transpersonal anxiety, existential anxiety, and shadow anxiety are different beasts indeed, and simply must not be treated the same. The indiscriminate use of a single therapeutic technique for all symptoms may have the most unfortunate effects.

It is also important to recognize the level from which a dream originates. Is it a nightmare dream, a terrifyingly direct message from the shadow? Or is it simply a hangover from the day, originating from the ego? Or deeper yet, a hangover from history, a "big dream" of archetypal import, messages from the transpersonal bands, hints from the gods themselves? The answer to this will determine which approach to the dream one will use: for example, Gestalt or Jungian (or both in proper sequence). Failure to recognize these differences might result in either impoverishment or inflation: archetype reduced to ego, or ego inflated to archetype.

Any slight appreciation of man's depth, of his pluridimensional awareness, of the spectrumlike nature of his consciousness, forces these considerations upon us—and they are extremely important considerations at that. For example, it may slowly begin to dawn on a person that he is leading a "life of despair." He might indeed simply be repressing some inner rage, so that here on the shadow level "m-a-d" has become "s-a-d," as most psychoanalytical thinkers might argue. This rage is usually connected with some sort of object loss, stemming from infantile loss of accustomed mother love—the so-called anaclitic depression. Yet, on the ego level, he might be totally out of touch with his body. Or yet again, he might have actually seen the cramp of the secondary dualism, the spasm at the existential level, the avoidance of death which is the root of all man's motivations in time. Or has he indeed looked into the very face of the transpersonal dweller on the threshold, and so knows deep within that his coming rebirth demands his instant death (as the mystics of all ages have told)? Can we be so callous and so insensitive as to dare throw them all into the same "therapeutic bag"?

In this regard, the question might arise as to what effect, if any, therapeutic procedures on the upper levels (shadow, ego, existential) have or might have on a person's development on or toward the lower levels (transpersonal, Mind). Although an extended discussion of this topic is beyond the scope of this chapter, the following may be said. The descent of the spectrum of consciousness can be described as a process of surrendering exclusive, narrowed, and partial identifications so as to discover broader and more encompassing ones down the spectrum. To the extent an individual can let go of his exclusive attachments on the upper bands of the spectrum—and this, in essence, is the aim of upper level therapies—his descent is thereby facilitated.

Theoretically, in totally healing the major dualism characteristic of any given level, the individual would be expected to necessarily, and quite spontaneously, descend to the next level. For example, in healing and wholing the split between persona and shadow, the individual—almost by definition—has descended to the ego level. In fully healing and wholing the split between ego and body, the individual has spontaneously descended to the existential level, and so on. Once on the new level, the individual will likely become more sensitive to that level's characteristics—its dreams, its dualisms, its class of "dys-eases," its potentials for growth, its needs. This phenomenon of spontaneous descent, which is *potentially* inherent in everyone, is an almost exact analogue of Maslow's hierarchical needs—that is, neurotic needs (shadow level), basic needs (ego and existential levels), and meta-needs (transpersonal bands). Mind has no needs for there is nothing outside it. As soon as an individual clears up one set of needs, the next set spontaneously emerges, and failure to satisfy these emergent needs will result in a different set of problems (grumbles and meta-grumbles, etc.).

Thus, on the shadow level, the basic needs are not satisfied. Through repression, alienation, or some other projective mechanism, the individual fails to recognize the nature of his basic needs. And since, as is well known, one cannot get enough of what one does not really need, a whole battery of insatiable neurotic needs develop. If, on the other hand, these neurotic needs can be understood and displaced, so that the underlying basic needs can emerge, the individual can begin to act on them so as to find thereby his way to a larger fulfillment. He also finds his way to a lower level of the spectrum. And by the time the individual reaches the existential level, an entirely new set of needs, the meta-needs, begin to emerge, carrying with them a call, sometimes a demand, to transcendence.

Acting upon these meta-needs initiates one into the world of the transpersonal bands; shunning them throws one into the grips of a meta-pathology. That these meta-needs correspond to a transpersonal reality is clearly announced by Maslow himself:

> Meta-motives are, therefore, no longer *only* intra-psychic or organismic [i.e., egoic or existential]. They are equally inner and outer.... This means that the distinction between self and not-self has broken down (or has been transcended). There is now less differentiation between the world and the person.... He becomes an enlarged self, we could say.... To identify one's highest self with the highest values of the world out there means, to some extent at least, a fusion with the non-self.[21]

Keeping in mind that this partial fusion of organism and environment is a fusion without confusion, Maslow's quote may be taken as perfectly descriptive of the transpersonal bands.

In light of the above, it would not be reckless to conclude that therapeutic measures on the upper levels of the spectrum may indeed facilitate the descent to the lower levels. This does not mean that a descent to the transpersonal bands or the level of Mind always *requires* upper-level therapy, even in the cases where it is indicated. It might certainly help, but may not be mandatory since lower level therapies may in a real sense reduce the work to be done on the upper levels. If this were not the case, meditation practices would probably never be useful to a neurotic unless he had undergone something akin to complete psychoanalysis.

Every major sacred or spiritual tradition maintains that human consciousness is in some sense a pluridimensional arrangement, manifesting through *maya* the infinite play of the Ultimate. Further, where every spiritual tradition has described the levels of pluridimensionality, these levels are in substantial agreement with those outlined in the spectrum (e.g., the Buddhist *vijnanas*, the Hindu *kosas*, Gurdjieff's "vibratory levels," etc.). I have only extended the *psychologia perennis* by suggesting that not only do these levels apparently exist, as maintained by the perennial psychology, but also that pathology can occur on any of these levels (except, of course, on the level of Mind), and thus the great contribution of Western psychologies lies precisely in addressing themselves to *these* pathologies. Of course, the West is now extending its interest to some of the deeper levels of the spectrum, but this will not annul the work to be done on the upper levels, work in which the West has historically excelled.

Thus it is possible to see the grand complementarity of Eastern and Western approaches to consciousness and "psychotherapy." On the one hand, the overriding concern of the Eastern explorers of consciousness (and by "Eastern" we really mean the *psychologia perennis* in general, geographically East or West being irrelevant) has always been with the level of Mind, and thus they gave little, if any, attention to the pathologies that could develop on the other levels. This is understandable, for the perennial psychology maintains that *all* pathology stems from ignorance of Mind. Thus, although they were perfectly aware of the various levels of the spectrum, and although they mapped them in detail, they felt that "curing" a pathology on any of these levels was not much more than a waste of time, for the root ignorance of the subject–object dualism would still remain. The West, on the other hand, has been—at least since the seventeenth century—almost completely bereft of even the least conception of the perennial philosophy, and hence, when the study of psychopathology began to develop in this metaphysical vacuum, Western scientists had no choice but to seek out the roots of neuroses and psychoses in one or more of the "upper" levels of the spectrum (such as the ego or biosocial levels). It is suggested that on their own levels they are *all* correct, and taken together they form a complementary approach to consciousness that spans the entire spectrum.

NOTES

1. Huxley (1944).
2. Schroedinger (1964), p. 21.
3. Deutsch (1969), p. 28.
4. G. S. Brown (1972), p. 104.
5. Benoit (1955), pp. 33–34.
6. N. O. Brown (1959), p. 91, 100.
7. Ibid., p. 159.
8. Putney & Putney (1966).
9. Perls, Hefferline, & Goodman (1951), p. 116.
10. Lowen (1967).
11. Hanna (1974).
12. Cf. Mead (1964).
13. Cf. Whorf (1956).

14. Fromm, Suzuki, & Martino (1963), pp. 98–99, 104.
15. Jung (1960), pp. 310–11.
16. Coomaraswamy (1943), p. 33.
17. Jung (1968), p. 110.
18. Maslow (1972), pp. 115–16.
19. Cf. Laing (1967).
20. Eliade (1969), p. 89.
21. Maslow (1971).

2
Exploring Mind: Form, Emptiness, and Beyond

John Welwood

Form is emptiness, emptiness itself is form;
emptiness is no other than form,
form is no other than emptiness.

Heart Sutra

In every crescendo of sensation, in every effort to recall, in every
progress towards the satisfaction of desire, this succession of an
emptiness and fulness that have reference to each other and are one
flesh is the essence of the phenomenon.

William James

I would like to explore the question of "what is mind?" without
promising any kind of systematic analysis or objective definition.
Rather, I would like to pursue the question from an experiential
point of view which may yield some useful new insights.

First, there seem to be two common Western assumptions about
mind: (1) The mind is often thought of as a separate substance or
system, apart from other aspects of human being, such as body,
spirit, heart, matter. This concept of mind as having a real existence
that can be defined separately from the bodily totality poses
innumerable problems for Western philosophy and psychology.
From an experiential point of view, such a definition of mind has
little meaning, for there seems to be no evidence that we can
experience any purely mental realm apart from our embodied

existence. Even fantasies and dreams always refer back to the body and our involvements in life contexts. (2) Mind is often associated with the differentiated, substantive parts of the stream of consciousness: definite thoughts or perceptions, or the faculty for having such discrete experiences. Thus mind is popularly a synonym for thinking or the faculty of thinking. Although Freud changed this notion with his concept of the "unconscious mind," he identified this unconscious with a set of "mental acts": unconscious instincts, wishes, emotions.

Instead of trying to observe or define mind objectively as something apart from this very process of observing, let us instead refer to mind as the very rich, immediate environment in which we live. This lived environment is so close and immediate that it is very difficult to analyze it from the perspective of a hypothetical external observer. Mind, as this subjectively lived environment, is the medium through which we know the so-called "objective world," and provides the potential for shaping and modifying this world.

The next question from an experiential point of view might be: what is going on in this environment and how is this environment experienced? Perhaps what is noticed first is the ongoing, overlapping sequence of differentiated mind-moments: thoughts, perceptions, feelings. These are like the specific objects in an environment. But the total environment is itself larger than any specific object and provides a kind of background or landscape in which these specific moments stand out. Trying to observe mind as a global background is like standing on a flat landscape in which we can see in all directions. The entire scene cannot be seen at once, for at least 180 degrees of it will be behind the observer's back. But though all of it cannot be seen, it is possible, nonetheless, to *feel* what it is like to live in that landscape, this being analogous to a felt sense of mind as environment. In this sense mind is a kind of pure awareness that underlies thought, perception, and feeling, continuing even when they are not present.

Then there is a more subtle aspect of the mind process that may take some direction or training to observe: inarticulate gaps or spaces within or between discrete thoughts, feelings, and perceptions. These can be termed undifferentiated mind-moments. So mind as a whole refers to the differentiated and undifferentiated moments, as well as the encompassing background environment-awareness in which the interplay between them occurs.

FORM AND EMPTINESS IN THE STREAM OF THOUGHT

Let us look more closely into the interplay between differentiated and undifferentiated mind-moments. In the stream of consciousness, thoughts, feelings, and perceptions overlap, follow upon, and change into one another. Distinct thoughts can be isolated as separate discrete moments by means of focal attention, which can single out figures against the background of the larger mind-landscape. What generally tends to be overlooked are the spaces between thoughts, the undifferentiated, preverbal moments. For instance, at the end of a sentence, there is a natural cadence, marked by a punctuation mark when written out, that allows a split-second sensing of the direction of the next sentence. Or between the words of the sentence itself, there are often halts and gaps (often covered verbally by "hm" or "ah") that allow us to sense or scan our meaning in a way that is different from the more linear focal attention of discursive thinking.

William James was particularly interested in these undifferentiated moments in the stream of consciousness, which he called the "transitive parts." He understood the inherent paradox of trying to focally observe these transitional spaces between articulated thoughts:

> Now it is very difficult, introspectively, to see the transitive parts for what they really are. If they are but flights to a conclusion, stopping them to look at them before the conclusion is reached is really annihilating them. . . . The attempt at introspective analysis in these cases is in fact like seizing a spinning top to catch its motion, or trying to turn up the gas quickly enough to see how the darkness looks.[1]

The difficulty of focally apprehending these undifferentiated spaces may lead to ignoring or denying them as important aspects of the mind process:

> If to hold fast and observe the transitive parts of thought's stream be so hard, then the great blunder to which all schools are liable must be the failure to register them, and the undue emphasizing of the more substantive parts of the stream.[2]

Thus focal attention, man's analyzing capacity, can easily fall into error when it fails to recognize its interdependence with the prearticulate aspect of mind that can be experienced fleetingly in the transitive moments of the stream of consciousness.

So far we have seen that there are gaps or transitional moments in the thought process that are difficult to apprehend through focal attention. If we look closer, it becomes evident that each differentiated moment of thought or perception *actually takes on its specific quality by virtue of these spaces surrounding it*, just as the objects in a room can only be appreciated in the proper context, with the proper element of spaciousness around them. The most beautiful antiques mean nothing in a cluttered room. Thus the spaces allow the forms to stand out as the particular forms that they are, and constitute the surrounding context or penumbra against which the given form assumes its particular meaning. As James points out, when we hear a clap of thunder, we cannot separate this experience from the previous moment of silence that it has interrupted:

> Into the awareness of the thunder itself the awareness of the previous silence creeps and continues; for what we hear when the thunder crashes is not thunder *pure*, but thunder-breaking-upon-silence-and-contrasting-with-it.... The *feeling* of the thunder is also a feeling of the silence as just gone.[3]

Similarly, in music, the meaning and contour of a melody derive from the intervals between the notes. A single tone by itself has little meaning, and as soon as two tones are sounded they are automatically related by the shape of the space or interval between them. The interval of a third has a totally different feeling-quality to it than does a fifth. When sounding these intervals, the notes themselves are of secondary importance, for any pair of notes the same interval apart will sound rather similar. Music serves as a good analogy for the interplay between form and emptiness as part of the larger environment of mind. Form is emptiness: the melody is a pattern of intervals between the tones. Although a melody is usually conceived as a sequence of notes, it is just as much a sequence of spaces that the tones simply serve to mark off. And emptiness is form: nonetheless, this pattern of intervals does make up a definite, unique melodic progression that can be sung and remembered.

Normally, an overreliance on focal attention ignores the spaces around thoughts, the felt penumbra that gives thoughts their meaning-context. Thus there is a danger of identifying mind with thought alone:

> ...like one who should say a river consists of nothing but pailsful, spoonsful, quartpotsful, barrelsful, and other molded forms of water. Even were the pails and the pots all actually standing in the stream, still between them the free water would continue to flow.[4]

This overemphasizing and solidification of thoughts to the exclusion of the open spaces within the mind-environment leads to a personal identification with the thought process. The troublesome equation, I = my thoughts about reality, can lead to a narrowed "self-sense" and an anxiety that is connected with defending these thoughts as one's territory. The familiar tendency is to assume that one is the originator and possessor of one's thoughts, rather than seeing them as ephemeral phenomena in the larger environment of mind.

So far, then, this discussion has dealt with "emptiness" as absence of form, an undifferentiated moment of consciousness without formal characteristics, which nonetheless serves an essential psychological function as the prearticulate matrix of thought-feeling-perception, as the space around them that allows them to stand out for what they are. This is the first of three types of emptiness to be explored here.

FELT MEANING

The vivid, living meaning of thought does not lie in its verbal-syntactical form. The words, "this is my house," could mean any number of things, depending on the felt context in which the words are thought or spoken. This context is what Gendlin calls "felt meaning":[5] how things affect me, how I am pre-reflectively relating to things before I formulate that relation in discursive thought. Felt meaning is what is inwardly referred to when someone asks, "How do you really feel now?" In order to answer this question, it is necessary to let go of all our quick, easy verbalizations and quietly refer to our felt sense of ourselves. Perhaps our eyes roll upward, we pause, sigh, mumble, or sit down—anything that will give us time to reflect on the felt background of our state of being. At some point each of us usually is able to discover what it is that we really feel, and this results in a sense of recognition, "Oh yes, that's it." A return to focal attention then allows us to articulate or elaborate various aspects of this complex of felt meaning.

As Gendlin has shown, felt meaning guides our present action and speech in an implicit, background way. Thought, imagery, and action are ways in which we try to formulate and express these inarticulate meanings.

Emptiness in this second sense goes beyond absence of form, or no-thing-ness, to refer to this "diffuse richness" of our felt involvement in life situations. Thus, when the "mind goes empty" or we meet an "empty gaze," what *may* be occurring is an inward reference to a rich context of undifferentiated felt meaning. According to James, "A good third of our psychic life consists in these rapid premonitory perspective views of schemes of thought not yet articulate."[6] What appears as a gap in the stream of thought may reveal a continuum of undifferentiated feeling. "The feeling of an absence is *toto coelo* [wholly] other than the absence of a feeling."[7] In order to discover and know these feelings, it is helpful to know how to look at them and relate to them properly—to relax focal attention and shift over to a more diffuse attention that can allow the seeing of things in their holistic complexity *all at once*. Creative thinking, action, decision making, and artistic endeavor are related to seeing holistically. As Mozart remarked of the process of composing music, "The best of all is the hearing of it all at once."[8]

So far, then, we have explored the interplay of substantive mind-moments and the undifferentiated spaces surrounding them in the stream of consciousness. Thoughts and perceptions have been described as deriving their full meaning from their relation to the spaces around them. Diffuse attention directed at these spaces makes it possible to discover an ongoing process of felt meaning that provides the living context for thoughts. This felt meaning, which appears as a gap or emptiness to focal, discursive mind, may become articulated as specific feelings that express the ways in which the individual lives and relates to his life situations.

THE LARGER ENVIRONMENT OF MIND

Is mind totally bound up in the felt relationships between the individual and his personal life-situations? If the relative formlessness of felt meaning can be articulated into specific feelings, what about the absolute spaciousness that is spoken of in Buddhist psychology as *sunyata* (emptiness)? Does *sunyata* simply refer to the undifferentiated quality of felt meaning that can never be grasped discursively, or does it refer to an aspect of mind beyond felt meaning?

The practice of meditation is one of the well-known methods for exploring the larger environment of mind. Normally during meditation there is an awareness of differentiated thoughts and perceptions, as well as the more global currents of felt meaning (like whitecaps and swells on the ocean). But occasionally there is a moment of deeper awareness: a momentary flash of nonpersonal awareness free of thought and feeling, a glimpse of a spacious quality of mind in which the boundaries of self and other are relaxed, and one's separateness is not felt so distinctly.

> Sometimes in meditation there is a gap in normal consciousness, a sudden complete openness. This only arises when one has ceased to think in terms of meditator, meditation, and the object of meditation. It is a glimpse of reality, a sudden flash which occurs at first infrequently, and then gradually more and more often. It may not be a particularly shattering or explosive experience at all, just a moment of great simplicity.[9]

These gaps seem to be windows opening onto a spaciousness that is without self-interest. There is simply an openness of mind in which things are seen purely for what they are without reference to personal projects or strategies. In Buddhist psychology, this empty quality of mind is seen as a person's true nature, always present in some way, and constituting the basis for real freedom, compassion, and peace. This then is a third sense of emptiness, here signifying a fuller sense of attunement that is free to realize itself because it is not *caught in* or *attached to* the daily struggle of striving and seeking. As the late Zen master Suzuki Roshi points out, it means not holding on to thoughts and purposes:

> When you have something in your consciousness, you do not have perfect composure. The best way toward perfect composure is to forget everything. Then your mind is calm, and it is wide and clear enough to see and feel things as they are without any effort. The best way to find perfect composure is not to retain any idea of things, whatever they may be—to forget all about them and not leave any trace or shadow of thinking. But if you try to stop your mind or try to go beyond your conscious activity, that will only be another burden for you. . . . Do not try to stop your mind, but leave everything as it is. Then things will not stay in your mind so long. Things will come as they come and go as they go. Then eventually your clear, empty mind will last fairly long.[10]

This passage makes two important points about the empty quality of mind. First of all, it is not an escape from reality, an ignoring of things and retreating inside oneself. Forgetting everything means simply not dwelling on thoughts past the point where they refer to what is immediately real. Then the mind is empty of struggle, which allows for seeing things as they are, unclouded by preferences and beliefs about how they should be. Secondly, trying to empty our minds is futile, for this very striving continues the struggle to achieve some purpose.

Is there a practice that can help in the discovery of the larger awareness beyond the discrimination process that seems to be continually tied to habitual patterns? The path suggested by Buddhist teachers lies in working with what is already happening, in this case the processes of thought and feeling. It seems that empty mind is present in the midst of the busy, confused mind:

> When I say "working with" irritation, I don't mean to suppress irritation or let go of irritation. But trying to become part of the irritation, trying to feel the abstract quality.... When we are able to become completely one with irritations or feel the abstract quality of the irritation as it is, then irritation has no one to irritate. So it becomes a sort of judo practice, the using of irritation's energy as part of your basic development.[11]

Going into the turbulence of emotions is like entering the eye of a hurricane. The surrounding winds may be very powerful, but persevering effort makes it possible to arrive at a clear opening in the midst of the storm:

> Any moment, wherever you are, driving a car, sitting around, working, talking, any activities you have—even if you are very disturbed emotionally, very passionate, or even if your mind has become very strong, raging, overcome with the worst possible things and you cannot control yourself... if you really go into it, there's nothing there.... There is nothing to throw away—even the most negative emotions are useful. The more you go into the disturbance—when you really get in there—the emotional characteristics no longer exist. Then this becomes proper meditation.[12]

Perhaps what Tarthang Tulku is referring to in the above passage is the way in which emotions open up and change when they are given full attention. For example, what may appear to be a fairly solid,

dense feeling of anger starts to shift and break up when it is looked
into more closely, which gives a feeling of opening and relief. The
emotion may become transparent, itself a window on a more
fundamental organismic process of change. This kind of experience
reveals an interesting paradox. From the level of discriminating
mind, there is a distinction between form and emptiness,
differentiated and undifferentiated mind-moments, so that they
appear to be two different aspects of mind. But if one experientially
stays with a thought or feeling, and goes deeply enough into it, it loses
its formal solidity and it becomes possible to discover one's own
organismic process.

> When you have pain or unhappiness, or any problems, just stay
> within the thought.... When you are emotionally upset, stay with
> the emotion. You do not need to escape or deny or hide from your
> feelings.... Just go into the center of the thought without trying
> to evaluate it. Just be the thought and completely accept it without
> grasping or holding on to it. Gradually a new awareness will
> develop inside this experience.... Emotions become the fuel of
> meditation.... The more "heated" we become, the more energy we
> have. But if we go directly into the center of the emotion, there's
> nothing there! We can transmute this samsaric mind because the
> mind itself is emptiness—not a conceptual emptiness... but an
> experience that becomes total openness, total honesty with each
> situation...direct seeing, total freedom from obscurations, com-
> plete receptivity.[13]

Even in the midst of an intense emotion, there are flashes of a
clear, empty space. For example, anger might be interrupted by
flashes such as, "Oh, I'm not really angry," or "This doesn't matter
that much." It seems that we could not be confused in our thoughts
and emotions unless we already had some sense of how things fit
together, just as the jumble of pieces in a jigsaw puzzle only has
meaning in relation to a prior whole picture that they were part of.
Here then is a deeper sense in which form is emptiness. In the core of
thought itself there is complete openness and clarity. Analogously, at
the core of "solid" matter, there are immense spaces in which the
electrons orbit the nucleus of the atom. Just as thoughts serve to
focus the undifferentiated background of mind, so it appears that
subatomic particles are but intense condensations of an energy field.
Buddhist psychology provides a picture of mind that curiously

resembles the quantum physics view of matter, with thoughts being analogous to the basic particles of matter:

> In these "quantum field theories," the classical contrast between the solid particles and the space surrounding them is completely overcome. The quantum field is seen as the fundamental physical entity; a continuous medium which is present everywhere in space. Particles are merely local condensations of the field; concentrations of energy which come and go, thereby losing their individual character and dissolving into the underlying field.[14]

Just as in physics, matter and space are two aspects of a single unified field, so in Buddhist psychology thought and the space around thought are aspects of the larger mind-environment.[15] Suzuki Roshi calls this larger background "big mind." If small mind is the ongoing discrimination process that draws on the undifferentiated context of felt meaning, then big mind is the background of both of them, pure presence in the world. Big mind is the limpid medium that encompasses and underlies thought, just as water surrounds and allows the fish to be what it is.

> The mind which is always on your side is not just your mind, it is universal mind, always the same, not different from another's mind.... It is big, big mind.... Your true mind is always with whatever you see.... So you see, the mind is at the same time everything.... When the fish swims, water and fish are the fish. There is nothing but fish. Do you understand?[16]

This level of clear mind in which self and other are not separate, but two poles of a single continuum, is also referred to in Tibetan texts as "Mind-as-such."[17] It refers to the larger environment of mind that can never be grasped as an object of thought and at the same time is the basis of thought, that which makes thought possible. Although the gaps between the dots on this page are in one sense nothing, in another sense they act as they ground that allows the dots to stand out as separate entities:

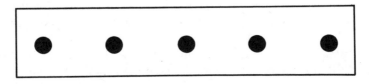

In this figure the three aspects of mind noted above are illustrated: separate forms, spaces around them, and the background environment in which form and emptiness occur. Can any one aspect be separated and meaningfully held independent of the whole?

Big mind may be beyond the span of focal attention, but it is not some article of metaphysical faith. Quite the contrary, in the words of a Tibetan text, "The nothingness in question is actually experience-able."[18] It can be discovered in an act of unitive knowledge, with a holistic awareness that does not try to pinpoint or analyze it as separate from anything, but rather knows it as "all of this."

In Buddhist psychology and practice, enlightenment is connected with the living realization of the encompassing mind. Mind in this sense is a psychological no-man's-land—a free, open reality without reference points, property boundaries, or trail markers. It is simply what allows things to stand out as they are in all their clarity. As a Tibetan text puts it,

> Since the foundation of sentient beings is without roots, the foundation of Buddha-knowledge is equally without roots. This rootlessness is the root of enlightenment.[19]

NOTES

1. James (1950), pp. 243–44.
2. Ibid., p. 244.
3. Ibid., p. 240.
4. Ibid., p. 255.
5. Gendlin (1962, 1978).
6. James (1950), p. 253.
7. Ibid., p. 252.
8. Quoted in James (1950), p. 255n.
9. Trungpa & Hookham (1974), p. 8.
10. S. Suzuki (1970), p. 124.
11. Trungpa, chap. 10, p. 128 of this volume.
12. Tarthang Tulku (1974), p. 181.
13. Tarthang Tulku (1975), pp. 160–61.
14. Capra (1975), p. 210.
15. For further discussion of this point, see Welwood (1977).
16. Suzuki (1970), p. 130.
17. Guenther (1975).
18. Guenther (1959), p. 54.
19. Guenther (1956), p. 269.

3
A View of Mind

Tarthang Tulku

Whatever our background or interests, whether religious or scientific, philosophical or psychological, it seems very important for us to understand the nature of mind. At first, mind seems so familiar, simple, easy. But the more we investigate and observe, the deeper and more mysterious mind becomes. If I enjoy something, it is through mind. If I suffer confusion, delusion, or frustration, it too is through mind. If I am enlightened, it is my mind that is enlightened. Since mind may manifest in all these ways, it seems essential for us to understand this mind.

The mind is actually very peculiar and unpredictable. It manifests many different forms and faces, and so we sometimes label it "consciousness" and sometimes "awareness." We might use many different words to describe the scope of its influence or to discuss its apparent functioning, but finally, it is very difficult to make mind tangible or to give it shape and to say solidly, "This is exactly what mind is."

Mind is also very precious. The more deeply we investigate it, the more we can discover a most comprehensive, universal kind of truth-knowledge. Therefore, the Buddha, the enlightened ones, the great teachers, and all those who have attained this knowledge first

This chapter is an edited transcription of a talk given by Tarthang Tulku at the Tibetan Nyingma Institute in Berkeley, California, February 1976.

observed their own mind. They did not blindly follow someone else's ideas but explored their minds to greater and greater depth until they discovered that the most valuable possession we have in this world is the human mind.

Our minds are, in a sense, already completely illumined, capable of seeing truth directly, but we fail to realize this. Instead, our tendency is to dissect each experience with our interpretations rather than experience the present moment directly, totally, and fully. In the same way, to describe mind we must always relate it to some other concept: for example, mind is like this, or consciousness is like that, awareness is good, ego is bad. We try to trap the mind into an imaginary net created by our interpretations of the external world. But as long as we attempt to discover mind through a series of images or concepts *about* mind, we may only be pointing to the mind that "thinks," the mind that sorts out information computer-style, or the subjective mind which is really just a reflection of the self-image.

A close analysis of the mind can illuminate the subtle details involved in discovering and distinguishing the various patterns and movements of mind. According to the Buddhist way of looking, however, mind is not just "being aware of" an object. Mind is much more than a collection of images, thoughts, and concepts. According to Buddhist psychology, the mind manifests over fifty specific mental events and at least eight different states of consciousness, but even these comprise just the surface level of mind. In the West, for example, it seems that when anyone talks about "mind," it is "mind-sensing" that is meant—relating to a series of perceptual processes such as seeing, hearing, smelling, tasting, touching, and conceptualizing. These are six types of "sense-consciousness" through which we perceive ourselves as a complex of thoughts, feelings, expectations, and physical sensations. Further, our cognitive images, interpretations, and concepts support an inner quality of very subtle, subjective "feeling-tones" which represent an accumulation of certain residues, memories, and conditioned habit patterns to which we react positively, negatively, or neutrally. Beyond this level of perceptual processes and interpretations—which corresponds roughly to the "subconscious" and which is always experienced by a subject   there is a more pervasive substratum of consciousness, termed *kun-gzhi* in Tibetan,* which is a kind of intrinsic awareness which is not involved

*The Sanskrit term is *alayavijnana*. See introduction (Ed.).

in any subject-object duality. Normally, however, we tend to label certain selective elements of our experience and categorize them in terms of a "subject" which perceives some "object" external to our "consciousness." But this sensory-intellectual awareness is not what Buddhism means by *mind*, for mind as such is not limited by any conceptions or ideas we might have about it.

Mind itself has no substance. It has no color and no shape. It has no form, no position, no characteristics, no beginning, no end. It is neither within nor without; it cannot be discovered as this or that thing; it is not mixed together with other things, yet it is not apart from them. This mind cannot be discovered, invented, destroyed, rejected, or accepted. It is beyond reasoning and so-called logical processes, beyond time and beyond all existence.

Through meditation, therefore, we try to understand the mind. In the beginning, we may focus on mind conceptually—what is mind? For some people this analysis is very valuable. It is an opportunity to ask questions, to search for answers, to watch the self-image, and to recognize certain personal problems. When we sit in meditation, for example, we can definitely see that we have thoughts and concepts. We can watch thoughts begin and end, and we can notice the interval between thoughts. We can clearly see how we process information from our senses, and how thoughts and emotions lead to judgments and negative attitudes. When the mind becomes still, thoughts are like drawings on water—before you finish, they flow away. Some people can see the thought as it arises; like snow in California, it's gone before it touches ground. This is one form of meditation in which we watch, observe, and analyze the patterns, inputs, outputs, and movements of the mind.

Each "type" of meditation has a different focus, depending on the development of the individual. Some people, for example, do not need to analyze their experience or the content of their thoughts. It is not necessary for them to engage in abstract thinking, read many books, or conceptualize very much; they can very simply and directly meditate. In meditation, the mind simply observes the natural process of the mind—beyond words and concepts, within the immediate, direct, and present moment of the experience.

Being aware of the "present" in this way does not necessarily involve an intellectual or conceptual analysis. This "present" is a different, more immediate type of mind-awareness. In everyday language, "awareness" generally means to be aware of some "thing." This is commonsense awareness, or "consciousness," which accumulates sensations, perceptions, images, feelings, thoughts, emotions, concepts, and cognitions. The meditative state of awareness, however, does not exist in consciousness. There is no need to look, imagine, think, or conceptualize in any particular way. As a living experience, natural awareness is simple and direct, open and responsive without concepts, words, images, or interpretations. Awareness takes place within the very first moment, not before and not after. It is immediate and spontaneous. There is no other "thing" to obscure the moment—neither a subject nor an object, neither time nor space.

This awareness cannot be interpreted conceptually, but is a natural openness that takes place when the mind is left to function freely, on its own, with no hindrances, interruptions, or distractions. The "field" of awareness is completely open "space," but this space is neither "outside" the body nor "inside" the mind. It is neither mental nor physical, and yet, at the same time, there is a deep, integrated sense of stillness, openness, and balance. This natural awareness becomes complete self-acceptance and generates a fresh new outlook all of its own. At the same time, the natural movement of this awareness eliminates all obstacles so that situations emerge clearly, just as they are, and the natural expression of this awareness provides the perspective which makes all positive action possible. In meditation, we are first trying to "pin down" mind, to hold it so that we can observe it. But finally, more advanced meditation says, "Let it go, give it up, cut it out. Just relax, without effort, completely natural. Just *be*, without holding, without concepts, without thoughts." This is the natural state of mind which is our own self-healer.

What we commonly believe to be mind, therefore, is not really "mind," but only the manifestation of various forms of "consciousness." Still, there is nothing we can point to and call "mind," and there is no way we can talk about or illustrate the nature of mind itself. But the deeper we investigate mind, the more we can find that every single thought and concept has a very special nature and quality. Problems and emotions become much easier, and we uncover more beauty, more energy, more clarity, and more joy. We can find this beauty or special quality within any kind of emotion or regular activity. Within our direct experience we can observe something interesting—a kind of knowledge, awareness, calmness, stillness, or balance, so that each moment becomes very unique and valuable.

4
The Meaning of Everything

Arthur J. Deikman

When I once told a friend it was my intention to explain consciousness, he exclaimed, "But consciousness is everything!" After thinking about it, I agreed with him. Thus my title, for I will present a model of consciousness that explains what pure awareness is, what the self is, and the "I" feeling, and the mystical experience, and meditation, and other phenomena as well. It is a serious attempt because this is what truly interests me. By its nature, it is also grandiose, for it is hard to see how one man can accomplish it all. However, I can make the attempt, and other people can complete the job.

AWARENESS

Upon reflection you will find that thoughts can cease for a brief while, that there can be silence and darkness and the temporary absence of images or memory patterns—any one component of our mental life can disappear, but awareness itself remains. Awareness is the ground of our conscious life, the background or field in which these elements exist. It is not the same thing as thoughts, sensations, or images. To experience this, try an experiment now. Look straight ahead and be aware of your conscious experience—then close your eyes. Awareness remains. "Behind" your thoughts and images is awareness. The distinction between awareness and the contents of awareness is crucial to the discussion that follows.

THE BIOSYSTEM

All around us is a world of structure. Brilliant, various, complex, the forms of our life surround us, and through them and in them we live. Most of these forms appear to be abiding structures or objects, like our bones, that are formed or are born, and disintegrate or die. We ourselves seem to be objects, and we think using a language that defines and creates relationships between objects. However, as we examine ourselves and other "objects" more closely, we begin to see them differently. Gardner Murphy[1] has pointed out that our concept of biological boundaries is a function of the particular time and size scale employed. Apparent boundaries are sensory phenomena in terms of those scales; they are not absolutes. For example, we are in constant exchange with the surrounding environment through respiration, eating, and elimination. Radioisotope studies have established the fact that our bodies are in a state of continual turnover of materials; we are not the same collection of atoms that we were a year ago. Bertalanffy summarizes, "As a result of its metabolism, which is characteristic of every living organism, its components are not the same from one moment to the next. Living forms are not in being, they are happening."[2] Bones and muscles are reinterpreted: "What are called structures are slow processes of long duration, functions are quick processes of short duration. If we say that a function, such as the contraction of a muscle, is performed by a structure, it means that a quick and short process wave is superimposed on a long-lasting and slowly running wave."[3] Activity, change, process—these are the "substance" of our bodies, of our world, of the universe. Gradients, not boundaries, determine form.

Furthermore, our individual organisms exist within a meshwork of higher levels of organization that ultimately includes all individual life forms and our planet itself. A swarm of bees furnishes an example of two levels of organization—each bee is an individual, but the swarm functions together as an organism in its own right. Its individual members cooperate in fulfilling a function possible only for the swarm, but at the same time necessary to the members. That swarm is part of a larger biosystem unity that includes the flowering plants that the bees pollinate. As you begin to picture the dazzling spectrum of organizational hierarchies that make up our biosystem and the cosmic system of which it is a part, it is not hard to perceive that we are part of one system that extends throughout the universe. In this view the biosystem is a whole, and the distinction between what is usually called biological (organic) and the inorganic is neither necessary nor basic. In what follows I shall use the term biosystem to refer to the entire range of world components that we apprehend through our sensory apparatus.

AWARENESS AND ORGANIZATION

As I noted earlier, a major problem in thinking about consciousness has been the mixing together of awareness with mind functions, such as calculating, sensations, memory, perception, and symbol formation. It is plausible to assume that mind functions are performed in the brain, which is the thinking organ. On the other hand, I would like to suggest that awareness, as distinct from the contents of awareness, is not a special form of sensation, with a particular receptor organ or some other neurological system responsible, nor is it any kind of neural response at all. Rather than being the product of a particular neural circuit, awareness is the *organization* of the biosystem; that is, awareness *is* the "complementary" aspect of that organization, its psychological equivalent.

COMPLEMENTARITY

Niels Bohr introduced the term *complementarity*[4] to account for the fact that two different conditions of observation yielded conclusions that were conceptually incompatible, i.e., light behaved like a particle on one occasion and like a wave on another. He suggested that there is no intrinsic incompatibility because the two aspects were functions of different conditions of observation, and no experiment could be devised that could demonstrate both aspects in a single observational condition. Similarly, the special characteristic of mental life, e.g., freedom from space considerations, is in apparent contradiction with the space characteristics of physical objects. The two realms of the mental and the biological are separate spheres of observation, and may be said to represent complementary aspects of the biological system that constitutes an individual. The conditions of observation of the physical world are those of the sensory apparatus (vision, hearing, touch, smell, taste), whereas the mental is "observed" by the nonsensory (memory, thought, imagery, and "intuitive" processes).

ORGANIZATION

Questions that arise immediately are: "What is meant by organization?" and "If awareness or consciousness is the complementary aspect of organization, what is it that is organized?" Let us say that an organism is "any thing or structure composed of distinct parts and so constituted that the functioning of the parts and their relation to one another is governed by their relation to the whole" (Webster's 2nd, unabridged, 1961, p. 1719). Relation is "any aspect or quality that can be predicted only if two or more things are taken together" (ibid., p. 2102). Thus, we are talking about elements that are mutually interdependent. In this connection, Bertalanffy has specifically defined the characteristics of the biological organism: (1) the organism is a complex of elements in mutual interaction; (2) the behavior of an individual element is influenced by the state of the whole organism; (3) the whole exhibits properties absent from its isolated parts; and (4) a biological organism is a basically active system—it has an autonomous activity, and is not basically reflexive or basically reactive.

Are the elements that are organized mental or physical? This question is dualistic and assumes a separation of mind and matter. In terms of the hypothesis I am presenting, the answer would be that the elements organized are both mental and physical, because the mental and the physical are hypothesized as being "complementary" aspects of the biological system.

On the biological side, the elements of the person system range from such low-level elements as chemical entities to the higher-order, more strictly biological elements of muscles, nerves, bones, and skin, and to the still higher-level components of respiratory, digestive, vascular, and motor systems. On the psychological side, ideas, affects, and sensations are at one level, and memories, thinking, and self-concepts are at a higher level. On the biological side, the organization of these elements is life; on the psychological side, the organization is awareness.

Thus, when I state that awareness *is* organization, I do not mean that consciousness is the "experience" of organization. The latter phrase implies a separate system that senses consciousness, the way we see light and smell odors. Rather, I mean to say that awareness is the complementary aspect of organization—it is organization, itself, in its mental dimension.

LOCALIZATION

The biosystem is a totality embracing our entire planet and the solar system. Awareness is the organization of that continuous system. It follows that awareness is not localized. The awareness that each individual believes to be his own is, in fact, an awareness that extends throughout existence, for it is the organization of reality. Since our thought contents are localized by the particular groups of perceptual and cognitive systems that constitute individual persons, we have taken for granted that the awareness that underlies our mental processes is localized as well. For example, our visual activity is usually experienced as being identical with awareness. However, if you close your eyes, you will recognize that your awareness and your visual field are not the same. Try it now. Once again, close your eyes and ask yourself what constitutes your awareness. With your eyes closed, you will tend to identify awareness with sounds and body sensations. If next you imagine these sounds and sensations to be absent, you will appreciate the fact that awareness is something other than sensations or thoughts. The sense that my awareness is my own is due to mixing the sensations and thoughts, which are indeed personal, with awareness itself, which is universal. Expressed in the more abstract terms I used earlier, the conclusion is that our individual centers of organizing activity are located within the general field of organization that is awareness.

ACTIVE ENERGY

Let us now go a step further and consider a departure from traditional assumptions concerning matter and energy. It is a basic axiom of contemporary physics that energy has no direction nor structural tendency of its own. Toulmin[5] has discussed the historical development of this concept of inert or passive matter, and has shown it to be an assumption. Continuing from his discussion, I propose that matter is intrinsically active in the direction of increasing organization. By this I mean that progressive organization is a basic characteristic of matter, like mass. As a corollary, increasing organization is the intrinsic aim of energy.

Such a concept is not compatible with our ordinary assumption that matter is purposeless, inert, and passive. Since the seventeenth century, we have looked at the elements of reality and expected to find that events are the product of preexisting vectoral forces, acting on inert entities. Only man seems to have prefigured goals toward which his actions tend. We regard it as erroneous and primitive to give to inanimate or lower animate forms the characteristics of our own mental life. However, we have not really been able to avoid doing so, because our analysis of the physical world is based on the psychological. For example, the concept of force is derived from our experience of our own willed action. At the same time, because we associate aim and direction with our own will and desires, the notion that energy might have an intrinsic aim (as postulated by Freud for mental energy) appears very strange, for that would make energy "human."

Likewise, our belief in the passivity of matter and the directionless nature of energy resides in our experience with inanimate objects: a stone does not move unless we push it. This assumption of inertness works well for analyzing problems within a particular spatial class and a particular time span. Because of these temporal and spatial limits, we may not be in a position to observe the "activities" of inanimate objects. However, if we increase our time scale and widen our spatial scale, it might appear that inanimate matter moves toward a goal similar to the animate. For example, from a long-term scale we are aware of what appears to be a direction of change that produces life forms. Increasing diversity and increasingly complex organization appear to be a trend that is discernable biologically, sociologically, and psychologically. We have given the name "evolution" to the phenomenon. That this phenomenon has been apparent to man for a long time is witnessed by the ancient Vedanta and Buddhist texts, as well as by the more recent conceptual efforts of Darwin, Erikson,[6] Bertalanffy, Piaget,[7] Polanyi,[8] Teilhard de Chardin,[9] and Spitz.[10]

VARIABLE AWARENESS

If awareness is organization and thus extends throughout the universe, present in varying degrees everywhere, why is it that sometimes awareness is vivid and total (as in phases of meditation), but at other times is absent, for example, when we are intent on an intellectual calculation or absorbed in a conversation or a movie? Traditionally, psychologists have tended to handle such problems by falling back on the searchlight model. The field of our attention is likened to the field of a searchlight that illuminates one area after the other. But if awareness is the searchlight and we can be aware of being aware, what illuminates the searchlight?

The problem can be solved if we define mind functions as organizing activities. Thus, perceptual processes organize stimulus inputs into series of gestalts, and thinking activity organizes events in terms of meanings of different kinds—philosophical, arithmetic, and symbolic. Let us now compare the biosystem to a pond of water. When the system is quiet, not occupied with the organizing activities of various mental functions, the surface of the pond is smooth, still, and reflective. At such times we exist in pure awareness, in a state of relationships, of organization. When the organizing activity of thought functions take place, the surface of the pond becomes transformed into patterns of ripples, as if a stone had been thrown into the quiet water. When the activity ceases, the surface of the pond is smooth and reflecting once again. We do not have to postulate a superobserver of both awareness and thoughts if we recognize that awareness depends on the state of the pond, or biosystem; thought functions are the organization's activity. There is no experiencing agency; the "experience" *is* the state or the activity, as the case may be.

One may ask, "If awareness is coextensive with everything, why is it that we can lose consciousness?" The answer is that when we lose consciousness, the individual receptor-organizing region ceases to function. Awareness, itself, does not cease, but the thought organization, including memory, of the individual person ceases to operate. When that happens, there can be no local (individual) articulation or memory of awareness. At such times, awareness cannot be known in that location. To put it in slightly different terms, the individual person is the means whereby reality articulates itself.

Mystics have stated that through mankind, God is able to know Himself. Perhaps what basically has blocked our understanding of such pronouncements has been our automatic assumption that the feeling of awareness is as localized as our personal perceptual system. However, once we discriminate between the general awareness and local mental contents, the puzzling concepts of mystics become more clear.

It should be noted that, in terms of this model, the awareness of a tree is not different from our own, but continuous with it, because awareness is the organization of the entire system. Awareness probably cannot be *known* or articulated in the system of the tree, but the awareness of the tree is not less intense or less rich than our own. We are not *more* aware because we are more complex; awareness is not a quantitative function, not a mind-stuff that accumulates as forms become more complex. Rather, awareness is the mental aspect of the organization of the entire biosystem. It is "known" only in those locales whose systems of organization permit "knowledge" of awareness.

Ordinarily, we do not recognize "our" awareness for what it is. The awakening to the true nature of this awareness constitutes the enlightenment of a host of mystic disciplines. As illustrated by the Zen monastery, these disciplines all feature techniques, conditions, attitudes, and living conditions designed to bring about a subsidence of the thinking activities that take the place of awareness. These thinking activities are individual, in that they are the activity of the individual center of organization of each individual person. Insofar as the person is activated to individual goals, thought activity persists and is dominant. However, the cultivation of selflessness can decrease the goal activity of the individual. Individual activity then subsides relative to the general field of organization—awareness itself.

The classical meditation disciplines were developed as a means of heightening awareness by subduing thought activity. Meditation, properly done, facilitates a shift from individual-centered activity to the general field of organization. Here, too, giving up individual striving (e.g., for spiritual advancement) can be a special problem. Furthermore, although it is not too hard to fill one's mind completely with a particular percept, such as breathing sensations, it is hard to have that perception and not work at it, not apply the mind to it, not be exercising the mind muscle, as it were, on that percept. When this active attention or concentrating can cease, then the sense of personal boundary that is associated with the individual's organizing activity fades away, and limitless awareness grows clear, vivid, and dominant. It is this limitless awareness that constitutes the unity experience of the higher mystical states.

THE "I" FEELING AND THE SELF

The self is that collection of attributes that identifies me as a particular human being. "Myself" is my body, my memories, my personality, my fears, my assets—all the things that constitute who I am in the eyes of others and of myself. We can understand the self as being a particular field of organization for the individual. The limits of the self are the experienced limits of the individual; those based on sensory perception, language, and the space-time of the object world. The self is all those things that I consciously include in the zone of my personal organization.

But what shall we make of the "I" feeling? Is it just another sensation, some spurious illusion based on a synthesis of sensory impressions? Try and locate the feeling or sensation inside yourself that corresponds to the word "I." For example, if you say such phrases to yourself as "I am going to go on reading this paper" or "I want a new car," the referent to the "I" is the feeling of intention, of will, of urge, or of desire. This "I" of "I want" is a tension along a particular axis, a force impelling in a particular direction, the intensity of which varies, but the basic quality of which remains the same. The "I want" feeling is the organizing force, itself, acting in the specific locus or node of an individual organism. Each of us is a circumscribed area of organizing activity, expressing the same organizing tendency or force that I have hypothesized to be a basic attribute of mass/energy. Awareness is the organization of the system but the organizing force, itself, specifically active in our own local region, is what we experience as the "I" or "I want."

However, there is another type of "I" that we can notice. This "I" emerges in periods when our urges do not dominate our awareness. Then "I" feels like an abiding, resting awareness, featureless and unchanging, a central something that is witness to all events, exterior and interior. It is the "I" of "I am." This "I" is identical with awareness. In most cases it is awareness circumscribed by the beliefs and assumptions that form actual barriers separating local awareness (local organization) from universal awareness (universal organization).

Beliefs and assumptions act as barriers because they are mental activities, action currents transforming the still water of awareness into waves and eddies. To extend the metaphor even further, it would seem that some type of spatial correspondence exists such that the belief that one is part of all mankind locates the delimiting barrier at a "wider" periphery than the belief that one is totally separate from other persons. This effect of a belief occurs because the psychological event is an event in the biosystem, not an event isolated in a "mental" world. Thus, a belief has a substantial existence, although that existence is not to be defined as physical. The physical and the mental are both aspects of the biosystem; they are a translation or manifestation of an entity that is basic to both. Reality is neither one nor the other.

OVERVIEW

Organizing activity takes place continuously and throughout the universe because it is a basic characteristic of mass/energy. Each person is a manifestation of that same activity, as if he were an eddy in a river. The organization of the entire system is awareness. We confuse our local mind-functions with the general awareness and believe we are separate selves. To the extent that we separate ourselves conceptually from other people, we perform an action that actually delimits our awareness by forming a biosystem barrier that interferes with the experience of oneness. Caught in the illusion of separateness, we engage in actions that bring suffering to ourselves and others.

In those cases in which, by means of an arduous discipline, a powerful drug, or an extreme life crisis, the delimiting barriers are temporarily dissolved, the individual awareness becomes the general awareness. These events of barrier dissolution constitute the phenomena of mystical experiences, provide the basis for religious metaphysics, and introduce into our lives the reality of the transpersonal.

NOTES

1. Murphy (1956).
2. Bertalanffy (1952), p. 124.
3. Ibid., p. 134.
4. Bohr (1958).
5. Toulmin (1967).
6. Erikson (1950).
7. Piaget (1954).
8. Polanyi (1958).
9. Teilhard de Chardin (1959).
10. Spitz (1959).

II
The Question of Personal Identity

Introduction

Careful attention to one's experiencing not only may begin to open up a sense of a wider awareness, but also may bring into question the nature of one's personality—who and what one is. Whereas Western psychology has traditionally accepted the reality of our conventional self-identity, Eastern traditions all point to a way of knowing and being that is not dependent on this "smaller self." Of course, the Eastern traditions often differ in their view of this wider sense of being. Hindu traditions speak about *atman*, a larger self beyond the ego, which is not a self in the conventional sense, but rather the essence of reality within us, our basic nature. Buddhism, by contrast, speaks of *egolessness*, meaning that reality is directly available to our perception and intelligence without having to be interpreted through our personality or filtered through our self-centered concerns. But in any case, the Eastern traditions seem to be pointing in a similar direction: it is the preoccupation and extreme concern with oneself that creates the bitter human legacy of misery, confusion, violence, and neurosis.

The great difficulty that most Western psychologists have with the Eastern notion of transcending self stems from their assumption that self-transcendence would lead to one of two states, neither of which our culture regards as wholesome: (1) psychosis or regression, the loss of one's boundaries, such that one lives in a continual state of panic and insecurity about threats to one's existence; or (2) asceticism, in which one totally abandons the demands of ordinary life, including passion, pleasure, and successful participation in social and economic realities. In fact, however, neither of these two options must follow from a proper understanding and realization of what the Buddhists call egolessness.

Transcending the preoccupation with self need not lead to psychosis or other-wordly asceticism because it does not cancel out the ordinary level of functioning. One can still function as an ordinary person, one can still pursue ordinary life aims, but one need not identify with and fixate upon one's *ideas* about this self. One may realize that the notion of self is simply a convention which, like language, is good for some purposes, but very inadequate for other purposes.

As Abraham Maslow realized in the later years of his career, beyond the basic needs for food, shelter, companionship, and even self-actualization, human beings also have a need for what he called *self-transcendence.*[1] A Buddhist might add that the reason human beings have this latter need is because self-transcendence is their very nature in the first place—experience already transcends the self and self-limited concerns. William James would seem to concur with this statement in his analysis of how the structure of experiencing is always a going *beyond*:

> We live, as it were, upon the front edge of an advancing wave-crest....Our fields of experience have no more definite boundaries than have our fields of view. Both are fringed forever by a *more* that continuously develops, and that continuously supersedes them as life proceeds.[2]

Some people may require a whole lifetime to recognize this need for self-transcendence, having to fulfill all their "lower" needs first, until they realize that no matter how many personal needs are satisfied, they still remain restless, seeking something more in life. Or it may be possible to realize the reality of egolessness on the spot, as an immediate, ongoing fact. This latter realization seems to be the point of the Eastern disciplines.

As William James so masterfully showed,[3] a close attention to the process of experiencing fails to reveal the ego or self we think ourselves to be. Wilson Van Dusen's opening chapter in this section points in a similar direction, with a very sensitive phenomenological study of what goes into such a simple act as wanting to say something. By looking into this phenomenon closely, one discovers that neither is one in control of what one wants to say, nor do one's words ever convey the full process of experiencing that is going on at any moment. If the individual is transcended by his very experience in every direction, if one cannot even grasp one's own consciousness and experience, then how can one claim to be tied to a self-identity at all?

Thomas Hora takes this problem beyond the questioning stage and points out that we act out symbolically in our bodily life the illusory reality of a separate self. Insofar as this self-concept is out of touch with the way reality works, beyond concepts, it imposes disabilities on the human organism, which show up in physical and mental disease. Hora also points beyond the emphasis developed in humanistic psychology on "self-actualization" toward the necessity for a "realization of reality," which is the basis for genuine art, understanding, and love.

Washburn and Stark very clearly describe the nature of the illusion involved in belief in an ego. They point out that it is egocentricity, the habitual attempt to create a sense of solid existence and self-importance that creates the project of identifying with an ego, a limited and defined image of oneself. Such an attempt is bound to fail and produce great suffering in that the nature of consciousness itself is an open, reflecting awareness which can never be reduced to any fixed content of consciousness such as the self-image.

Tarthang Tulku explores more experientially how the attachment to self-image works. He points out how the self-image creates many emotional and psychological disturbances, and indicates how it is possible at any moment to step out of this attachment and to experience oneself in a more open and balanced way.

In the final chapter of this section, Ken Wilber and I explore the similarities and differences in the way the ego is viewed in Western and Eastern psychology. Reducing the Freudian notion of ego strength to its simplest terms, we suggest that psychoanalysis and Buddhism both attempt to heal the splitting of life experience into two alienated halves, I and It. However, although Western clinical psychologists may recognize how this split leads to neurosis within the intrapsychic domain, they generally do not take account of a more basic split between self and world, which limits one's ability to contact the full richness of life. It is suggested that the Buddhist understanding of egolessness allows a fuller attunement with life, and that meditation is important for helping one to realize what egolessness is. This question leads into the third section, in which the role and function of meditation is considered.

NOTES

1. Maslow (1969). See also Roberts (1978).
2. James (1976), pp. 34-35.
3. James (1950), chapter 10.

5

The Mystery of Ordinary Experiencing

Wilson Van Dusen

Let's see—I am puzzled what to say. My fingers are clamped over my mouth and I stare at the things in my study with a hard feeling of determination. My head feels hot, as it does when I'm concentrating. What am I to say about ordinary experiencing? I scan several notes scattered on my desk. Still the fingers clamped over my mouth and the feelings of hard determination. Bits of ideas come to consciousness. "Why not start out with—an example of ordinary experience? No. That moves too fast. It sweeps over a number of mysteries as though each was understood." I sit back in my chair and swallow. Now a single finger is clamped over my lips. "I'll have to do both—show the range of things, and then show how each is not fully comprehended."

The whole tenor of this experience was set by the felt need to write. The fingers *clamped* over my mouth were a spontaneous outward representation of my state. The tone of the state was hard, determined. Yet I did not know what to say. The hard gesture reflected the determination (clamped) as well as not knowing what to say (lips covered). Later, when I was more nearly ready to write, there was only one finger guarding the mouth. Staring at the things in the study, searching notes, and scanning ideas that came to me all had the same implications. My response to a felt problem (how to write of ordinary experience) was rapidly and spontaneously represented in a number of ways (hand on mouth, staring, searching notes, checking ideas coming to me, hot head, feeling of hard determination). What I could not see at first later emerged as a conflict in directions—whether to describe the whole flow of experience or to capture one bit of it accurately. The response to the conflict was to move back in my chair (association—sit back and take another look) and swallow (association—try to digest this). The resolving of two trends into one came as I clamped one finger over my mouth. The solution was to accept both trends as part of one.

What I have briefly described was an ordinary experience. The first thing to note is that it represents itself spontaneously and simultaneously on several levels at once—gesture, bodily sensations, inward feeling, actions taken, ideas emerging, self-reflection, and decision making. This in itself is quite remarkable. We are something that can represent itself in several ways simultaneously. This occurs whether we pay much attention to these ways or not. In fact, we often focus on one ("I wonder what I should say?") and hardly notice the other representations. In other words, though we exist on several levels simultaneously, we may choose to focus on one or more of these as the real, main, or only level.

This limiting of self to a single prominent level is done so commonly that many forget the greater complexity of experience. Because we explain ourselves in verbal terms, the verbal level has become preeminent. In the above instance, if asked, "What are you doing?" I would have been inclined to answer, "Just working on a problem." The verbal answer is coded shorthand for a complex process all of whose parts are not necessarily even known. The reliance on the verbal as the main or only level of internal processes leads some to think that thought is just unspoken words. Let us focus closer on them.

Phenomenology represents a serious effort to capture human experience just as it is. When the effort of phenomenology is focused on a tiny portion of human experience it acts like a psychological microscope. When I focus the microscope on the formation of words in my head, the bit I would choose is the sudden appearance of ideas. What is it really like when an idea becomes conscious enough that it can be said to myself internally, or externally spoken of?

"I am now formulating this sentence." I felt the general tenor of this sentence before I had finished writing the one before it. It felt like a simple declarative beginning—almost too simple, rather naked and alone. I began to hear it inwardly before it was set down. It was as though I were listening to someone speak. The tenor of the words was felt before they were said, the laying out of meaning was there before they were spoken in my head, and they were said in my head before they were written. These are like successive waves of clarification, each one running over the one before. The whole process took perhaps less than a second. The ending of the sentence also trailed off in a slightly scary feeling. It was as though the gap from the end of one sentence to the next was a little frightening until the next one came.

Focus your own phenomenological microscope on the simple process of thinking up a sentence. See if the process isn't something like the following:

There is a feeling of a need for something.

There is a background feeling it is coming.

The feeling becomes a presentiment of meaning.

The felt meaning germinates into internal speech.

The internal speech lays out a sentence—the end of which is felt while the first part is being heard.

If the sentence is to be spoken, the not-yet-spoken parts are going through stages of being felt, emerging understanding, being heard, spoken.

After the sentence there is a trailing off of feeling, meaning, like an afterglow.

All this may seem like pedantic detailing. Yet it has profound implications. What I would normally think I thought up is really the result of a more complex growth of feelings into words. The feelings are mine, I guess. I have so little idea of their nature, structure, origin, or future directions that it is perhaps presumptuous to say they are mine. It might be more accurate to say I am theirs!

Furthermore, if we sort through the catalog of processes we have cleverly named as existing in people's experience, all of them stem from feeling. Attitudes are a more or less permanent feeling toward things. This feeling-attitude tends to condition response. Action is preceded by feeling. We will see later in the hypnogogic state that feeling can be seen shaping words or images. Fantasy tells the story of feeling. Logical processes are a kind of guardedness and structuring of feeling. Memory is very much based on feeling.

It might help clarify the whole catalog of internal processes if they were seen as points in a continuum of differentiation. The vaguest feeling is the undifferentiated end of the continuum. Specific thoughts, words, memories, images, acts are the multiple outputs of the differentiated end of the continuum. These multiple outputs are related (words in my head are related to words said are related to acts, etc.). Essentially it is the underpinnings, the undifferentiated source of these endproducts, that is most elusive to us. We more or less identify with the differentiated endproducts. Some identify with these products to the exclusion of their feeling source. As we look closer at processes that primarily represent the life of feeling (fantasy, hypnogogic state, dreams), we have more difficulty identifying with this feeling base as our own making. When the feeling base handily spins off symbolic ideas and images it becomes even more difficult to name it as our own doing. Yet, if it is not fully our own doing, then neither are its products (our thoughts, actions, etc.).

The issue is where one will pin one's personal identity. What can one say "Yea, that is myself!" to? If I say, "I make these words," then I must defend control over the whole feeling process underlying them. Yet we will see later that feeling can also speak symbolic ideas that few even understand! It is enough to indicate clearly at this juncture that the I—what I really call me-mine and take responsibility for—is best not limited yet. It is a fundamental issue. This is no minor, simple question. One fundamental answer that emerges from the study of many myths, religions, and one's own experience is: let the personal identity be everything and nothing simultaneously. When one carefully explores the boundaries of personal identity they expand beyond all expectations. The broadening of these boundaries may well be the root of wisdom.

When some feel the necessary humility of leaving open their identity, they feel to have a name, to say I, reflects a lack of wisdom. I can bear a name, and sign checks for convenience, and yet not feel bound by this punctilious boundary of self. The book has a cover and a definite title, and yet may talk of remote worlds. We are such books that we can be circumscribed by titles and yet understood as not circumscribed at all. The title is not the limitation, but the way we conceive of our self is.

A very simple and ordinary example that disturbs the conception of our boundaries is the way we are made up of our ancestors. One can conceive of one's hereditary parents and grandparents almost like curious assigned data or a social security number. Yet a careful examination of personal experience shows individuals to be at least partly shaped by their parents and significant others. The perceived parent, the one experienced and lived with, is introjected and woven into the fabric of one's experience. This is both the perceived parent and the real parent. Insofar as the mother is well perceived, it is more of the real mother that is introjected. The individual is also shaped around what the parents transmitted genetically. Beyond the obvious eye and hair color, and the like, we don't know how much of our psychic experience is involved in this transmission. An individual is also shaped in part by the cultural traditions and even subtle mores of the groups he has lived with. In view of this, it would be more accurate to say that, at least in part, we are the confluence of many others. All those "others" can never be fully catalogued. The confluence of their influences is part of the vast, unknown, undifferentiated background world of the individual. The differentiated individual is the resultant. We are coming under the influence of many others by our increasing participation in the media. How much we are shaped by the cultural matrices we exist in is only now becoming clear with the growth of anthropology and sociology.

However we split it, the boundaries of the self are relatively vast and unclear. But for appropriate convenience we set them at the skin. What is inside the skin is mine, outside it is other. Since I perceive and react to others and am really compounded of others in several ways, this skin boundary should be viewed as a useful fiction. It is the same as saying a book is bound by its covers. This is true enough if one wants to take the most limited view of the book, but it overlooks its contents, where they came from and the effects they might have on the worlds of others.

The apparently simple issue of what is the boundary of the individual is best left open. Any closing of it is an artificial limiting of our conception. The individual is at the confluence of heredity, parents, significant others, his culture, language, schooling, and the media. He is transcended by these, and in many real respects he is their resultant. When we look closely at the simplest of human experiences we find the so-called individual also transcended within by sensations he doesn't plan and by feelings that seem the general background and source of his experiencing. Consciousness is the running, moment-by-moment bit of clarity and awareness at the confluence of these forces. One's own words emerge out of a sea of feeling—meaning—presentiments. We are the meeting place of at least a number of transcendencies. The discovery of this should not be a matter of great pride or despair. It is just things as they are.

I once worked with a man in a legal experiment on the effects of the drug LSD. We were in a relatively barren hospital room. It took me a while to discover that the man was going around the room quietly naming things. "That is a chair," he would say to himself. Under LSD everything had become too lively and a little frightening. He pinned them down and limited their existence by naming them. He might as well have said, "You are *only* a chair." I fear our hanging an identity on the sequential confluence of transcendent experiences does about the same thing. Naming implies that we have comprehended, circumscribed, delimited, put down. Naming the chair doesn't mean I really understand how it is made or what it is. It says, in effect, you are of the class of things I've seen before. Of course self or personal identity is also of the class of things I've seen before—whatever it is!

But watch my fingers writing. Theoretically I know how they move. Brain to nerve to muscle, etc. Brilliant. I theoretically understand how I move! Yet secretly I don't really understand brain, nerve, or muscle. Practically speaking, do I know how I move? Well, let's see. I feel the finger pressing the pencil, moving it over the paper. The movements are very fast, but barely able to keep up with inner speech. I pause a moment, resting the hand, watching to see what else will come out of inner speech. I seem to be just this sequence of experiences: feeling, to inner speech, to finger movements. I am this coming together, whatever it is! This confluence seems to be conscious of the meeting. The confluence is experiencing is consciousness. I am the confluence that is consciousness that is experiencing what is here. Yet when this consciousness examines in detail any aspect of its experience it does not fully comprehend or rule it.

Our experience has flowing into it more than we generally understand. It is the same with our body. Though we live in it, move it, and indeed are it, we don't fully understand a single organ of it, nor indeed a single cell. Whatever this experiencing is called man, it is only beginning to open up the nature of its experience because it is transcended at every hand. Though it can name experiencing or consciousness, these too it does not understand.

If you have followed my arguments, you may have several possible reactions:

1. You can't really see that anything transcends you. In which case I would charge you to examine fully a single thought as it emerges. If your thoughts are too fast for you, try to slow them down, and examine several hundred of them. If you get handy at that, then examine examining. Tiring of that, try to hold one thought in mind for five minutes and record all the places your mind wandered off to and try to see the blanknesses that precede wandering.

2. You are puzzled that I seem to call into question conventional ideas of the boundary of personal identity. It will not be nearly so difficult or threatening to explore the further operations of mind if the boundaries of self are left open.

3. You feel bothered, or better yet crushed, by the idea that you are transcended at every quarter. One becomes accustomed to this, and, like open boundaries, it removes impediments.

So much for very ordinary experience that represents itself and exists on many levels, in many ways easily and spontaneously—whatever *it* is.

6
Beyond Self

Thomas Hora

When the ancient Chinese scholar Yen Hui was considering becoming court advisor to the ill-famed ruler of his time, he came to his teacher Chuang-tzu for advice. Chuang-tzu warned him that he is in great danger of being beheaded unless he learns "mind-fasting." Heedful of the advice given him, Yen Hui retired to practice "mind-fasting" in accordance with his teacher's instructions.

Three years later, Yen Hui returned to his teacher saying that he thinks he is ready for his assignment. The master challenged him to prove it. Whereupon Yen Hui said: "Before I disciplined myself in mind-fasting as you instructed me, I was fully conscious of being Yen Hui. Now that I have perfected myself in the discipline, I realize that from the beginning there never was a Yen Hui."

The master said: "Yes, you realized 'hsu,' which translated means 'Emptiness.'"

James Legge, *The Texts of Taoism*

Voodoo is a primitive tribal method by which illness, suffering, and on occasions even death is inflicted upon a condemned individual. This is accomplished by sticking pins into an effigy doll. The amazing effects of this method demonstrate the vulnerability of man in whose consciousness the *body as the "I am"* represents primary reality. In the consciousness of the victim the voodoo doll becomes an extension and a representative of the *self*, and whatever happens to this image is experienced by the victim personally and directly. This to such extent that medical science has been found in some instances to be helpless in counteracting the "spell." Voodoo is effective as long as there is a shared belief in the reality of assumed notions. The voodoo doll is the shared symbol of the victim's self.

Symbols are representations of man's notions about Reality. *Symbols are products of man's desire to give form to that which forever must remain formless.* In human consciousness the body tends to be a symbol of the self. Body sensations thus become symbolic thoughts (dreams) about reality of the self. Human thinking is prevalently dedicated to proving the reality of one important basic assumption. Namely, that man exists as a separate and self-sustaining entity in time and space. In other words, human thinking is prevalently preoccupied with *self-confirmation.* This type of thinking is always circular and it circles around its own hypothetical center.

Bodily sensations tend to reveal in symbolic fashion self-confirmatory desires. The body becomes the symbolic manifestation of thought mistaking itself for reality. In other words, the body reveals man's inclination to view reality from that center which calls itself the self.

The question may be asked: What is that center around which the self-centered man is centered? Where is this center located? What does it consist of? And how does it come into being?

The self is a conceptual center of being, built up from accumulated assumptions about the nature of reality as mediated by the sensory apparatus and discursive thought. Concepts are statements *about* reality. They have no reality of their own and their location is in that unknown place which is called memory and mind. Thus the self, or the "I am" can neither be localized nor does it have actual reality of its own. Yet ordinary man spends most of his life in an unceasing effort to confirm this abstraction as a concrete reality. The need to confirm the reality of the self is in itself evidence of a lurking doubt existing in the awareness of man.

It is, then, this disquieting, lurking doubt which underlies the ubiquitous human inclination toward self-assertiveness. When self-assertive man becomes aware of the suffering which he brings upon himself and others, he attempts to behave in self-restraining or self-effacing ways. However, self-restraint is but the assertion of the self against itself. Therefore it only leads to further suffering. For both, self-assertiveness and self-restraint are both ignoring what really is by being preoccupied with what "should be." *Ignorance is that mental activity which ignores what really is.*

In contemplating human existence and social life as an endless scramble and struggle with the problem of self-confirmation, one is faced with a fountain of despair, conflict, and suffering.

The tragic element of the human condition is rooted in that cognitive deficiency which underlies the desire of man to confirm his self as reality. Since the self is that which "should be," it is not possible to confirm it constructively. For only the confirming of *what really is* can be constructive. The effort at confirming what "should be" is therefore destructive of reality. Consequently it is pathogenic. *Disease is that shadow which the "I am" casts upon existence.* For "I am" to be reality the world must be destroyed. The acute psychotic experience of world destruction is the birth of the delusion concerning an autonomous, exclusive "I am."

One young man, teetering on the brink of a psychotic break, was so involved in self-confirmatory preoccupations in the form of grandiose boasting that when he tried not to boast, he became plagued with painful erections. When the erections were understood as vicarious boasting on a sexual plane, he lost his erections but began to feel cramps in his lower extremities. When these were understood as body language saying "I am," these also left him. At this point, he began to feel a need to tighten his shoe laces repeatedly to keep himself "together," that is, to feel himself as a self.

Suffering is the consequence of that cognitive deficiency in man which gives rise to self-confirmatory desires. Self-confirmatory strivings keep man in a state of ignorance by inducing him to ignore that which really is. Physical suffering is the body's way of being in the process of confirming itself. The "body-mind" speaks directly prior to verbal language. Language is one step removed from the event of self-confirmation taking place in the organism.

As long as artistic expression is of self-confirmatory nature, it is not truly creative and has little integrative value. True art is expressive of reality. Which does not mean that it is of necessity realistic in the conventional sense of the word. True art illumines the hitherto unseen. It broadens man's consciousness and cognition. It is therefore integrative both for the artist and the observer. Creativity has its meaning in illuminating man's relationship to his ontological ground. The creative artist helps man to see and worship.

When man becomes aware of the suffering inherent in idolatry of the self, or the other, or of what "seems to be" and what "should be," he discovers that "self-realization" is an altogether misleading idea, both in art as well as in psychiatry. *Health is contingent not on self-realization but on realization of reality.*

Selfishness, indifference, and inconsiderateness are revealed as consequences of insufficient cognition prevailing in common man. Self-centered man calculates, plots, and schemes his own self-confirmation. In the process he unfailingly hurts and harms himself and others. It seems that most human suffering reveals the presence of self-centeredness and calculative thinking.

Enlightened man transcends his self in "seeing the truth of what is." In this process of losing himself he finds that which is real. He heals, that is, he becomes whole (holy) in his "at-one-ment" with reality. The seer becomes the seeing and the seeing becomes the seen. Love is thus *re-cognized* (rediscovered) to be a mode of cognition. *Love is found to be that intelligence which forever reveals itself as understanding.*[1]

In the experience of understanding the true nature of reality is revealed. In it there is neither "self" nor "other"; there is only the all-transcending timeless process manifesting itself in that "field of phenomena" which man is the medium of.

Self-centered consciousness does not discern the ground of being. Interpersonal consciousness is focused on the interaction of the self and the other. It equally fails to see that background without which foreground could not appear. The interpersonal focus ignores the truth of what really is because it is concerned with the relationship of the self to the other. It does not realize that the self is the same as the other, since the other is but an other self. In the realm of understanding there is neither "self" nor "other," there is only that which really is. *Love is self-less.* It is that *background of harmony* which is obscured but also revealed by the foreground of the discordant self.

NOTE

1. Hora (1961).

From John Welwood, ed., The Meeting of the Ways: Explorations in East/West Psychology (Schocken Books, 1979).

7

Ego, Egocentricity, and Self-transcendence: A Western Interpretation of Eastern Teaching

Michael C. Washburn and Michael J. Stark

Common to many Eastern religions and philosophies is a distinctive conception of the self and its possible transcendence. Specifically, the Eastern view holds that (1) attachment to a separate self or ego is one of the main roots of human misery, ignorance, rebirth, etc.; (2) this ego can be transcended; (3) to transcend it is to awaken to the illusion that sustains it; and (4) consciousness thus divested of the ego illusion is experienced as "empty" or "void" and for that reason open to union to or attunement with God, reality, the Tao, and so forth. These propositions offer a significant alternative to the conception of the self that is predominant in the West. For this reason it is our purpose to render them more accessible to a Western audience by presenting an exposition and defense of them in terms of contemporary Western philosophy and psychology.

EGOCENTRICITY

The Eastern view on ego, suffering, and transcendence is presented in terms of a theory of *egocentricity*.[1] Egocentricity is a system of beliefs, feelings, perceptions, and behaviors that arises when experience is centered in oneself in such a way that the world is viewed and assessed as it bears upon one's sense of identity and worth

74

as a unique individual. The egocentric is one whose life is guided by a need to prove, above all to himself, that he is someone, that is, that he has a unique identity, and, furthermore, that what he is is something of worth and importance. And the reason he acts in this way is because he has a deep-seated feeling that he lacks precisely what he is trying to prove. Egocentricity thus derives from a sense of deficiency: it is because a person is without a fundamental sense of his own (psychological) existence and value that he is compelled to prove himself in face of the world. This need to establish and defend the ego indicates that the ego is a function of egocentricity rather than vice versa, as might ordinarily be supposed.

Egocentricity is at the root of unnecessary suffering because it is based on false assumptions that lead relentlessly to unhappy conclusions. The egocentric sets out to accomplish impossible tasks and is bound to suffer the consequences. Moreover, egocentricity is a self-perpetuating system, since the possibilities for change that are consistent with it actually serve to aggravate the sense of deficiency that generates it. The only way out of this vicious circle lies in the "transcendence of the ego," which consists in seeing through the false assumptions of egocentricity. When this is accomplished, the self-defeating attempts to establish identity and worth cease, and, relieved of the chore of pursuing an illusion, one is freed to experience the world in an altogether new way.

THE PREMISES OF THE EGOCENTRIC SYSTEM

There are three premises upon which the egocentric system is based. The first holds that a person's identity and worth stand in need of proof. This premise indicates three things about the egocentric, namely: (1) that he senses that identity and worth, or being and value, are lacking in him; (2) that therefore he feels a need to establish them; and (3) that he assumes this can be accomplished by marshalling sufficient evidence in their support.

Although the first premise refers to both identity and worth without distinguishing between them, it is nevertheless important to note one difference, namely, that, of the two, identity is the more basic. This is evident from the fact that people, in striving to forge identities, are often willing to adopt unfavorable ones—that is, identities that bring the disapproval of others and an inner feeling of worthlessness—rather than feel as if they have no identity at all. The reason for this is that identity pertains to one's (psychological) *existence* as a person, and existence is a precondition of everything else. It is necessary to exist as a unique person before the question of value can even arise. Thus, although the struggles for identity and worth usually coincide, the former takes precedence when identity is seriously threatened.

The second premise of egocentricity states that identity and worth are established by winning the recognition and approval of other people. This assumption, which stresses the indispensability of the other, is properly a part of an overall outlook that is called *ego*centric, because in all cases the individual uses other people to achieve something for *himself*. What he seeks to achieve is a sense of being and worth, and he tries to establish this through intersubjective experience because he finds it wanting within his own intrasubjective experience. The egocentric's pursuit of recognition and approval is, then, his attempt to convince himself of his being and value by first convincing others.

The third premise maintains that happiness and fulfillment belong to the person who succeeds in establishing identity and worth. This premise constitutes a promise to the egocentric that his efforts have a purpose and reward. It thus provides him with a reason for being.

THE FUTILITY OF EGOCENTRICITY

We shall argue that all three premises of the egocentric system are false. Our identity and worth as individuals do not stand in need of proof. Nor are they the kinds of things that could be proved, regardless of the amount of confirmation that may be received from others. Thus it is incorrect to believe, as egocentricity promises, that happiness can be achieved by means of a quest for these things. Egocentricity is an impossible project; it cannot deliver what it promises, and it leads instead to repeated frustration, chronic anxiety, and, frequently, a sense of the futility of all efforts and the meaninglessness of life.

There are two reasons that help to explain the futility of

egocentricity, one subjective and the other intersubjective. The subjective reason lies in the nature of consciousness, which according to many Eastern schools is said to be inherently "empty" or "void." These terms are not meant to imply that consciousness is a negative reality or that it lacks an intrinsic nature. Rather, their function is to indicate something that, although a positive reality, is one that defies description in the usual sense due to its radical uniqueness. Definition and description ordinarily involve the listing of attributes that inhere in a substance. But this is not applicable in the case of consciousness, because it is not so much an entity with qualities as it is a *medium* for the reflection of qualities. In this regard it is like a mirror without reflections; it is in its own nature "empty" or "void" of distinct, differentiable properties. However, most people do not know their consciousness in this way, and they assume that the qualities of their particular selfhood constitute the entirety of their being. The reason for this is that consciousness, except under the most unusual of circumstances, is not experienced as distinct from the objects of its attention and identification. Without distinct properties of its own by which it might be marked off from its objects, consciousness is for all intents and purposes indistinguishable from them, at least so long as it continues to reflect them. But it is not for this reason reducible to any or all of its objects; for it not only possesses the power of attending to them and assuming their forms but also, and equally, the negative power of disengaging itself from them and divesting itself of their qualities and forms. Consciousness thus is never identical *to* what it identifies *with*, as it can shed itself of any of its past or present objectifications. And if it empties or voids itself of all of them, it can experience itself in its pure, unconditioned state.

Given that this is the nature of consciousness, it follows that no content of consciousness can be ontologically secure. This is so because all such contents require the attention or identification of consciousness for their existence; and these can never be certain because consciousness retains the power to alter its attention and to disengage itself from any of its identifications. What holds true of the contents of consciousness in general also holds true of the ego-centric's identity as a particular case. As a species of identification, it too is a content of consciousness—even though its individual features may refer to objects beyond consciousness. This means that the egocentric can never really *be* his identity, as his consciousness, although for the present entirely identified with it, nonetheless remains something more than it. Nor can he have any certainty with regard to his identity, as his consciousness can withdraw itself from it at any time. The egocentric's pursuit of a solid and sure identity cannot, then, succeed. His identity is but a content of consciousness and, as such, it is insecurely founded, resting upon something that is essentially "empty" or "void" in nature.

The intersubjective reason for the futility of egocentricity lies in the fact that the recognition and approval of others are necessary *but not sufficient* conditions of the egocentric's sense of identity and worth. They are necessary because the allied pursuits of identity and worth could not take place without them, but they are insufficient because they can never be supplied in great enough amount to bring these efforts to a successful completion. Egocentrics simply cannot get enough reinforcing attention from others, and they continue to feel in need of it regardless of the amount they may have received in the past.

Perhaps this point can best be made in terms of an analogy. The egocentric sees the world as a testing ground on which one seeks to establish a sense of existence and value as a person by winning the acceptance and positive regard of others. This perception requires that experiences be assessed as successes and failures, where "success" and "failure" are to be understood in a very extended sense. A success is anything that is perceived as indicating that an individual has being or value. It encompasses, therefore, any feeling, thought, or behavior that is the occasion for recognition or approval by others, or, derivatively, for self-acceptance or self-approval. Similarly, a failure is any event that is perceived as lessening one's being or value. Experiences perceived as failures constitute injury or, if severe, a sense of psychological death because worth and sometimes one's very being as a unique person are felt to be at stake. On the other hand, those perceived as successes maintain and even enhance one's identity and sense of worth, at least for a while. But the problem is that no success, no matter how impressive, nor any string of successes, no matter how long, is sufficient finally to establish a sense of identity and worth firm and certain enough to eradicate once and for all the egocentric's gnawing feeling of inner deficiency. What the egocentric really needs is an internal and unconditional sense of being and value. No amount of external confirmation of these can stand as an adequate substitute.

Life is full of examples that demonstrate the futility of the quest for recognition and approval. It is a common occurrence for people to use such expressions as "If only such and such, then I would be someone" or "If only such and such, then I would be happy." A possible life scenario might be: (1) if only I had more friends; (2) if only I were recognized as being a talented athlete, musician, student, etc.; (3) if only I had a college degree; (4) if only I could meet the right person; (5) if only I could get a good job; (6) if only I could get a better job (home, car, wife, husband); (7) if only I could make a name for myself; (8) if only my children were successful; and so on right up to the point of death. The assumption in each case is that if this one condition were met, then identity, worth, and therefore happiness, would be achieved. Yet when one of these conditions is met, rather than experiencing lasting satisfaction, a new condition arises that is seen as the one that will finally do the trick, and so on indefinitely.

SELF AND SELF-IMAGE

We have spoken of egocentricity in terms of both identity and worth. It is now necessary to incorporate these within the larger notion of the *self-image*, which is the set of all those features, whether real or imagined, in which the egocentric believes his identity and worth to reside.[2] It should be noted that this definition intentionally restricts the applicability of the concept of a self-image to egocentrics. Non-egocentrics possess an awareness of their selfhood, but this awareness does not amount to a self-image because they do not stake their sense of worth upon it, or upon any of its parts or contents. Furthermore, they are not attached to their conception of themselves and thus feel no need to defend it against challenge and change, as if their very (psychological) existence depended upon it. The egocentric, on the other hand, guards his self-image as if it were his life and sees it as containing any measure of value that he might possess.

The self-image is but a narrow and inaccurate reflection of the total self or organism. The latter includes all that one brings to, deposits in, and takes away from experience; and this is an open-ended, fluid, and frequently inconsistent set of features (e.g., qualities, potentialities, achievements, skills, weaknesses, feelings, insights, ignorance) that exist with or without the mediation of other people. The self-image, on the other hand, is the (relatively) closed, unchanging, and rigidly consistent set of features that the egocentric imputes to himself only in relation to his past, present, and projected interaction with others. The self-image thus is a subset (and usually a fairly small one) of the total self, containing within itself only those elements of one's totality that, because they are founded in intersubjective experience, can serve to enhance a sense of being and value. Furthermore, the self-image necessarily involves inaccuracy and distortion. The most obvious reasons for this are: (1) that the egocentric is prone to inflate or exaggerate aspects of himself that are reflected in those features of the self-image to which he is most strongly attached; (2) that he is liable to minimize or suppress from awareness aspects of himself that are in conflict with these favored features; and (3) that he tends to ignore or deny change and future possibilities because he clings to the self-image as to a hard-won possession. Another and perhaps more subtle reason is that the egocentric is blind to the limited scope of the self-image. He does not understand that it is an incomplete picture of himself and thus suffers from the distortion that results from forcing what is only a part to stand for the whole.

A second point about the relation of the self-image to the self is that the self-image is a response to the egocentric's sense of inner deficiency and incompleteness. The egocentric feels as though he lacks being and value within himself, and he therefore seeks to prove these in face of the world by attempting to win the recognition and confirmation of others. The product of this effort, including both its successes and failures, is the self-image. The self-image, then, is an interpersonally-grounded substitute for what the egocentric feels is missing within himself. It is a surrogate or puppet self, the function of which is to compensate for what he fears is a deficiency in his being. Indeed, the self-image is the very *ego* of egocentricity. It is the egocentric's attempt to produce a substantial self with a unique and justifying essence, in reaction to the deep-seated feeling that he lacks just such a thing. The egocentric thus treats the self-image as if it were the substance around which his conscious experience revolves and in which it is supported; and he believes that its central features express his unique essence and, hopefully, value.

But this, of course, is an illusion, precisely the kind of illusion to which Eastern schools refer when they speak of the ego, or at least of the sense of separate selfhood, as being a species of ignorance. The illusion or ignorance in question is a crucial instance of the (false) identification of consciousness with one of its contents. Consciousness not only takes on the form of this object, the self-image; but it also is mistakenly assumed to *be* this object. In this way, the real priority becomes inverted. The self-image, which is a mere content of consciousness, is wrongly elevated to the status of an entity that exercises consciousness as its power. But this identification and inversion can be overcome, for consciousness is always able to disengage itself from any of its objectifications. The transcendence of the ego is to be understood in this way. The ego is but the false identification of consciousness with the self-image. Its transcendence, therefore, requires only that this identification be broken asunder.

Most Eastern teachings maintain that the transcendence of the ego constitutes liberation not only from illusion but also from suffering, for when consciousness is freed from the ego-illusion, it simultaneously is disburdened of all the unhappy consequences that result from its futile defense in face of the world. Up to this point we have spoken of the futility and frustration of egocentricity only in very general terms. We shall now consider the specific ways in which it adversely affects life in the areas of feeling, perception, and action.

THE ADVERSE EFFECTS OF EGOCENTRICITY

There is no dimension of life experience that is not affected by egocentricity. It is manifested in a person's emotional life in a variety of ways—most obviously in the polar feelings of pride and self-contempt and less obviously, though just as importantly, in the underlying feelings of anxiety and despair.

Pride and self-contempt are inevitable correlates of the defense of the self-image, for the person who experiences life as a testing ground feels prideful when he meets with success and contemptible when he fails. Pride and self-contempt are reciprocally related; and the elation of success and the depression of failure tend to lead into each other time and time again.

It may sound odd to say that self-contempt is an integral part of egocentricity, as it is more common to think of egocentricity in terms of vanity and pride. Nevertheless, self-contempt is as much a part of the egocentric system as pride, because, like pride, it rests upon the premise that identity and worth stand in need of proof. But unlike pride, of course, it is the feeling that emerges when the proof is found wanting. In fact, self-contempt may even reflect the egocentric's actual condition better than pride, since it seems to confirm what he suspected from the outset, namely, that he is deficient in being and value. This supposition is supported by the psychological fact that, in most cases, failures are felt to be more devastating than successes are felt to be uplifting.

Pride and self-contempt, together with their kin, elation and depression, are the most obvious of the distinctively egocentric feelings. But there are other egocentric feelings and emotions that are every bit as important, even though their presence and causes are not as readily detectable. In particular, we are referring to anxiety and despair, both of which occur most often as subtle feeling-states in the background of conscious awareness. Though they rarely occupy the specific focus of attention, their persistence and pervasiveness make them at least as destructive to a sense of well-being as the other, more turbulent emotions.

Anxiety is an inseparable part of the egocentric's experience due to the precariousness of the self-image, which is inherently insecure, both from within and from without. Subjectively, the self-image is unsurely founded in consciousness; and intersubjectively, the ever-present possibility of failure means that its defense can never be a fait accompli. These factors conspire to produce a tense watchfulness and chronic disquietude. The egocentric may not be aware of this uneasiness at all times, because it is a constant medium for the more specific and intense feelings and emotions. But it breaks through to the foreground of awareness frequently enough, especially during those times when the self-image is more uncertain than usual because of assailment by threats, real or imagined.

The egocentric is unable to deal with anxiety effectively. Neither withdrawal from activity, nor stepped-up efforts to succeed, nor added precautions against failure provide permanent relief from anxiety, since none of these measures gets to its real source, that is, the inherent insecurity of the self-image. Continual anxiety and repeated frustration in attempting to alleviate it can lead to despair. Despair is the deep underlying feeling that there is no end to anxiety, that one's best efforts are of no avail, and therefore that life is essentially unhappy.

Despair is best described in contrast to depression, which also can be a part of the egocentric experience. In some ways despair is to depression as anxiety is to fear; for (1) neither despair nor anxiety have specific objects while depression and fear typically do, and (2) despair (like anxiety) is usually subtle and constant while depression (like fear) tends to be more conspicuous and episodic. Concerning the first of these parallels, the object or cause of depression is in most cases some definite setback to the egocentric's sense of identity or worth. Despair, on the other hand, is diffuse and involves a sense of hopelessness about life in general.

There is a glimmer of hope in the hopelessness of despair, for profound despair is an indication that a person at least has learned that the egocentric quest for identity and worth is an impossibility. The despairing person knows that the promise of egocentricity is a false one. The problem is that egocentricity is still equated with life itself, and because the egocentric quest is known to be futile and hopeless, he mistakenly concludes that life is also. The glimmer of hope is that the despair of the despairing individual will be so utterly without hope that it will awaken him to the possibility of life beyond the limits of egocentricity.

Given that egocentricity is the dominant way of relating to the world, it needs to be explained why most people do not appear obviously to be suffering in the grip of anxiety and despair. The answer to this apparent paradox is twofold. First, as we noted, anxiety and despair are often quite subtle and difficult to discern. They usually lie below the surface of the minute-to-minute fluctuations of emotion, constituting the background against which the other feelings and emotions are experienced. But of perhaps greater importance is the fact that most people really do believe that the egocentric system works and, if it does not seem to be working for them, they blame themselves and not the system. They assume that almost everyone else is doing acceptably well and rather than reveal what they take to be their own failing, they maintain outer appearances and in the process contribute to a universal illusion.

Egocentricity also has adverse effects upon perception, for the egocentric has a vested interest in seeing the world as conforming to the self-image. He thus tends systematically to channel and interpret information in a biased manner, prohibiting an accurate experience of self and world. Experience is measured against the self-image, and elements are deleted, modified, or avoided if threatening to it and emphasized or even imagined if needed to support it. The world is seen only as it appears in conformity with the conditions of the self-image. The world as it exists beyond these limits is necessarily hidden from view.

Egocentricity affects action too, because a person responds to the world in accordance with his perception of it, and since the egocentric often misperceives the world, the situations in which he acts may be quite different from what he takes them to be. Furthermore, egocentric action is restricted and repetitive, since possible actions are limited to those that coincide with the self-image. The tendency is to adhere to those ways of acting that in the past have brought perceived success and a sense of identity and worth. To the extent that the same narrow actions are repeated, it becomes difficult to adapt to changing conditions and life loses its freshness and intensity.

CONCLUSION

We stated at the outset that there are four propositions pertaining to the self that are central to most Eastern religions and philosophies, namely: (1) that attachment to a separate self or ego is one of the main roots of human suffering, ignorance, rebirth, and so forth; (2) that the ego can be transcended; (3) that to transcend it is to awaken to the illusion that sustains it; and (4) that consciousness thus divested of the ego is experienced as "empty" or "void" and for that reason as being open to union or attunement with reality or the divine. Having set forth the theory of egocentricity, we are now in a position to explain how these propositions are to be understood in terms of it.

Concerning the first proposition, we have seen how the egocentric outlook contributes to suffering by giving rise to such feeling-states as self-contempt, depression, anxiety, and despair. Its implication in human ignorance is evident in its distorting effects upon perception. And egocentricity also leads to constant repetition ("rebirth") of inappropriate behaviors; by calculating actions to guarantee conformity with the self-image, the egocentric is condemned to make the same errors over and over again.

The second proposition, that the ego can be transcended, finds its explanation in the fact that the ego to be transcended is but an effect, and not the cause, of egocentricity. The egocentric's attempt to prove identity and worth does not spring from an already existing ego-entity possessing an inflated sense of its own value. Rather, it arises from a felt lack of precisely such a thing. Just as a starving person centers experience in the stomach, so the egocentric centers experience in himself, which, at some level, he senses to be deficient in being and value. The ego that needs to be transcended is not, then, a given; it is a project, and an impossible one at that. The transcendence of the ego thus consists in the elimination of the cause of this project, and this is within our power because the cause is needless ignorance or illusion. To transcend the ego is to overcome the illusion that sustains it, and this is the point of the third proposition, to which we now turn.

In terms of egocentricity, the fundamental illusion is that the self-image *is* the self proper. This false identification must be thoroughly understood before it can be dissolved. Since it is rooted in the three premises of egocentricity, the falsity of these must also be understood, not merely on the level of the intellect but deeply within oneself. Specifically, one must come to understand (1) that well-being cannot be achieved by attempting to prove being and value, not only (2) because no number of successes can be sufficient to accomplish this, but also (3) because being and worth are not the kinds of things that stand in need of proof. Of these points, it is the third that is really crucial. Insight into the second by itself does not get one beyond egocentricity; in fact, it is likely to lead to despair. An understanding of the third point, however, marks a decisive break and the beginning of a radically new point of view.

Once the illusion of egocentricity has been dispelled, then, according to the fourth proposition, consciousness is experienced as "empty" or "void" and for that reason as being open to union with or attunement to reality or the divine. As we explained earlier, consciousness is "empty" or "void" in the sense that it is a pure reflecting medium rather than a substance with distinct properties. But an appreciation of this, its intrinsic nature, is not possible so long as the identification of consciousness with its objects persists. And there is one object, the self-image, that resists disidentification more stubbornly than all the rest. The egocentric refuses to empty himself of this basic identification because he (mistakenly) believes that his being and value reside in it. To give it up and fall into the "emptiness" of consciousness would be equivalent to extinction. But here the Eastern traditions insist that the fear of the "emptiness" of consciousness is not a fear of something that is in itself ontologically negative or necessarily unpleasant. It is, rather, fear of the unknown. The Eastern traditions are virtually unanimous in holding that the person who summons the courage and faces the void will not find empty nothingness, but rather empty fullness and openness.

Egocentricity can be transcended by those who dedicate themselves to it. When this is accomplished, the negative features that plague the egocentric condition give way and their opposites are rendered possible. The felt need to prove identity and worth is eliminated, allowing unconditional self-acceptance and affirmation. Anxiety and despair yield to tranquility and bliss. Perceptual distortion ceases and one begins to see the world beyond the limits imposed by the self-image. Action loses its rigidity and repetitiveness and becomes increasingly resilient, spontaneous, and creative. And in general, as the egocentric perspective is left behind a world-centered, rather than a narrow self-centered, perspective is achieved.

NOTES

1. Our conception of egocentricity owes an equal debt to Jean-Paul Sartre in philosophy and Carl Rogers in psychology. Specifically, we have learned, and appropriated, a good deal from Sartre's theory of consciousness and his notion of the fundamental project; and we are in debt to Rogers for many of the ideas contained in our theory of the self-image and its effects upon feeling, perception, and action. However, the conception of egocentricity presented here stands entirely on its own and goes well beyond these principal sources of inspiration.

2. This conception of the self-image is similar to Carl Rogers's notion of the self-concept, though it is fitted into a very different systematic and metaphysical context.

8
The Self-image

Tarthang Tulku

In the Tibetan tradition, consciousness is pictured as a physical reaction. What a human being is inside is the same as what he or she is outside in the physical realm. A human being *is* the embodiment of his consciousness. A person's characteristic behavior patterns—his obsessions, his dullness, his unhappiness, or his feelings of great fulfillment—are all manifested on the physical level. We may say that a person is really functioning properly as a human being when his consciousness is well-balanced.

If we observe our constant play of thoughts and ideas, we will find that we have many thoughts and many conceptions about who or what we are. Our thoughts are so much involved with a *self-image*. We expect ourselves to behave in certain ways. We see ourselves sitting in a certain way, or wearing certain kinds of clothes, or talking in a certain manner. These expressions of individual characteristics take on a separate form—a separate personality—which is different from who we actually are. First we create thoughts or thought-models which feed our consciousness. Then our consciousness immediately becomes involved in the world of our self-image. But when we examine it, the self-image doesn't show itself. It cannot be pinpointed as anything. It disperses: it is nothing. True, you may have

This chapter is an edited transcription of a talk given by Tarthang Tulku at the Tibetan Nyingma Institute in Berkeley, California, spring 1974.

concepts about a certain self-image you may have at a certain time, but there is no one particular self-image that outlasts any conceptions you may have about it.

We think and talk as though we could actually touch or see our self-image. However, two separate qualities are involved: our "self," or "me" or "I"...and our self-image. This "me" or "I" is involved with life in a multitude of ways. This "I" experiences and feels and sees things in a way which is very alive and immediate. When this "I" becomes filled with the self-image, the person begins to act as though he were someone else. For example, perhaps you are tremendously shy, or you feel very shameful, embarrassed, guilty, or generally dissatisfied—at this time the "I" is overcome with a very vivid, very alive sensation which is really only the activation of a personal drama, the self-image.

We can think, examine, meditate, and maybe make very clear to ourselves what kind of status we are giving to this self-image. Let us say you are watching your thoughts and emotions during some tremendous disturbance, some great sadness. Your mind is very agitated. At these times you might be able to observe that you are not actually the person who is experiencing this emotional state. You are not actually the person that is feeling great pain. These disturbances are being created through the operation of your self-image. But sometimes this is hard to see because you are so involved with the self-image you have created throughout your whole life. What is essential for you to see is that, during those particularly painful disturbances, you have the opportunity to step back and actually see the core of your self-image. In your daily experience, certain energies develop—a trembling or volcanic sort of consciousness, or a feeling of fear, anger, or tightness. What is creating this holding-strength is the self-image. But just like the self-image, this holding-strength does not really exist. Just as there is no abiding "self," or "ego," there is also no abiding self-image. True, the actual feeling is there, but its holding-power will be completely lost as soon as you have lost your interest in feeding the self-image. At that time you can have a totally different experience than what you had thought was possible in that previous state of painfulness.

In order to make ourselves more flexible, we must first learn to recognize this self-image. *It is not you.* All of this is a very big subject, but here we are talking about the self-image in a simple, practical way. For example, we are experiencing an emotional disturbance. Maybe we have feelings of very deep physical dissatisfaction. When you imagine or think about it, the thoughts and feelings are almost visible. Perhaps it is a sexual problem. Many people feel frustrated. They feel energy blockages. This may be due to a great deal of fantasizing which creates an image, an idea, which can never be experienced in reality. At the same time, a person may feel tremendous energy. But his energy is frustration-energy. He feels as if his energy is being drawn away—self-drowning, completely hopeless, a feeling of desperation. His emotions feel very thick, dense, dark, and confused—there is no light. This energy of frustration causes the person to want to cry, but he does not know why. He hasn't any reasons or explanations for this unhappy state. Energy is drawn up, then collapses completely. The person feels drowned in his own sorrow. There is no life, no light, no positive feelings. At this time, he has many fantasies, dreams, and expectations—but none of these things happen. Nothing comes alive. All that he experiences is the expression of what he would *like* to have happen. These kinds of feelings cause him to remain in his own realm, his own world. His self-image is keeping him there. But if he lets go of that energy, that holding-power, he can immediately separate himself from it: instantly he feels different. Something very different definitely happens, but a person may not exactly understand what it is unless he has this experience.

You can especially learn this awareness, or "looking," when you have obsessions or fantasies. You can see the restrictive self-image and separate yourself from it. Suppose you do not have any good friends and you feel very lonely. You want to be happy. You want to make your fantasy more vivid, more alive. You can almost see it, feel it, touch it. For instance, men, in their heads, do a lot of fantasizing about women's bodies, and the opposite is true for women. In this imagining, a person creates sensational feelings and generates much energy. You can feel that energy and vividly visualize it. Use this fresh energy to arouse your awareness to separate you from your self-image-making—and immediately look back at your situation. To recognize this energy before it consumes you, you must develop an awareness that can look back at the situation you have created. At this time the energy-strength is felt very differently—it is like two different worlds, two different kinds of energies. But when you step back, then you can use this fresh energy to see the world of your involvement with the self-image.

What we created initially was the self-image—we are perpetuating something we can never satisfy. We will never find any satisfaction because we are not feeding the right person, which is our real self. Instead, this nourishment goes to our self-image. Often it is very difficult for us to determine whether certain sensations arise from us or from our self-image. Let us say our sensations create enjoyable feelings of importance or goodness or security. But the self-image has a very grasping nature. Holding on to the enjoyment and trying to make sensations permanent develops feelings of tightness. This self-grasping is always making demands and causing us, finally, to be dissatisfied with our present experience. We can never *have* enough. So how do we work with the self-image? First, recognize the self-image, and second, jump away from it and look at it—because *the self-image is not you.*

We can find all sorts of rational excuses for our difficulties. But you must forget the rational side. You must understand that you are not happy because your feelings are very clouded. You feel uncertain, and a dark, heavy feeling dominates your whole being. You are not open because you are completely permeated by the self-image. We need to see this rigidity in ourselves and work to change our mental stance. For example, every time you think you are not happy, say, "I am happy." Say it strongly to yourself, even if your feelings are contradictory. Remember, it is your self-image and not you. Just as fast as a fish can move in the water, you can instantly change to a happy, balanced attitude. Keep yourself there. Believe yourself. Be open to that positiveness. Your whole inner situation can change, even if the external conditions do not change right away. If you want to feel positive and have satisfaction, then be open and flexible. *You have the choice.* When certain things are occurring in a way which you do not like, immediately, at that time, mentally change your concept. All you need to do is take a different perspective. When you do this, you will see the self-image creating disturbances. When you look back at the self-image, you don't want to see that your consciousness is dependent on so many conditions. So you need to understand that consciousness is really quite flexible.

Our consciousness does not have a diamondlike quality in its present form. It is not yet indestructible. So it is important to develop flexibility in our consciousness. We can practice changing from unhappiness: completely believe the unhappiness in your mind and feelings, and then change it...like a fish which can quickly change direction in the water. Its body has almost an electric swiftness and sharpness. This energy is very subtle. So in the beginning try to develop this skill of *changingness*. This skill develops acceptance, not in the heavy way—"I need to accept this"—but in a simple way, just feeling the experience happening. In this way you give yourself the choice to develop very effective or skillful changes whenever you are confronted with negative experiences. First, *be* the experience, completely accept it. Then jump to the positive side. How is it? You can clearly see the differences between the positive and negative experiences. Then you can almost experience both at the same time. Jump from one side to the other and then back again. Mentally jump. You will see there is no "from," there is only awareness.

This experience is like looking into a mirror. From this awareness you can see where you are now and how it was before. You can almost simultaneously feel two different atmospheres. Then you can make the choice to develop the self-image which makes you a prisoner, or you can stay with the positive side which is a feeling of lightness, fullness, and wholeness. No desiring, no unfulfillment. You yourself are balanced, and everything is interesting for you just as it is. You become no more and no less than what you are. You feel no impediments, no distractions, no obstacles. Your feelings and your mind no longer feel so divided. You do not feel agitated or restless. You do not feel you have to go somewhere, because you are feeding yourself directly, instantly. There is no dominating, conceptual self-image taking you away from the immediacy of your being. You feel complete just as you are. But when you are dominated by your self-image, you are not independent, you are not liberated. You feel pressured, under the control of some unidentifiable agent. You have chosen to allow yourself no choice. This is what the self-image perpetuates. As long as you are involved with your self-image, you have no real feeling of completeness. Once your consciousness is thinking in terms of the self-image, you are no longer free.

We must learn to deal with this self-image by first of all recognizing it for what it is and then acting differently. Our concepts and feelings create our consciousness, whether we are happy, sad, or indifferent. To change effectively we must accept certain ways or attitudes that may be different from ones we are familiar with. We need to learn to act differently. This is possible because there is nothing in us that is substantial. The "actor" is not solid. Even so, we feel we do not want to change. We may be unwilling to see situations differently. This is the strength of our self-image. We don't seem to want to give up this bondage, this *samsaric** suffering, because we feel we have to maintain our position as servant to our self-image. We seem to love suffering. We almost have to be in some kind of suffering in order to live out our life. These are all characteristics of our self-image. Even if we consciously say to ourselves that we do not want to suffer and we do not want to go through this—we still must go through these experiences. We must live them out. This is the difficult part.

Because the self-image does not really exist, it is very difficult to deal with. You cannot exactly catch it. But at the same time it dominates us and controls us and makes us miserable. We can say we don't want to be miserable. But unless we come to some conclusions about what makes us suffer, we are only playing a game with ourselves. We cannot gain anything spiritually, or intellectually, unless we come to certain conclusions about the cause of our suffering. Otherwise we cannot become enlightened. We will not be able to achieve anything positive unless we choose for ourselves an attitude that is balanced, happy, and satisfied. No matter what situation we find ourselves in, we have the choice of which way we would like to go. Mentally healthy, a balanced mind, feelings of satisfaction...these are humanly very acceptable and desirable. If we can succeed in these things—which is like looking for knowledge or wisdom—our whole life will have purpose. Otherwise, we are just very casually playing in *samsara*. If we want a healthy attitude, then we can decide.

---

*The term *samsaric* refers to self-created suffering which results from one's lack of understanding of reality. For further discussion of *samsara*, see p. 110 (Ed.).

9

On Ego Strength and Egolessness

John Welwood and Ken Wilber

The ego feeling we are aware of now is...only a shrunken vestige of a far more extensive feeling—a feeling which embraced the universe and expressed an inseparable connection of the ego with the external world.
Sigmund Freud, *Civilization and Its Discontents*

Wherever there is other, there is fear.

The Upanishads

The two notions of ego strength and egolessness express in a nutshell the difference between the approaches of Western and Eastern psychology. Western psychotherapists have emphasized the need for a strong ego, meaning by that maximal competence in dealing with impulses, conflicts, and environmental demands without lapsing into anxiety-ridden behavior or withdrawal from situations. On the other hand, the Eastern notion of egolessness, as developed particularly in the Buddhist tradition, attempts to go beyond the notion of a strong ego by stressing that ultimately there is no such thing as an ego, a separate self, and that full human life can only be realized in light of this basic fact of existence. Just as an Eastern person with only a superficial knowledge of Western psychology might misunderstand the therapeutic goal of developing ego strength, so too a classical psychoanalyst would probably view egolessness as an invitation to psychosis. In order to clarify this perennial East–West confusion, we need to discover (1) whether, underlying their differences in language and attitude, both traditions may be pointing to a similar mechanism that keeps us entrapped in an impoverished view of ourselves and our full potential; and (2) just how the two traditions actually differ.

THE I AND THE IT[1]

Let us begin with Freud, the undisputed father of Western psychology's attempt to understand human neurosis and promote human sanity. In a now famous passage from the *New Introductory Lectures*, Freud states that the therapeutic intent of psychoanalysis is "to strengthen the ego. . . ,to widen its field of perception and enlarge its organization, so that it can appropriate fresh portions of the id. Where id was, there ego shall be."[2] Viewed in its simplest terms, this *reclamation* (which Freud likened to the Zuyder Zee project) and integration of the lost or repressed aspects of the self ("Where id was, there ego shall be") remains to this day the major aim and goal of psychoanalysis and ego-oriented psychotherapies. Thus, in the widely-circulated text on *The Technique and Practice of Psychoanalysis*, Greenson noted: "Resolving the neurotic conflicts means reuniting with the conscious ego those portions of the id, superego, and unconscious ego which had been excluded from the maturational processes of the healthy remainder of the total personality."[3] Similarly, Fenichel stated: "The therapeutic task, then, is to reunite with the conscious ego the contents. . .which have been withheld from consciousness by countercathexis"[4] ["repressing forces"].

As succinct as these statements are, they nevertheless are couched in a highly technical language and a complex conceptual framework. The very complexity of the psychoanalytic framework— important as it otherwise is—has perhaps served to obscure and mystify an essentially simple and straightforward point. Moreover, Freud used the term *I* or *ego* in different ways within different contexts, which also served to obscure his message. On the one hand, Freud posited the ego as a "metapsychological" construct that served the explanatory role of accounting for the stability and reality-orientation of the psyche. He also spoke of the ego as an organization, as an inherent structural principle of the psyche. And finally, Freud occasionally lapsed into a language that indicated that the ego he was referring to could actually be *experienced*, as when he wrote: "Normally, there is nothing of which we are more certain than the feeling of our self, of our own ego."[5] This confusion between a phenomenological ego—a self-sense that can be felt—and a psychological organization with a postulated explanatory value, has made it difficult to clarify the psychoanalytic meaning of the ego, and to compare it to what Buddhism or Eastern psychologies might mean by the same word.

Let us, then, using one of Freud's simpler expositions of the question in *The Problem of Lay-Analyses*, examine the essence and core of what he seemed to mean by "developing ego strength" or "reuniting ego and id." (To an orthodox Freudian, the following discussion may seem oversimplified, but we feel that it is necessary to highlight this important thrust of Freud's work and bring clarity to the subject matter of this chapter.) Freud begins by explaining one major "part" of what he calls the "soul (psychical) apparatus":

> For argument's sake, let us accept the popular conception and assume that within us there is a psychical organization, recording sensations and perceptions of physical wants on the one hand, and releasing motoric actions on the other. This medium for establishing this definite cooperation we call the "I."[6]

Notice immediately that Freud uses the word *I*—not the word *ego*! In fact, in Freud's writings the term that his English translators rendered as "the ego" was actually *das Ich*, which is German for "the I." He used the pronoun *I*, not the noun *ego*. By looking to Freud's original terms, as Brandt has pointed out,[7] we recapture instantly a great portion of the basically simple and elegant message of Freud. The psychoanalytic ego is an extremely difficult concept to define. But all of us already have a sense of what Freud might mean by the I.

Having asserted that the I is one major aspect of the psyche, Freud goes on to describe the second major aspect:

> Aside from the "I," we perceive another region of the soul, much more extensive, much more impressive, and much more obscure than the "I," which we designate the "It."[8]

Notice that Freud does not use the word *id*. He instead uses the impersonal pronoun, the *It*, or *das Es* in German. Thus at bottom Freud seemed to be concerned with the conflicts between the I and the It. Freud is very explicit on the use of the pronouns the *I* and the *It* to denote the two major regions of the psyche:

> Doubtless, you will raise an objection against our intention to refer to these two regions or stages of the soul with simple pronouns, instead of giving them beautiful euphonious Greek names. However, in psychoanalysis, we prefer to remain in contact with the popular way of thinking, and attach commonplace terms to our scientific conceptions, rather than look upon such nomenclature in contempt.[9]

Freud then straightforwardly explains why he uses the term the *It*, which we of English tongue have learned to call the "id":

> The impersonal pronoun "It" is most appropriate for our purposes as is plainly proved by the fact that we frequently speak of something, averring that " 'It' came to me quite suddenly"; " 'It' gave me a shock"; " 'It' was stronger than I."[10]

Here then are the two major aspects of the human psyche: the I and the It. Freud explains:

> To all intents and purposes, the "I" is actually the front layer, the obvious, whereas the "It" is the inner layer, the hidden. To make it even more plain: The "I" is inserted between the reality of the outer world, and the "It," the latter constituting the soul proper, the essence of the soul, as it were.[11]

The It, then, is the hidden or veiled aspect of mind, and the I the obvious and apparent aspect. And yet, the I and the It started out as one, and ideally they remain as one: "There is no inherent opposition," Freud points out, "between the 'I' and the 'It,' both belonging together. In cases of normal health, it is practically impossible to distinguish between the two."[12] This ideal situation, however, is more the exception than the rule, for early in the development of most individuals, a more or less radical split occurs between the I and the It. The two factors fail to stay on friendly terms, but instead begin a rather prolonged and complex war. The goals of the I are pitted against the urges of the It. Initiated by the I, this war has the object of banishing or suppressing part of the It. Freud explains:

> And now, I ask you to visualize what would happen in case this "I" is actuated by an urge arising from the "It"—an urge which the

weak "I" would like to resist, because it feels that...this urge may
involve danger, may result in a traumatic situation, a collision with
the outer world.[13]

In this battle between I and It, something has to give. Neither side will
totally surrender its position, so one side simply has to be forcefully
restricted:

> The "I" makes an attempt at flight, deserting the specific part of
> the "It" and leaving it to its fate. It refuses all such assistance as it
> usually renders to urges arising from the "It." We refer to such a
> case as repression of urges by the "I.".... The repressed urge now
> goes its own way.... With its synthesis disturbed, a part of the "It"
> remains forbidden ground to the "I."[14]

This might seem a fitting end to the whole war between I and It.
The offending It is abandoned and expelled from the field of
consciousness, and the I is free to go its own way. However, such is
not the case: the It may be ordered off the field, but it doesn't leave
the territory, nor does it rest quiet in its exile.

> The isolated urge does not remain idle, however. Because normal
> gratification was denied it, it continues to compensate itself by
> engendering psychical derivatives which take its place and,
> connecting with other psychical activations, estrange them to the
> "I." Finally, in the form of an unrecognizable substitute, the
> isolated urge penetrates to the "I" and to consciousness, presenting
> itself as what is known as a "symptom."[15]

In other words, when the It is banished from consciousness, it may
take on the form of a symptom, and thus *force* its way back into
awareness in this disguised form. *The symptom becomes a new type
of It*, and as a symptom, "It" continues to plague the I. "This revenge
of the 'It' on the 'I,'" says Freud, "resulted in nothing less than a
neurosis."[16]

In this way, the sphere of the I becomes drastically reduced,
narrowed, and limited, for many energies and potentials have been
cast out and alienated. They have been turned from I into It, from self
into not-self, from dynamic energy to painful symptom. Something
that could and should be felt as part of oneself is felt and perceived as
an It, as not-I.

As a very simple example of this process, suppose that, in
response to some provocation, a hostile or angry impulse strongly

wells up in a person. If properly integrated, anger can be a workable form of mobilization of energy for overcoming obstacles and frustrations. But suppose that the individual in our example is one who, like many individuals in our society, has a great deal of difficulty handling anger effectively. Instead of relating to his anger in an integrated manner, he condemns it altogether. He senses that his angry impulses are absolutely dangerous, and thus attempts to deny the existence of any angry urges that might arise in him. So this anger is no longer I but It, no longer a true part of himself but a banished and outcast "other."

However, the anger does not simply vanish or evaporate! Rather, it continues to rise up again and again, demanding recognition from the I. Yet the I refuses to accept this It, and a battle between the two is under way. Oddly enough, our angry friend still continues to perceive these impulses. He senses that *somebody* is angry, but since it can't be himself, who could it be? It must be somebody else—anybody else—and so he must find a suitable candidate. Instead of seeing the anger as *his*, he seems to see it in other people. In technical terms, this process is called *projection*. He projects his anger onto others, thereby relieving himself of the responsibility for his own energies and turning them into an It out there.

By projecting his aggression outside himself, he starts to feel that all sorts of people, for no apparent reason, are angry at him, hostile, "out to get him." His friends and associates rightly deny this if he brings it up, but his feeling is insistent. It is insistent because it is *his* anger which boomerangs back to its true owner. Under these circumstances, he understandably starts developing feelings of anxiety or fear, because "everybody's out to get him!" He may even develop phobic symptoms, perhaps avoiding innocuous situations which he sees as dangerous.

Thus he has failed to discover in his angry impulses any positive intelligence or energy, which might have provided him with a more direct and satisfying way of relating with his world. Since he cannot accept his aggression, it has only one place left to turn—against himself. Instead of acknowledging his own aggression for what it is, he attacks himself and imagines others are doing it! Instead of the satisfaction of forcefully working with obstacles in the environment, he settles for a substitute satisfaction: he attacks himself, while maintaining a self-righteous indignation against the world. And what he seems to feel is no longer anger, but fear—fear of his own hostility which he now imagines to reside in others—and resentment of the ways of the world. He actually feels his aggression as fear, as external anger aimed at him. (Fear is what anger feels like on the outside, just as obligation is what demand feels like on the outside.)

If a person is openly aware of his own aggression (or desires, envies, or other personal tendencies), then he can more often than not exert a guiding influence over them. He is *responsible* for them, and they, in turn, *respond* to him. On the other hand, when personal tendencies are made into Its, these Its are quite beyond conscious control. They seem to come and go as they please, without any relation to, or consideration of one's overall life purposes. Freud pointed to this uncontrollability when he called these alienated aspects of oneself "derivatives of the It." We say, "This symptom, It annoys me." "It's an obsessive thought—I can't control It." "My desire to eat—It's stronger than I am." "This fear, It just overcomes me." And of every symptom or problematic feeling, we say, "I just wish It would go away." Thus even our language expresses this loss of acceptance of and responsibility for our own feelings, as Fritz Perls has pointed out:

> Look at the difference between the words, "I am tensing myself" and "There's a tenseness here." When you say, "I feel tenseness," you're irresponsible, you are not responsible for this, you are impotent and can't do anything about it. The world should do something—give you an aspirin or whatever it is. But when you say, "I am tensing," you take responsibility.[17]

In short, all these Its—symptoms, tensions, obsessions, upsets, dramas, scares—represent ways in which we torture ourselves with our own energies. In denying part of our experience, we surrender responsibility for it and lose the opportunity to integrate it as a dynamic aspect of ourselves. Our attempt to get rid of It has sadly failed, and we are left with bittersweet symptoms and funny puzzles about ourselves.

Jung described this same split in terms of an inaccurate self-image, which he called the *persona*, and an alienated, cast-out, projected It, which he called the *shadow*. As we shall see later, this is a form of the same mechanism that Buddhism speaks of as the root of suffering and human neurosis. It is the dualistic splitting of a unified field of experience and a subsequent fixation upon a limited part of the whole field as constituting the I. This leaves us with an impoverished self-sense, always under threat and subject to attack from an alien "other" which we refuse to accept as part of ourselves.

THE TASK OF PSYCHOTHERAPY: REUNITING I AND IT

Western psychotherapy has generally recognized that the end to the tormenting split between persona and shadow, I and It, individual and neurotic symptoms, lies in the direction of befriending, integrating, and taking back those parts of oneself that have been made alien and other. Taking back the It can be a difficult and prolonged task in therapy. The neurotic clings to his symptoms and to his restricted world on the one hand, while on the other hand he despairs about them and seeks some kind of salvation. Symptoms (as "substitute gratifications of neurotic pleasure") in fact provide a grim pleasure, in that they allow the I to affirm itself as separate from the much-despised It. The individual as persona, as isolated I, will defend his suffering as though it were his most prized possession. Of neurotics, Freud states:

> They complain about their sickness, at the same time exploiting it to the limit. As a matter of fact, if an attempt is made to cure them of their ailment, they will protect this most cherished possession of theirs with the self-same fervor with which a lioness defends her offspring.[18]

The individual entering psychotherapy for this kind of problem must learn to befriend the parts of himself which he has previously rejected. How and where is the It to be discovered once it has been cast out? Different therapies deal with this question in different ways. Often the It may be found in one's projections. Fritz Perls was most explicit on this point: "Much material that is our own, that is part of ourselves, has been dissociated, alienated, disowned, thrown out. . . . I believe most of it *is* available, but as projections."[19] Instead of populating the world with innumerable external persecutors, the individual may take back his projections and discover the hostile persecutor in himself. "We have met the enemy and it is us." He starts to see and feel the form of his harsh superego (in Freudian language), or his Controlling Parent (in Transactional Analysis language), or his torturing Topdog (in Gestalt Therapy language). With amazement he discovers how brutal he can be to himself.

At this point, he has moved from "It pinches me" to "I pinch me." He now faces the decisive step of putting an end to his self-torture by acknowledging his anger as a workable part of himself. He must learn, that is, to integrate the It (anger, in this case) in its true form as energy directed from self to the world. As he does so, the anger generally takes a less violent form, in that it is no longer constricted by its rejection as an It, an alien other. In befriending one's angry impulses, one enlarges one's sense of being alive, being human. Anger is no longer an alien territory that must be avoided, but becomes a form of energy that one can explore as a way of relating more positively to the world. In so doing, one regains lost potentials for being and for doing.

We could call these potentials that have been lost because of the dualistic sundering of one's experience into I and It, "forgotten potentials." Freud found that behind every symptom, behind every alienation of an It, there lay a lapse in memory, an amnesia pertaining to the It itself. We forget an It, and we forget that we have forgotten. This is, in effect, the definition of repression!

Thus an important aspect of therapy is to remember something forgotten. *Greater potentials are not so much created as remembered.* To be sure, a remembered potential very often needs to be channelled, exercised, trained, practiced, extended in development, utilized. But on the whole, it is not something new and novel that we must create from the ground up, but rather develops through the remembrance of parts of oneself that have been dismissed and therefore remain untapped. To remember is simply to re-member or re-collect, to *join together again* that which was dis-membered and fragmented, to make whole that which was split and disjointed. For the I to remember the It is to re-member the I and the It, to join them together once again "as it was in the beginning." In short, the key to tapping lost potentials is through acknowledging and befriending the parts of one's experience which one has labeled as "other," as It. "I have befriended the enemy and It is I." When the It is recognized as part of oneself, all the lost potentials of the It are thereby regained. Right there in one's symptom (e.g., fear, anxiety) and right there in one's projections (e.g., resentment, blame, external persecutors) lie the forgotten possibilities for relating directly and energetically to one's world, if one can simply re-member them.

This, then, is Freud's seminal contribution to the search of Western psychotherapy for uncovering lost potentials and for establishing a fuller relationship to one's experience. The inaccurate and impoverished sense of self can be expanded, enlarged, and enriched by befriending and taking back the It. This enriched sense of self seems to be what Freud meant by "ego strength."

THE TASK OF EXISTENTIAL-HUMANISTIC THERAPIES: REUNITING MIND AND BODY

However, although Freud skillfully described the mechanism of alienation, in which experience is split into I and other, he did not see certain wider implications of his work. For one thing, he himself was a victim of the dualistic mentality that he attempted to heal in his patients. He felt that the human world was severed in a number of ways that could never be fully healed, which left him with a basic pessimism about the human ability to transcend neurosis. Although he tried to remedy the consequences of the *intrapsychic dualism* of I and It, he accepted the inevitability of this inner split. He also perceived many wider dualisms, many other forms of I–It separation as an inherent part of human existence.

For example, he seemed to accept the rift between mind and body as irreducible. As Daniel Goleman points out, "From Freud on, mainline psychoanalytic practice, if not thinking, has focused on the intrapsychic to the exclusion of the body."[20] The conflicts that Freud studied were primarily mental, involving two parts of the mind or "psychical apparatus." A strong ego, although no longer debilitated by internal mental conflict, is still never fully at peace with the body or the world in Freud's view. The body and the world remain "other," another form of It beyond the purely intrapsychic "id." And they remain, in Freud's thought, quite alien to the ego. As Norman O. Brown points out, "One can see Freud's thought inhibited by a conception of Self and Other as mutually exclusive alternatives."[21]

Although it is common enough to feel a split between thinking mind and the wider organism, such a separation is but another form of the I–It dualism by which we identify with a more restricted self at the expense of our larger potentials. In fact, the re-membering of mind and body as a unified whole is one of the major thrusts of the existential-humanistic movement in psychology, encompassing such diverse formulations and thinkers as: "being-in-the-world" (Heidegger, Binswanger, Boss); "mind-body intentionality" (Rollo May); "organismic valuing process" (Carl Rogers); "felt meaning and preconceptual experiencing" (Eugene Gendlin); "bioenergetics" (Alexander Lowen). As Rollo May sums up this orientation: "Neither the ego nor the body nor the unconscious can be 'autonomous,' but can only exist as parts of a totality."[22] The alive body which is no longer considered an It is no longer a burden, no longer to be exploited or mortified. Instead, the body can become a moving presence, a rich source of lived meaning which expresses the life that is flowing through one. This integration of mind and body in a unified whole is perhaps the fullest sense of ego strength that has been developed thus far in Western psychology.

Yet the self which existential-humanistic psychology speaks of, though it is significantly wider than the narrow, distorted *persona*, the purely mental ego, is still largely identified with the individual mind/body organism. As such, it still represents a limited "I," which to some extent is still alienated from the "It" of the environment, other sentient beings, the cosmos and its universal principles. In Jacob Needleman's words, the self of Western psychology is still "too small, too egoistic, too introverted."[23] To the extent that this self is still separate from the whole world process, it must continue to experience what Rollo May and other existential thinkers have called "existential anxiety." This is a basic anxiety of the mind/body in relation to the world, and particularly in relation to death. Death manifests not only as a final biological fact but also as a moment-to-moment experiential reality in the continual possibility and threat of nonbeing. As May describes it, this anxiety is "an ontological characteristic of man, rooted in his very existence as such.... Anxiety is *the experience of the threat of imminent non-being.*"[24]

THE BUDDHIST VIEW OF EGO

If we accept May's characterization of existential anxiety as an inevitably recurring feeling in the face of the unknown, that which transcends the self, and finally, death, then we may begin to see the importance of a sense of egolessness for the complete realization of human potential. Although psychotherapy may help develop a relative kind of sanity by stopping the war between different parts of oneself (persona vs. shadow, ego vs. body), it is questionable whether complete human sanity and wholeness can be fully realized so long as one maintains and defends one's identification with ideas of oneself as a separate identity. For the identification with *an image of self*, an idea of who and what one is, a fixed idea of one's virtues and limitations, sets up a boundary which requires *maintaining defenses* against whatever may threaten these ideas. It is precisely the maintaining of defenses against expanding one's horizons that is the essence of neurosis, as understood in all psychological schools. Thus, complete sanity seems impossible without a radical giving up of identification with all ideas about oneself, which is to say, enlightenment itself, as it has been described in the world's great spiritual traditions.

In order to understand what Buddhists mean by egolessness, it is first of all important to realize that they do not mean by "ego" quite what Western psychology generally means by the term. They do not mean a postulated psychological structure that accounts for effective worldly functioning and coping. They do not mean something that has any actual existence, as Freud seemed to think that "the I" did. Ego in the Buddhist perspective refers to an activity, a tendency that keeps recurring at every level of experience. It is the activity of *identifying* with the objects of consciousness (i.e., thoughts, feelings, perceptions) and *grasping* anything that maintains this identity. This identifying and grasping activity splits the world over and over again into an I and an It. This ego activity is seen very concretely in one's style of living. This attempt to maintain a solid self-image by fixating certain parts of one's experience takes place on many levels, from grosser kinds of trying to secure material possessions to subtler kinds of holding on to ideas, feelings, concepts, beliefs, habitual styles of relating to the world.

The Buddhist use and understanding of the term *ego* thus differs from the Freudian ego in the following ways:

1. The Buddhist usage refers *both* to the mechanism of splitting experience into I and It *and* to an impoverished sense of self that follows from this split. In this perspective, it is clear that the ego is

nothing that has real existence, but is an attitude that is manufactured, and to that extent, illusory. For Freud, however, the I is a real and necessary part of the "psychical apparatus."

2. From a Freudian viewpoint, the lifting of ego's repressions leads to a healthy, strong ego. However, from the Buddhist viewpoint, ego is the result of a falsifying act; therefore, a strong ego cannot be an end goal. The goal is rather to see through the falsification of experience. However, a Buddhist would probably not argue with the prerequisite of a healthy ego for the path of liberation from false views of life, *if that means being able to function effectively and not being debilitated by inner warfare.*

In other words, the spiritual path does not seem to require a destruction or breakdown of the Freudian notion of a healthy ego. Rather, it is concerned with transcending the ego by realizing a more encompassing awareness which is not tied to any idea of self. A Buddhist would not suggest destroying one's functional ego—clearly, that could be psychotic—but rather would suggest, beyond developing conventional ego strength, completing the process of "reclamation of It" by fully realizing a way of being that is expansive and open, without attachment to boundaries.

3. Freud saw the ramifications of the I–It split in only one domain, the intrapsychic realm. From a Buddhist perspective, since "ego" refers to an activity rather than an intrapsychic domain, this I–It split may be discovered at other levels of experience as well. For example, the identification with the mind, the mind/body organism, or even conceivably many kinds of "transpersonal witnessing," or "cosmic consciousness" can all be manifestations of the ego tendency. Any level of experience may be turned into one of ego's territories.

Ego in the Buddhist sense, then, arises from the act of holding oneself separate from the totality of one's experience at any moment, and identifying with that separate part of an originally undivided experiential field. The totality of one's experiencing at any moment includes the whole world around one, both physical and social, and yet one habitually identifies with one's limited notion of "me," and then acts to support and protect that notion in every possible way. Normally we have forgotten that we do this, just as the phobic personality has forgotten his own anger which is projected externally as a threat. What we are left with, as "normal neurotics," is not so much the all-pervasive anxiety of the phobic, but the all-pervasive "symptom" of self-consciousness, the feeling of watching and judging our lives as spectators. We have lost our direct and naked contact with our own immediacy and presence as part of the total world process. Since we feel separate from our lives, from the world, from the naked power of life itself insofar as it threatens our sense of identity, we feel an underlying background deficiency or impoverishment. So we grasp and hold on to ideas and things that prop us up or reassure us that we exist and are important.

THE DEVELOPMENT OF A SEPARATE SELF-SENSE (EGO)

How do identification and grasping create this separate self-sense which we normally consider to be who we are? Buddhist psychology has studied a sequence of five major stages in this process, which is said to reoccur from moment to moment. These stages of ego development are known in Buddhism as the five *skandhas*, and will be outlined here as they have been presented in particular by Chögyam Trungpa.[25]

In the Buddhist view, ego is seen as developing out of a basic ground of open awareness, which is beyond personal characteristics or strivings. This open awareness is so groundless that panic arises: "What is this all about?" "Who am I?" "How can I keep from slipping into nothingness?" This panic provides something to hold on to, becoming the basis of ego. To deal with this basic panic a stable center, a fixed reference point of "I-ness" develops. This is known as the first *skandha*, the "birth of ignorance."

The second stage of development occurs once self and other have become separate, with the corresponding territories of this and that, here and there. This second stage is called *feeling*, and refers particularly to judging situations by *feeling out the territory*. Now that the world is an It, out there, separate from me, the question arises: "Is it a hostile, friendly, or neutral territory?"

The third stage, the *skandha* of *perception-impulse*, involves strategies for dealing with situations as one has set them up, namely passion, aggression, and ignorance. Passion in this sense refers to one's strategy for dealing with desirable situations—hunting, seducing, possessing, incorporating. Aggression is a rejection of threatening situations. And ignorance in this sense is an active avoidance which allows one not to have to face things directly.

A further step in self-armoring comes with the fourth *skandha*, known as *conceptualization*. One builds up elaborate schemes of interpretation, rationalization, and belief that are more sophisticated versions of the cruder strategies of passion, aggression, and ignorance. However, as the defense system becomes more complicated, one also becomes further enmeshed and trapped in one's version of reality.

Finally, ego gains consummate sustenance and continuity in the fifth *skandha*, where all the previous stages come together as the *stream of consciousness*—the ongoing flow of thoughts and feelings that reaffirms one's notion of who one is and how one sees the world. This stream of consciousness includes not only explicit thoughts and emotions, which jump about erratically, but also the implicit background or undergrowth of felt meanings that shape our thoughts. Ego maintains its hold through the continuous process of mental chatter and inner dialogue. The *I* is born in the first *skandha* and becomes a fully-developed self-concept (a "me") in the fourth *skandha* of conceptualization. Now with the fifth *skandha*, ego tries to maintain itself through the perpetual dialogue between I and me that accompanies most of our waking consciousness. This inner dialogue keeps us from waking up to the openness of awareness that exists independent of our thoughts. We always have thoughts happening to fill in the little gaps in mind's fabric, and these thoughts, built on strategies of passion, aggression, and ignorance, automatically reinforce our separate self-sense.

William James presents an illuminating impressionistic analysis of how the self-sense is reinforced by the stream of consciousness:

> Now can we tell more precisely in what the feeling of the central active self consists?. . . First of all, I am aware of a constant play of furtherances and hindrances in my thinking, of checks and releases, tendencies which run with desire, and tendencies which run the other way. Among the matters I think of, some range themselves on the side of the thought's interests [passion], whilst others play an unfriendly part thereto [aggression]. The mutual inconsistencies and agreements, reinforcement and obstructions, which obtain amongst these objective matters reverberate backwards and produce what seem to be incessant reactions of my

spontaneity upon them, welcoming or opposing, appropriating or disowning, striving with or against, saying yes or no. This palpitating inward life is, in me, that central nucleus [of the ego].[26]

James goes even one step further in the Buddhist direction by recognizing that beneath these dynamics of consciousness, which *seem* to indicate the existence of an ego, there is no substantial self to be discovered beyond a series of purely bodily processes:

But when I...grapple with particulars, coming to the closest possible quarters with the facts, it is difficult for me to detect in the activity any purely spiritual element at all [i.e., any central self]. Whenever my introspective glance succeeds in turning around quickly enough to catch one of these manifestations of spontaneity in the act, all it can ever feel distinctly is some bodily process, for the most part taking place within the head.[27]

The undergrowth of the five *skandhas* may be discovered by simply attending carefully to one's thought process, as in meditation. For example, if one were to observe one's stream of consciousness in regard to one's lover, one would likely find: a succession of jumbled emotions and thoughts (fifth *skandha*); mental categories that this person has been sorted into (fourth *skandha*); impulses and strategies for attracting, resisting, or avoiding the other (third *skandha*); a feeling of how one basically stands in relation to the other, either in a positive, negative, or neutral light (second *skandha*); and, most fundamentally, a separation of oneself from the person, treating him/her as *other* (first *skandha*).

Thus the Buddhist analysis of ego development is compelling and relevant in a direct and personal way. It sees the project of maintaining a solid self-sense as the basis of ordinary consciousness and behavior. This project is the basis of all forms of I–It dualism, which gives rise to passion and aggression. Thus the Buddhist analysis makes sense out of these driving forces, while allowing for a way of transcending their compulsiveness as well. Psychoanalysis, on the other hand, posits passion (*eros*) and aggression as irrational instincts that are always just *there* as primary brute facts, as aspects of It. And it sees ego as a later development whose function is to deal with these irrational drives. Freud's notion of these instincts as primary givens led to his famous pessimism about the human condition, in that ultimately he could see no way to integrate them fully into the human world.

THE RELATIONSHIP BETWEEN EGO AND EGOLESSNESS

If ego is seen as a way of fixating, grasping, and holding on to contents of consciousness, this holding on is not quite like a barnacle on a rock—it is not a *continuous* holding on. If one could hold on to something without interruption, one would gradually become joined with what one is holding on to, just as a barnacle becomes part of the surface of a rock. The holding on of ego is somewhat different. It is an active, but *intermittent* grasping. It is like the grasping action of the hand that makes a fist. If the fist remained clenched all the time, it would cease to be a hand, and would become a different kind of bodily organ. A fist by definition is the *action of clenching* the open hand. Just as a fist can only form out of the neutral basis of an open hand, the grasping of ego can only assert itself out of non-ego, out of a nongrasping awareness. Without this neutral nongrasping ground to arise from and return to, ego's activity could not occur. This neutral ground is what is known in Buddhism as *egolessness*, open nondual awareness, the *ground* against which the *figure* of ego's grasping stands out. Ego in this sense presupposes egolessness. They are two sides of a coin.

Egolessness provides the ground for ego to arise and to subside, both of which actually occur all the time. Theologian Harvey Cox is quite wrong when he says, "There is no basis whatever in our Western experience for understanding what the Buddhists mean by egolessness."[28] We continually have little glimpses of egolessness in the gaps and spaces between thoughts, the transitive moments of consciousness.* Ego is being born and dying at every moment, in that every moment is new and open to possibility. Ego-centered thoughts are continually arising out of a more open, neutral awareness which surrounds them and eludes their grasp. We continually have to let go of what we have already thought, accomplished, known, experienced, become. A sense of panic underlies these births and deaths, which creates further grasping and clenching. Ego, in some sense, *is the panic about egolessness*, arising in reaction to the unconditional openness that underlies every moment of consciousness.

Identifying with an image of ourselves is an attempt to give ourselves some hold on things, some security. Experience may

---

*The transitive moments of consciousness are discussed in chapter 2.

change, but (at least, so we hope) the experiencer endures. As the poet Apollinaire wrote, *"Les jours s'en vont, je demeure"* (The days may pass, but I remain). But the experiencer gets in its own way, so that we rarely feel in direct contact with things. The experiencer cannot tolerate its continually impending deaths. Existential anxiety is an indication of an impending death. Despair is the dawning realization that the I is nothing, instead of the solid identity it tried to hold on to, that the I has to let go and die again, that there is no support for this continual game, that the I is dangling in thin air and bound to fall again.

SAMSARA AND KARMA

This continual round of births and deaths is understood in two ways in Buddhist thought, as *samsara* and *karma*. *Samsara* refers to the illusory nature of the whole process, in that ego is not an actually-existing thing. Nothing is born or dies except one's thoughts: here I am again, here I go again.

But if ego is illusory, how is it that I still think I am the same *me*? *Karma* refers to the relative continuity between successive births of the idea of self, the transmission of tendencies from one thought or mind-moment to the next. No single mind-moment could ever be completely independent of what went before or what follows after. As James pointed out, insofar as thought proceeds through time, each present moment, even as it slips away into the past, is related to what preceded it upstream and what follows it downstream. This is the karmic sequence. James echoed the Eastern notion of *karma* in his analysis of how thoughts inherit and transmit a chain of seeming ownership:

> It is a patent fact of consciousness that a transmission like this actually occurs. Each pulse of cognitive consciousness, each thought, dies away and is replaced by another....Each later thought, knowing and including thus the thoughts which went before, is the final receptacle...of all that they contain and own. Each thought is thus born an owner, and dies owned, transmitting whatever it realized as its self to its own later proprietor.[29]

Since each pulse of consciousness leads into the next, ego is recreated with every thought that attempts to fix or hold on to some segment of reality. Who I think I am now will determine to a certain extent who I will become. The succession of *karma* appears inexorable.

It would seem then that there is no way off the karmic wheel. Indeed there seems no easy escape from ego. For who is it that desires escape? The desire to escape from oneself or from one's *karma* is itself another grasping thought, another moment on the wheel that keeps it turning in its inevitable progression. In fact, the desire to escape keeps one tied to the wheel ever stronger, for the grasping quality of this desire is the essence of ego. The way out must lie in some other direction.

MEDITATION

It seems that trying to get rid of ego grasping only reinforces a dualistic mentality, and that we need to see how it is that we keep perpetuating our isolation. A powerful tool for doing this is the practice of meditation. Meditation, properly practiced, does not try to get rid of ego and its alienation, but rather creates a situation in which one can see how one manufactures and maintains both the identification with a self-image and the inner struggle this entails. The practice known variously as "just sitting," *zazen*, mindfulness, and bare attention is characterized by attending to the breath while allowing thoughts to arise and pass away. If ego is like an opaque curtain tensely stretched tight and obscuring our vision, returning attention to the breath is like poking a small pinhole in this fabric, thereby allowing just a little bit of light or fresh air to move through. It is as though the interaction of tension and the pinholes causes the holes to get larger, until the fabric finally tears apart. To try to get rid of ego directly would be like pulling all the harder on the curtain, which is self-defeating because it only increases the tension.

CONCLUSIONS: EGO STRENGTH AND EGOLESSNESS

The basic fact of egolessness in no way precludes the development of effective functioning in the world, which the Freudians would call "ego strength." What it implies, rather, is that we can stop identifying with manufactured ideas about our unique, separate identity, and all that this entails in lost potential for fully realizing what it is to be alive. We can stop doing this because of the more primary fact that the essence of human nature, the basis of mind, is completely open and spacious. Mind can identify with a smaller image of itself, a limited self-concept, only because it is a wider, suprapersonal background to begin with. To realize the full impact of egolessness through a practice such as meditation does not mean that one runs a danger of psychoticlike distortions of identity boundaries. One remains perfectly aware of the conventional boundaries of where this organism leaves off and the world or other organisms begin. But this conventional sense of self is seen as just that—a convention—that may be played with rather than anxiously maintained in a serious, heavy-handed manner. One is no longer chronically anchored in that role. Formerly, one could not drop this facade, either for others or—and here is the pathological problem—oneself. One's personality per se is not particularly maladaptive or problematic unless it is totally fixated upon and identified with.

Egolessness also implies the dissolution of the tendency to treat any part of one's total life-environment as an It. Not identifying with I implies that there are no more separate Its, that all sentient beings and the world are an extension of one's own body and to be treated as such. Thus compassion and social concern may be realized in an intimately personal way. The identification with ego is always to some extent narcissistic, as even Freud seemed to recognize when he said, "the development of the ego consists in a departure from primal narcissism and results in a vigorous attempt to recover it."[30] To overcome the I–It split inherent in the identification with ego also implies that one no longer "represses" one's awake intelligence, one's open and clear awareness. Nor does one project it outwardly onto gods, demons, charismatic leaders, culture heroes, or other external beings to whom one might normally sacrifice one's own intelligence.

Finally, in the realization of egolessness is entailed an acceptance of death. Letting go of any form of fixation, identification, attachment is a form of death. Having undergone the death of one's fixation on a separate identity, one can then face death in all its forms more readily. The meditative life-style includes death as a part of life itself. The realization of 'egolessness thus allows the transcending of both Freud's conflict between the erotic life-impulse and the death instinct, as well as the existential anxiety described by May and others as a response to the threat of nonbeing. Seeing that defending a self-image is unnecessary, one is freed from the fear of life. Seeing that being and nonbeing cannot be separated, one is freed from the fear of death. Because one no longer must maintain a life-project based on proving, justifying, extending, or immortalizing one's personal identity, one may breathe more deeply, appreciate death as a recurring and renewing event in one's life, and embrace life in all of the forms in which it presents itself.

NOTES

1. For a fuller elaboration of this analysis of Freud's thought, see Wilber, "Where It was, I shall become," in Walsh & Shapiro (1979).

2. Freud (1933), p. 112.

3. Greenson (1967), p. 26.

4. Fenichel (1972), p. 570.

5. Freud (1961), p. 65.

6. Freud (1927), p. 55.

7. Brandt (1966).

8. Freud (1927), p. 55.

9. Ibid.

10. Freud (1927), p. 56.

11. Ibid., p. 57.

12. Ibid., p. 71.

13. Ibid., pp. 73–74.

14. Ibid., pp. 74–75.

15. Ibid., p. 75.

16. Ibid., p. 76.

17. Perls (1969), p. 107.

18. Freud (1927), p. 121.

19. Perls (1969), p. 67.

20. Goleman (1971), p. 9.

21. N. O. Brown (1959), p. 50.

22. May (1969), p. 224.

23. Needleman (1975b), p. 16.

24. May (1958), p. 50.

25. Trungpa (1973), pp. 121–132.

26. James (1950), p. 299.

27. James (1950), p. 300.

28. Cox (1977), p. 139.

29. James (1950), p. 339.

30. Freud (1959), p. 57.

III
Meditation

Introduction

Many of the contributors to this book have suggested that the potential for living one's life in an open and wakeful way (which the Eastern traditions refer to variously as enlightenment, awakening, liberation, nirvana, objective consciousness, egolessness, etc.) is not just a philosophical or religious belief, but rather may be experienced directly. Moreover, this wider potential is not solely the province of the mystic or the spiritual adept who has retired from the everyday world. It has been suggested that this potential is available to everyone, and may actually be glimpsed in little ways right in the midst of one's ordinarily busy and confused mind-spaces.

To expand one's attention beyond its ordinary distracted and self-centered concerns is not easy, particularly amid the demands and constraints of most people's daily activities. Thus the Eastern traditions stress that to realize one's wakeful mind and to integrate that realization into one's daily life, a form of practice or self-knowledge discipline is necessary. The most common form of self-knowledge discipline in Eastern traditions is the practice of meditation. Meditation is a procedure that allows one to investigate the process of one's own consciousness and experiencing, and to discover the more basic, underlying qualities of one's existence as an intimate reality.

Of course there are many different styles and types of

meditation. Many different practices have been called "meditation," ranging from concentration exercises, contemplation of spiritual ideas, the use of mantras, visualization, and so on. In order to clearly present the relevance of meditation for understanding major psychological issues in one's life, in this book we will focus on one major type of meditation.[1] It is a type which has been characterized as "receptive," "formless," or "opening-up." There are many styles that this particular type of meditation has taken, being known variously by terms such as mindfulness and insight (*shamatha-vipashyana*), *zazen*, choiceless awareness, and self-remembering. This kind of meditation has been characterized by one observer as:

> ...the practice of open, nonreactive attention. Experience is witnessed nonselectively and without interference or interpretation. Continuous alertness is also required....The meditator... must maintain attention in order to avoid becoming fascinated by, caught up in, or carried away by whatever may arise in his awareness.[2]

This practice often involves sitting quietly and attending to one's breathing, while neither indulging in one's thoughts as they appear nor suppressing them, but simply letting them arise and pass away. In this way, the meditator gradually begins to become more familiar with the patterns of his or her own mind. Probably the most obvious fact that one immediately encounters when beginning to practice this kind of meditation is not "cosmic consciousness" so much as the churning, restless quality of one's thinking. This thinking-fantasizing process seems almost nonstop at times, and often feels quite painful to sit with. This more familiar level of mind is fully recognized and acknowledged by the Eastern psychologies, and its patterns have been studied in great depth within certain traditions.[3] Eastern psychologies are not solely concerned with the open and unconditioned dimension of mind, but also with this ordinary level of thoughts, emotions, and fantasies in which we seem to spend most of our lives. Furthermore, it is of great interest and importance in certain Eastern traditions to understand the interrelationship between these two levels.

Probably the initial inspiration for the practice of meditation, at least in the case of such people as the historical Buddha, was the unsatisfactoriness of this normally restless, confused state of mind in which attention is "hijacked" by one preoccupation after another.

The more one meditates, in fact, the more unsatisfactory these ordinary preoccupied, fixated states of mind seem. However, the meditator also may begin to find open moments in his experience which seem to beckon him onward to discover a more clear and accepting kind of awareness. This almost gravitational pull of a greater, more open awareness results in what is often called in the Eastern traditions a *path*.

This path of developing deeper awareness seems to be the basic point of a self-knowledge discipline, which can be distinguished from religious practices that require belief in a deity or a divine plan. Chögyam Trungpa makes this distinction between meditation as a self-knowledge discipline or a religious practice in his chapter. He also characterizes meditation as a process of simplifying one's life, neither trying to attain some ideal nor trying to get rid of anything.

It seems that the goal of meditation, properly understood, is not separate from the actual process that one goes through by following the practice. This is what is meant by the saying "The path is the goal." In other words, instead of seeking some kind of "spiritual reward" as the motivation for meditating, one finds that the process of growth and transformation is inherently valuable. Claudio Naranjo's discussion of this point is quite clear and illuminating, as he points out certain elements that many different kinds of meditation have in common.

Robert Ornstein's review of research bearing on the selective quality of ordinary consciousness, which normally acts in an *automatic* way to *screen out* information, clarifies how it is that meditation may actually work to "open up" awareness.

In the chapter which concludes this section I explore how meditation throws light on that part of our experience which depth psychologists have traditionally called "the unconscious." If what is unconscious are wider ways in which the mind/body organism lives and structures experience, then this understanding has important clinical implications about the nature of psychopathology. Perhaps psychotherapy cannot be separated, in the final analysis, from the path of developing greater awareness, which has traditionally been the province of the spiritual traditions. This theme, which is only briefly touched on at the conclusion of this chapter, leads into the final section of the book, in which new approaches to psychotherapy in light of the Eastern psychologies are explored.

NOTES

1. No doubt many of the ways in which this type of meditation is discussed in this section will also apply to other forms of meditation as well.

2. Washburn (1978), p. 46.

3. Particularly the *abhidharma* literature of Buddhism. It is odd that such an all-pervasive aspect of human experience as this continual thought-fantasy chatter has been so little studied in Western psychology.

10

An Approach to Meditation

Chögyam Trungpa

Meditation seems to be the basic theme of spiritual practice. It is a vast subject and one that is very loosely defined, so there is a tremendous possibility of distorting it, adding our own version to it. Therefore, it seems quite important to take a look at meditation scientifically in the way it applies to our spiritual practice.

There are all sorts of concepts about meditation. One involves trying to establish communication with a divine power and using exotic techniques to tune into this power. This particular style of meditation could be defined as a religious practice. Another way of approaching meditation is as a spiritual practice rather than a religious one, working with the perceiver rather than focusing on external divine forces of any kind.

Do such things as divine forces exist or not? Does a God exist or not? The answer is that it is not certain until we work with the perceiver of that particular energy. In the Buddhist form of meditation we try to look at the perceiver of the universe, the perceiver which is self, ego, me, mine. In order to receive guests, we have to have a place to receive them. It is possible, however, that we may not find it necessary to invite any guests at all. Once we have created the place where guests are welcome, we may find they are there already.

This chapter is a transcription of a lecture given at the Washington Conference, Association for Humanistic Psychology, September 1971.

The practice of meditation is based, not on how we would like things to be, but on what is. We often do not have a proper understanding of what we are, of what we are actually doing. Instead our attention is focused on the possible end-product of the processes we are involved in. Spirituality should be taken very seriously, very honestly. This means it should not partake of that exotic quality which is filled with promises. From the beginning it should be concerned with the actuality of who is involved in the practice.

In the tradition of Buddhism, each person in the lineage of teachers develops a self-understanding which adds to the tradition. The process is like handing down a recipe for bread. In each generation the bread is exactly like the original bread, but possibly more flavorful because of the added experience of the bakers involved in the handing down. In each generation the bread is fresh, delicious, and healthful.

One might say, how can I know that these experiences are valid for me? I can't say that they are particularly valid for particular individuals unless I have a personal relationship and understanding with them. But certainly the process of working on one's psychological states from a fresh point of view is valid. What I have to say about these psychological states is that they are purely one's own experience. Studying and learning about them is more of a confirmation than new information.

There is a need to be realistic and critical about what we are. We must not be spiritually gullible. Often we find that what we are is not attractive; we find looking at ourselves discouraging. But looking at ourselves is not finally discouraging; rather it develops the ability to be more realistic. We always ask a question when there is uncertainty. Questions would not arise at all if we did not have the creative ground of uncertainty within us. The questions we ask already contain the answers in embryonic form. In other words, they are expressions of the answers. The answer may turn out to be negative and disappointing, causing us to hate ourselves, but nevertheless, we will have discovered something real.

This self-disillusionment seems to be the starting point of meditation practice. The starting point is dissatisfaction, the absence of a dream or wishful thinking. It is something realistic, down to earth, and direct.

Ego starts from bewilderment; bewilderment or dissatisfaction or not knowing how to step to the next solution. Finding a solution, we haven't actually found it, because we're not exactly certain to whom the solution applies. There is, therefore, a basic suspicion of the nonexistence of ourselves, a basic confusion. Somehow that basic bewilderment or confusion is the working base.* From that confusion, basic bewilderment, or basic paranoia, whatever we call it, arises the attempt to communicate further in order to establish our ego.

Each time we try to establish our so-called reality, the basic paranoia becomes larger and larger; for establishing relationships with the apparent phenomenal world makes demands, requires energy, and the facing of overwhelming situations. When the phenomenal world becomes greater and more powerful than us, there is automatically a feeling of bewilderment. As we continually feel bewildered, we do our best to establish our pattern. In a materialistic sense, we try and become a rich, respectable, or powerful person. In a spiritual sense we try and adapt to a basic discipline. Finding a basic discipline could be a process which enriches the ego or the self. Even if we follow a spiritual rather than a worldly life, if we don't have the basic understanding of why we are trying to accumulate, we are still materialistic in outlook. This is what is known as psychological or spiritual materialism.**

What we do, what we collect doesn't matter. The style of the collection is based on the notion of developing a fundamental health which should be seen as basic ego trying to relate to things as sedatives. Any kind of spiritual practice based on that attitude could be extremely dangerous. One can attain a state that could be called spiritual egohood.

We have a problem there. The question is, how can we approach spirituality otherwise? Is there any possibility of approaching it in another way at all? You might say, please don't say no, please tell us some more. Well, that's it in a sense. Once we realize that there is no

---

*Basic bewilderment or primal ignorance about who we are and what we are supposed to be doing gives rise to the grasping attempts of ego to establish a solid identity. Trungpa calls this bewilderment the "working base" here because it is also a vulnerable, questioning attitude which may lead to awakening if it is not totally suppressed by ego's attempts to solidify itself and pin things down through fixed concepts (Ed.).

**For a further discussion of the phenomenon of spiritual materialism, see Trungpa (1973) (Ed.).

way out from this end, we want to break through something; we want to step out more, to jump. Jumping or leaping is a very dignified thing to do. It is being willing to be an explorer on the biggest scale, willing to be a samurai in the widest sense, willing to break through, to be a warrior. It seems that the question begins from that point when we actually want to break through something. That leap consists, of course, of giving up goal, aim, and object at the same time. What we are doing in this case is stepping out of even the basic bewilderment; not trying to creep around from underneath or by the back door, but stepping out completely.

We find that in spite of the willingness to explore, we still have the basic bewilderment within us and we have to work with that. This involves accepting the basic bewilderment or paranoia as it is. That is the working base. That basic psychological state consists of layers of psychological facades of all kinds. The basic bewilderment is overwhelmingly stupid, and yet intelligent in that it plays its game of deaf and dumb cunningly. Beyond the bewilderment, ego develops certain patterns of emotions and sensations. When emotions are insufficient to fortify the ego, we apply concept, the conceptual process of labeling and naming things. Things having names and concepts attached to them help us domesticate the bewilderment or confusion. Beyond that, ego collects neurotic thoughts, neurotic not in the sense of mad, but in the sense of irregular. Thoughts in this case change direction all the time and are on very shaky ground. A single thought pattern never develops. Rather, one thought overlaps another—thoughts on spirituality, sexual fantasies, money matters, domestic matters, etc., overlapping all the time. That is the last stage of ego development.* In a sense ego is systematically well fortified.

Bewilderment, as we have said, is reinforced by processes developing at the emotional level. Emotion in this case is the basic magnetizing quality which is passion or the basic repelling quality which is aggression. The next level comes in when the emotions cease to function as impulsive processes. At this point, we need an analytical mind to reinforce them, to put them in their proper place, to confirm their right to be there. The analytical process creates concepts. Concepts are scientifically, mathematically, philosophically, or spiritually worked out.

*This is the process of the five *skandhas*. See also chapter 9 (Ed.).

Concepts and emotions are very crude spokes of the wheel. There is a gap between the two, an area of not knowing where we are, a fear of being nothing. These gaps could be filled with thoughts of all kinds. Discursive thoughts, grasshopperlike thoughts, drunken-elephant type thoughts, all fill the gaps of not knowing what we are, where we're at. If we want to work on that particular base, the idea is to not collect any new things, new subjects.

Further collecting would be inviting invasion from the outside. Since the whole structure of ego is so well fortified against attack, an external invasion is not going to destroy the ego at all. In fact, it is going to reinforce the whole structure because the ego is being given more material with which to work. Meditation practice is based on an undoing, unlearning process. It is an infiltration into this well-fortified structure of the ego.

Beginning meditation practice works purely on dealing with thought processes. It begins there because these thought processes are the last fringes of ego's development. Working on them makes use of certain very simple techniques. The techniques are very important and must be very simple.

Presenting exotic techniques tends to emphasize the foreign quality rather than the familiar, "homey" quality that is most desirable. The technique most often used in the Buddhist tradition is awareness of breathing or walking. These techniques are not ways of developing concentration, tranquility or peacefulness, for these qualities cannot be forcibly developed. All of these things are beyond achievement if they are sought after.

The other way of approaching the practice is the gamelike approach. The game is that the path and the goal are the same. You are not trying to achieve anything, but are trying to relate to the path which is the goal. We try to become completely one with the techniques (breathing, walking, etc.). We do not try to do anything with the technique but identify and become one with it. The beginning level of any of the traditions of meditation could be said to be a game, a trip of its own. It's purely imagination; we imagine ourselves meditating. It's another type of dreaming. One has to accept that dreamlike quality and work along with it. We can't start perfectly and beautifully, but if we are willing to start by accepting our neuroses and basic chaos, we have a stepping stone. Don't be afraid of being a fool; start as a fool.

The techniques of meditation practice are not designed to reduce active thoughts at all. They provide a way of coming to terms with everything that goes on inside. Once we have accepted what goes on in our mind as neither good nor bad, but just flashes of thoughts, we have come to terms with it. So long as we regard the mind's activity as a foreign invasion, we are introducing another new element to the chaos and are feeding it more. If we accept it as part of our ego development, ego structure, and don't evaluate it or put any labels on it, we come much closer to seeing the interior.

After the thought processes, the next barrier is the pattern of concepts. We should not try to push away the concepts, but try to see them realistically. Concepts are based on irrelevant evaluations. There is nothing which is absolutely good or bad. Once we cease to plant the seed of evaluation, the conceptual processes become a neutral and open ground.

The next process is that of emotion: love, hate, etc. A problem arises when we tend to become too ambitious in terms of dealing with emotions—particularly those involved with the spiritual practice. We've been told to be kind, gentle, good people. Those are the conventional ideas of spirituality. When we begin to find the spikey quality in ourselves, we see it as antispirituality and try to push it away. That is the biggest mistake of all in working with our basic psychological patterns. Once we try to push the biggest problems away and look for a dramatic cure for them, we are constantly pushed back, defeated all the time. The idea is not to seduce ourselves into trying to create a utopian spirituality, but to try and look into the details of the peak emotions, the dramatic qualities of the emotions. We don't have to wait for situations which are regarded as big and meaningful to us; we should make use of even the small situations in which these emotions occur. We should work on the small or minor irritations and their particular emotional qualities. Do not suppress or let go of irritations, but become part of them; feel their abstract qualities. The irritations then have no one to irritate. They might fade away or become creative energy. If we are able to work brick by brick with those smaller, seemingly insignificant emotions, at some point we will find that removing each brick has taken away the whole wall.

We tend to be involved with ambition in spiritual practice. There's no hope if we become too ambitious in any way. Once this occurs and we try to achieve something very quickly, we are forced to remove the awareness of knowing the situation as it is now. Ambition seduces us into thinking of something that we want to achieve in the future. We become too future-oriented, missing the point of a given situation. Our greatest opportunity is in the present moment and we begin to lose it. However, feeling that the future is an open situation is what meditation practice actually is. Relating with the present situation removes the basic bewilderment that we have discussed, the fundamental heart of the whole ego structure. If we are able to relate with the actual situation as it is, without referring to the past or future, then there are flashes of gaps, possibilities of approaching the present situation. That freshness or sharpness, the penetrating quality of knowing the present situation, brings in a way of looking at the bewilderment with clarity and precision. If we're trying to achieve something in terms of spiritual ambition, that ambition itself becomes a hangup.

The only way to relate to the present situation of spirituality or the neurotic state of the moment is by meditation. I don't mean sitting meditation only, but relating with the emotional situations of daily life in a meditative way, by working with them, being aware of them as they come up. Every situation then becomes a learning process. These situations are the books; they are the scriptures. You don't need more than that. Books and sacred writings become purely a source of inspiration. We have to realize that we already have within us the potential of developing spirituality before we read the books or regard them as part of our collection.

By undoing the successive layers of facades, we begin to discover that the precision and sharpness we spoke of is there already. We don't have to develop it or nurse it. It's just a question of acknowledging it. That is what is known as faith and devotion. The fundamental meaning of faith is recognizing that precision, clarity, and health are already there. That is the psychologically wealthy way of looking at situations. You see that you are already rich, that you don't have to search for something else or introduce a new element.

We say that the sun is behind the clouds, but actually it is not the sun but the city from which we view it that is behind the clouds. If we realized that the sun is never behind the clouds we might have a different attitude toward the whole thing.

QUESTION AND ANSWER SESSION

Q: For me you made it very clear—the neutral ground of our concepts. But when you talked about emotions, you introduced another word—working on the "small irritations," which is somewhat different.... I would like to hear you elaborate on the small emotions.

A: Well, the seemingly smaller irritations are not really small, but "small" is a way of viewing them. We view them as being insignificant things—such as the little bug crawling up your leg or a drafty window blowing at your face. Little details like that are seemingly insignificant because they have less concepts from your point of view. But they still do have the irritating quality in full flesh. So the way to deal with it is that you have a tremendous opportunity there, because you don't have that heavy concept, so you have a very good open approach toward working with that irritation.

When I say "working with" irritation, I don't mean to say suppress irritation or let go of irritation. But trying to become part of the irritation, trying to feel the abstract quality. You see, generally what happens when we have irritation is that we feel we are being undermined by irritation, and we begin to lose our own basic dignity; something else overwhelms us. That kind of power game goes on always. That is the source of the problem. When we are able to become completely one with irritations or feel the abstract quality of the irritation as it is, then irritation has no one to irritate. So it becomes a sort of judo practice, the using of the irritation's energy as part of your basic development.

Q: Am I reading you right when you say the effect of meditation begins when one empties oneself from preconceived ideas and notions, and one must empty oneself before one can be filled?

A: Well, I wouldn't say that is the aim of meditation particularly, but that is the by-product of meditation. In actual practice you don't have to achieve anything, but you try to be with the technique.

Q: We have a pattern of becoming one with whatever it is that concerns one and going with it; and in the process it is no longer a problem. I understand Buddhism also contains this thinking.

A: I think so, yes. But the whole point is not trying to solve the problem. It's having a friendly, welcoming attitude to the problem.

Q: I'm amazed that so many of our so-called modern concepts—breathing, etc.—Buddhism has used for thousands of years. I had the pleasure of being with a Buddhist monk in Bali and found that all my "original" thinking was already contained within Buddhism.
A: Well, it's something basic, the voice of basic sanity. I mean, you can find it anywhere, in any tradition if it faces reality. It doesn't necessarily have to be Buddhist.

Q: Is meditation a continuous process of dynamic living?
A: Definitely. Without ambition, of course.

Q: When one is liberated, when one has practiced meditation in the proper way, without ambition, and one reaches the goal, how does one live? What is the nature of his being?
A: Well, the actual nature of that being is quite dangerous to talk about.

Q: Why is it dangerous?
A: Well, that could be a temptation.

Q: An attempt to go there artificially?
A: Or unwise.

Q: Can't we discuss it?
A: I would say the continual process of living becomes more real. You are actually in touch with more real reality, the nakedness of reality where there is natural confidence without a framework of relativity. So I would imagine that that state of being, from a personal psychological point of view, is extremely free. But not being free about anything, but just being free, being true.

Q: Is there ecstasy and rapture?
A: I don't think so, because then you have to maintain that ecstasy. It is a state which doesn't involve any maintenance.

Q: What are the prerequisites before one begins to meditate?
A: That you are willing to meditate, willing to go into discipline or practice—a conviction which could be a false conviction at that time, but it doesn't matter.

Q: How does one go about escaping from the belief in the analytical mind in order to begin?
A: Well, it seems that in terms of meditation the literal quality of the

technique automatically brings you down, because there is no room for any sidetracks at all. It is quite an absurd, repetitive, ordinary technique, quite boring often; yet somehow you are put into a framework where an instinctive understanding of relating with the technique, rather than an intellectual one, begins to develop.

You see, the problem is that analytical mind cannot be freed by another aspect of analytical mind until the questions of analytical mind are dissolved. This is the same as the method of "Who am I?" in Ramana Maharshi's teaching. If you regard "Who am I?" as a question, then you are still analyzing yourself, but when you begin to realize that "Who am I?" is a statement the analytical mind becomes confused. One realizes there is something personal about it. Something instinctive which is freed by the actual living situation. The disciplined technique of practicing meditation amounts to putting yourself into an inconceivable situation in which the analytical mind doesn't function anymore. So I would say that the disciplines of the Buddhist teachings are largely a way of freeing oneself from analytical mind. Which has a dream quality. Analytical mind is close to the clouds, while the instinctual level is much closer to the earth. So in order to come down to earth, you have to use the earth as a means of bringing you down.

Q: Could you give us some examples of the meditation practices?
A: Generally in the Buddhist tradition the first step is working on the breathing—not concentrating, not contemplating, but identifying with the breath. You are the technique; there is no difference between you and the technique at all. By doing that, at a certain stage the technique just falls away, becomes irrelevant. At that point your practice of meditation is much more open to meditation in action, everyday life situations.

But that doesn't mean that the person should become absorbed in the state of meditation in the vague sense at all. You see, the basic meditation is being, I suppose we could say. But at the same time it is not being dazed by being. You can describe being in all sorts of ways. You could say being is a cow on a sunny afternoon in a meadow, dazed in its comfort. You could think in terms of an effort of being, trying to bring some effort to yourself to be being. That is to say, being with the watcher watching yourself doing. Then there is actual being—we could call it "actual"—which is just being right there with precision and openness. I call it panoramic awareness, aerial view. You see a very wide view of the whole area because you see the details of each area. You see the wide view, each area, each detail. Black is black and white is white, everything is being observed. And that kind of openness and being is the source of daily practice. Whether the person is a housewife or secretary or politician or lawyer, whatever it may be, his life could be viewed that way. In fact, his work could become an application of skillful means in seeing the panoramic view. Fundamentally the idea of enlightenment—the notion or term "enlightenment" or "Buddha" or "awakened one"—implies tremendous sharpness and precision along with a sense of spaciousness.

We can experience this; it is not myth at all. We experience a glimpse of it, and the point is to start from that glimpse and gradually as you become more familiar with that glimpse and the possibilities of reigniting it, it happens naturally. Faith is realizing that there is some open space and sharpness in our everyday life. There occurs a flash, maybe a fraction of a second. These flashes happen constantly, all the time.

11
The Domain of Meditation

Claudio Naranjo

The word *meditation* has been used to designate a variety of practices that differ enough from one another so that we may find trouble in defining what meditation is.

Is there a commonality among the diverse disciplines alluded to by this same word? Something that makes them only different forms of a common endeavor? Or are these various practices only superficially related by their being individual spiritual exercises? The latter, apparently, is the point of view of those who have chosen to equate meditation with only a certain type of practice, ignoring all the others that do not fit their description or definition. It is thus that in the Christian tradition meditation is most often understood as a dwelling upon certain *ideas*, or engaging in a directed intellectual course of activity; while some of those who are more familiar with Eastern methods of meditation equate the matter with a dwelling on anything *but* ideas, and with the attainment of an aconceptual state of mind that excludes intellectual activity. Other authors distinguish concentration from meditation, regarding the former as a mere drill for the latter.

The distinction between ideational versus nonideational is only one of the many contrasting interpretations of the practices called meditation. Thus, while certain techniques (like those in the Tibetan Tantra) emphasize mental images, others discourage paying attention to any imagery; some involve sense organs and use visual forms (mandalas) or music, and others emphasize a complete withdrawal from the senses; some call for complete inaction, and others involve action (*mantra*), gestures (*mudra*), walking, or other activities. Again, some forms of meditation require the summoning up of specific feeling states, while others encourage an indifference beyond the identification with any particular illusion.

The very diversity of practices given the name of "meditation" by the followers of this or that particular approach is an invitation to search for the answer of what meditation is *beyond its forms*. And if we are not content just to trace the boundaries of a particular group of related techniques, but instead search for a unity within the diversity, we may indeed recognize such a unity in an *attitude*. We may find that, *regardless of the medium* in which meditation is carried out—whether images, physical experiences, verbal utterances, etc.—the task of the meditator is essentially the same, as if the many forms of practice were nothing more than different occasions for the same basic exercise.

If we take this step beyond a behavioral definition of meditation in terms of a *procedure*, external or even internal, we may be able to see that meditation cannot be equated with thinking or nonthinking, with sitting still or dancing, with withdrawing from the senses or waking up the senses: meditation is concerned with the development of a *presence*, a modality of being, which may be expressed or developed in whatever situation the individual may be involved.

This presence or mode of being transforms whatever it touches. If its medium is movement, it will turn into dance; if stillness, into living sculpture; if thinking, into the higher reaches of intuition; if sensing, into a merging with the miracle of being; if feeling, into love; if singing, into sacred utterance; if speaking, into prayer or poetry; if doing the things of ordinary life, into a ritual in the name of God or a celebration of existence. Just as the spirit of our times is technique-oriented in its dealings with the external world, it is technique-oriented in its approach to psychological or spiritual reality. Yet, while numerous schools propound this or that method as a solution of human problems, we know that it is not merely the method but *the way in which it is employed* that determines its effectiveness, whether in psychotherapy, art, or education. The application of techniques or tools in an interpersonal situation depends upon an almost intangible "human factor" in the teacher, guide, or psychotherapist. When the case is that of the intrapersonal method of meditation, the human factor beyond the method becomes even more elusive. Still, as with other techniques, it is the *how* that counts more than the *what*. The question of the right attitude on the part of the meditator is the hardest for meditation teachers to transmit, and though it is the object of most supervision, may be apprehended only through practice.

It might be said that the attitude, or "inner posture," of the meditator is both his path and his goal. For the subtle, invisible *how* is not merely a *how to meditate* but a *how to be*, which in meditation is exercised in a simplified situation. And precisely because of its elusive quality beyond the domain of an instrumentality that may be described, the attitude that is the heart of meditation is generally sought after in the most simple external or "technical" situations: in stillness, silence, monotony, "just sitting." Just as we do not see the stars in daylight, but only in the absence of the sun, we may never taste the subtle essence of meditation in the daylight of ordinary activity in all its complexity. That essence may be revealed when we have suspended everything else but *us*, our presence, our attitude, beyond any activity or the lack of it. Whatever the outer situation, the inner task is simplified, so that nothing remains to do but gaze at a candle, listen to the hum in our own ears, or "do nothing." We may then discover that there are innumerable ways of gazing, listening, doing nothing; or, conversely, innumerable ways of *not* just gazing, not just listening, not just sitting. Against the background of the simplicity required by the exercise, we may become aware of ourselves and all that we bring to the situation, and we may begin to grasp experientially the question of attitude.

While practice in most activities implies the development of habits and the establishment of conditioning, the practice of meditation can be better understood as quite the opposite: a persistent effort to detect and become free from all conditioning, compulsive functioning of mind and body, habitual emotional responses that may contaminate the utterly simple situation required by the participant. This is why it may be said that the attitude of the meditator is both his path and his goal: the unconditioned state is the freedom of attainment and also the target of every single effort. What the meditator realizes in his practice is to a large extent how he is failing to meditate properly, and by becoming aware of his failings he gains understanding and the ability to let go of his wrong way. The right way, the desired attitude, is what remains when we have, so to say, stepped out of the way.

12
The Esoteric and Modern Psychologies of Awareness

Robert Ornstein

What are the general effects of the practice of meditation on awareness? If we are to determine the aftereffects of meditation on awareness, it would be useful to review some aspects of the psychology and physiology of consciousness. Though we should not expect that the practice of meditation will necessarily change every aspect of ordinary consciousness, we may be able to determine more clearly the effect and aftereffect of meditation in terms of our knowledge of the psychology and physiology of consciousness.

Contemporary psychology provides several different viewpoints from which to characterize awareness. Some are completely independent of one another, some are complementary, some intersect.

We normally consider that the single function of our sensory systems is to gather information about the world: we see with our eyes, we hear with our ears. Gathering information is certainly a major function of sensation, but sensory systems also act in just the opposite way. Our ordinary awareness of the world is selective and is restricted by the characteristics of sensory systems. Many philosophers have stressed a similar view, but only recently has precise physiological evidence been available. Huxley and Broad have elaborated on Bergson's general view of the mind as a "reducing valve." In *The Doors of Perception* and *Heaven and Hell*, Huxley quotes Dr. D. C. Broad, the eminent Cambridge philosopher:

The function of the brain and nervous system is to protect us from
being overwhelmed and confused by this mass of largely useless
and irrelevant knowledge, by shutting out most of what we should
otherwise perceive and remember at any given moment, leaving
only that very small and special selection that is likely to be
practically useful.

And then Huxley comments:

According to such theory each one of us is potentially Mind at
Large. But insofar as we are animals our business is at all costs to
survive. To make biological survival possible, Mind at Large has
to be funneled through the reducing valve of the brain and nervous
system. What comes out at the other end is a measly trickle of the
kind of consciousness which will help us to stay alive on the
surface of this particular planet. To formulate and express the
contents of this reduced awareness man has invented and endlessly
elaborated those symbol-systems and implicit philosophies that we
call languages. Every individual is at once the beneficiary and the
victim of the linguistic tradition into which he has been born—the
beneficiary inasmuch as language gives access to the accumulated
records of other people's experience, the victim insofar as it
confirms him in the belief that reduced awareness is the only
awareness and as it bedevils his sense of reality, so that he is all too
apt to take his concepts for data, his words for actual things. That
which, in the language of religion, is called "this world" is the
universe of reduced awareness expressed, and, as it were, petrified
by language. The various "other worlds" with which human beings
erratically make contact, are so many elements in the totality of
awareness belonging to Mind at Large. Most people most of the
time know only what comes through the reducing valve and is
consecrated as genuinely real by their local language. Certain
persons, however, seem to be born with a kind of bypass that
circumvents the reducing valve. In others temporary bypasses may
be acquired either spontaneously or as the result of deliberate
"spiritual exercises" or through hypnosis or by means of drugs.
Through these permanent or temporary bypasses there flows, not
indeed the perception of everything that is happening everywhere
in the universe (for the bypass does not abolish the reducing valve
which still excludes the total content of Mind at Large), but
something more than, and above all something different from, the
carefully selected, utilitarian material which our narrow individual
minds regard as a complete, or at least sufficient, picture of
reality.[1]

Huxley writes more elegantly and less quantitatively than do most researchers and theorists in the fields of psychology and physiology, but much modern work in these disciplines tends to support the same general view that ordinary awareness is a personal construction. If awareness is a construction and not a "registration" of the external world, then by altering the nature of the construction process our awareness can be changed.

The normal view outside of the philosophical tradition, psychology, and the esoteric disciplines is that we experience *what exists,* that the external world is completely and perfectly reflected in our subjective experience. This idea is quite impossible to maintain even at the simplest level if we consider the many different forms of energy that impinge upon us at any moment. Sounds, electricity, light waves, magnetism, smells, chemical and electrical impulses within ourselves, thoughts, internal muscular sensations, all constantly bombard us. An appropriate question on the nature of our "ordinary" consciousness should be one that reflects a view quite different from the common one. How do we ever achieve a stable consciousness in the face of all this fantastic amount of stimulation?

There are two major ways in which we "make sense" out of the world. First, we use our sensory systems to discard and to simplify the incoming information, allowing only a few of the possible dimensions of sensation into our awareness. Second, we further sort the amount of information that does come in along a very limited number of dimensions, out of which we construct our awareness. These dimensions have been called in psychology "unconscious inferences," "personal constructs," "category systems," "efferent readinesses," or "transactions," depending on the writer's style and his level of analysis.

Quite obviously, each individual receptor is equipped physiologically to receive information only within certain limits. We wouldn't expect our eyes, for instance, to respond to the low bass note of an organ, or our ears to the taste of noodles. The eyes are "tuned" by their physiological structure to receive only a certain limited frequency range of stimulation and to send messages to the brain when energy in the appropriate frequency range reaches them—and so with the ears, the tongue, etc. That sensory receptors function to reduce the incoming information can be better understood if we study animals who are lower on the phylogenetic continuum and whose receptors discard even more information than do our own. It is difficult, otherwise, to conceive of the amount of stimulation to which we ourselves do not respond. We can then say that the function of our receptors and sensory systems is not only to gather information but to *select* and discard it.

If we consider more and more complicated organisms, their capacity to "retune" their sensory systems becomes greater. If the visual field of a human is turned around by wearing inverting lenses, he can, in a few weeks, perform actions as complicated as riding a bicycle through town. As we consider more complicated animals, more and more advanced all the way up to man, their nervous systems seem to be more computerlike—machines, to be sure, but ones that can alter the relationship between input and performance by a change in the "program." The higher mammals can be regarded as machines that are capable of "retuning" themselves in accordance with alterations in the external environment.

We can easily demonstrate this computerlike, higher-level selectivity and tuning. At a party or at a place where several people are talking at the same time, we close our eyes and listen to just one person speaking, then tune him out and listen to another person. We are able to do this, to listen to one person's speech and then suppress it as it comes into our ears and hear another person's speech that we have previously ignored. It is very easy to do. We shouldn't really be surprised since we tune ourselves continuously to suit our needs and expectations, but we are not usually aware of it. When we perspire during the summer we like the taste of foods that are more salty than usual. We don't think consciously that we need salt and we should take more salt in our foods; we *simply like* foods that at other times we would consider quite oversalted.

Some examples from our everyday existence show how we become more sensitive to portions of our environment when we are in need. When we are hungry we see more restaurants, see more food, smell more aromas than when we are not. When we are awaiting someone we immediately notice anyone who resembles the other person, in his hair color, general appearance, clothes, or because he is coming out of the door through which we expect the person to arrive. When we are interested in the opposite sex, we perceive them differently than when we are not. When after a meal our need for food has diminished, so does the attractiveness of food. We are able continuously to reprogram and reconstruct our awareness, based, at least in part, on our intent.

A major way in which we create our awareness is by tuning out the constancies in our environment. While we are learning a new skill, like skiing, all the complex adjustments and motor movements are somewhat painfully in our awareness. As we progress, as skill becomes "automatic," the movements no longer enter consciousness. Compare the first time you tried to drive a car, especially one with a gear shift, with how it feels to drive a car now, after you've learned. When we drive to work the first time, everything appears quite new and interesting—a red house, a big tree, the road itself—but gradually, as we drive the same route over and over, we "get used" to everything on the way. We stop "seeing" the trees, the bridges, the corners, etc. We become "automatic" in our response to them. When we enter a room and a fan is turning, creating a buzzing sound, we are aware of it for the first few moments and then the sound seems to go out of awareness.

Many of the producers of the objects we buy take into account that we constantly need new stimulation, and that we adapt to and tune out the old. When we buy a new phonograph record, we play it over and over again for a period, then leave it on the shelf unplayed. We get bored, the record no longer seems "new"; it is out of our awareness—on "automatic." Most of the market products are periodically changed slightly (automobiles, for instance), so that we begin to "see" them again, and presumably buy them.

In psychology and physiology, the phenomenon we have described is termed "habituation." The "response" in this case is one of the physiological components of the "orienting reaction" to new stimuli, the reaction that involves our registering of input. The physiological indicators of such reaction include EEG, heart rate, and skin resistance. Suppose we measure the resistance of the skin, for example, and repeat a click every five seconds. The first tone will cause a sharp drop in skin resistance. There will be less skin resistance change caused by the second tone, still less by the third, until, depending on the parameters of the particular experiment, the skin resistance no longer drops with each click. The response of the skin to this stimulus has been "habituated." When, after hearing for a while the sound of a clock ticking, we then turn the sound off, we no longer show the "orienting" or registering reaction. This does not merely involve a simple process of raising the threshold for stimuli entering into awareness and thus tuning the click out. Our computer is capable of a more sophisticated selective tuning. It is true that if we substitute a louder click, we will begin to hear it again. And if we substitute a *softer* one, the orienting reaction also returns and we will hear it again. If we change the interval between the appearances of the tone—if it appears a little bit later than we expect, or a little bit sooner, even slightly—the tone returns to our awareness, and the orienting reaction reappears.

Karl Pribram has pointed out another example of this phenomenon, which he called the "Bowery El" effect. In New York City an elevated railroad once ran along Third Avenue. At a certain time late each night a noisy train would pass through. The train line was torn down some time ago with some interesting aftereffects. People in the neighborhood called the police to report "something strange" occurring late at night—noises, thieves, burglars, etc. It was determined that these calls took place at around the time of the former late-night train. What these people were "hearing," of course, was the *absence* of the familiar noise of the train. We have a similar experience, although much simpler, when a noise that has been going on suddenly stops.[2]

If we look at the same object over and over again, we begin to look in the same way each time. We do this with the constancies of our world, our ordinary surroundings—the pictures in our house, the route we drive every day, etc. Charles Furst has studied the effect of repeated viewing of the same picture on the way we look at it.[3] He found that eye movements tend to become more and more stereotyped as the same visual stimulus is presented. When we see a new image our eyes tend to move in a new pattern around it, but as we see it again and again, like the rooms in our house, we tend to look in a fixed way at fixed portions of it and ignore or tune out the rest. The "Bowery El" effect, the "Furst" effect, and the more precise studies on habituation suggest that we tune out the recurrences of the world by making a "model" of the external world within our nervous system, and testing input against it.[4] We somehow can program and continuously revise or reprogram conception or models of the external world. If the input and our model agree, as they do most often with the constancies of the world, then the input stays out of consciousness. If there is any disagreement, if the new input is *even slightly* different, slower, softer, louder, a different form, color, or even if it is absent, we become aware of the particular input once again. This "programming" forms an additional reducing valve behind the fixed reducing valves of the senses.

Perhaps the most clear and striking trend in the psychology and physiology of perception in the past few years has been our increasing understanding of the interactive and constructive nature of our "ordinary" awareness. One of the leaders in this investigation, Jerome Bruner, has emphasized that perception involves acts of categorization.[5] As we become experienced in dealing with the world, we attempt to make more and more consistent "sense" out of the mass of information arriving at our receptors. We develop stereotyped systems or categories for sorting the input that reaches us. The set of categories we develop is limited, much more limited than the richness of the input. Simple categories may be "straight," "red," or "animal." More complex ones may be "English," "rectilinear," or "in front of." In social situations categories may be personality traits. If we come to consider a person "aggressive," we then consistently tend to sort all his actions in terms of this particular category. Personality traits seem to exist mainly in the category system of the perceiver.[6]

Our previous experience with objects strengthens our category systems. We expect cars to make a certain noise, traffic lights to be a certain color, food to smell a certain way, and certain people to say certain things. But what we actually experience, according to Bruner and to others, is the *category* which is evoked by a particular stimulus, and *not* the occurrence in the external world. Bruner and his associates conducted an extensive series of studies on the effect of category systems on awareness. In his review "On Perceptual Readiness," he suggests that "correct" perception is "...not so much a matter of representation as it is a matter of what I shall call model-building."[7]

Since we can tune ourselves on the basis of our category systems, there must be physiological mechanisms that allow us to tune our awareness. Pribram and Spinelli have set out to demonstrate an analogue of this process on the physiological level.[8] They recorded from cells in the frontal cortex of the brain while stimulating other areas, and showed that the pattern of the receptive fields to external stimuli can be altered by the brain. These and other experiments demonstrate that the output system of the brain (efference) has an effect on the input (afference), the brain "selecting its input."

Some have gone so far as to maintain that consciousness depends *solely* upon the output of the brain, regardless of which input keys off a given output. Roger Sperry emphasized this point,[9] and after him Taylor and Festinger have provided some experimental demonstrations of this idea. Their statement that awareness depends solely on the output regardless of the input is not at all inconsistent with Bruner's contention that the category activated will determine awareness.

We ordinarily speak of "seeing an image" on the retina of our eyes. More properly, we do not really "see" with our eyes but, rather, with the help of our eyes. The eyes and other sense organs should be considered information selection systems. We can trick the eye, for instance, in several ways. If we press on our eyelids with our eyes closed, we "see" a white light, and yet there is no physical light energy present. What we have done is to cause the cells in the retina to fire by pressure instead of by their usual source of stimulation, light energy. The cells in the retina fire and send signals up to the brain. Messages from the retina are interpreted as light by the brain, no matter how the message was brought about, and so we are tricked into "seeing." There are times when we do not even need our eyes to "see"—for instance, when we dream at night, or in the case of hallucinations, there is no light energy reaching our eyes.

We can understand, then, that seeing is not a process which takes place *in* our eyes, but, rather, *with the help* of our eyes. It is a process that occurs in the brain and is determined by the category and output systems of the brain. Vision is a process that is fed only by the input that comes through our eyes, and our awareness is constructed from this input and from our past experience.[10]

Our eyes are also constantly in motion, in large eye movements (saccades) as well as in eye tremors (nystagmus). We blink our eyes every second, move our eyes around, move our heads, our bodies, and we follow moving objects. The view of an object is never constant, and the very receptive fields on the eyes are changing all the time. Yet our visual world remains very stable. We can walk around a horse, for instance, and although our view is constantly changing— we sometimes see the tail, sometimes the back, a side view, a three-quarter view, a straight front view—we always see the same horse. If we "saw" an "image" on our retina, the visual world would be different each second. We must then *construct* our awareness from the selected input sorted into categories and in this way achieve some stability of our awareness out of the rich and continuously changing flow of information reaching our receptors.

We might briefly review some of these general characteristics of our awareness. Our senses receive information from the external world but, for the most part, are built to discard much of the continuously changing stimulation that reaches them. We also possess the ability to restrict further and modify the information that reaches awareness, by "reprograming." The brain selects and modifies input. We build "models" or representations of the world based on our past experience. We can, therefore, tune our awareness on the basis of past experience, expectation, and needs. We use this ability to tune out the constancies of the world, the clock ticking, the route over which we normally drive, our living room, an old phonograph record. Our experience is therefore an interactive process between the external world and the continuously revised models of our categories. We can select input, tune ourselves to relevant input, categorize, and finally construct our awareness from these and from our past experiences, our associations, thoughts, and emotional state.

The current work in American academic psychology provides a useful means of understanding normal awareness as a constructive process. One dimension, though, that is lacking in the current characterization is an analysis of the continuous flow of awareness. The writers cited provide a useful series of metaphors for the frame-by-frame components of awareness, but this is a segmented analysis. There is no doubt that at any instant our awareness is a construction based on past experience, but a more general characterization of the continuing nature of our awareness is needed. A more suitable metaphor was given by William James in his *Principles of Psychology*. He considered awareness a stream, continuously flowing, continuously changing direction. James said:

> Consciousness then does not appear to itself chopped up in bits. Such words as chain or train do not describe it fitly, as it presents itself in the first instant. It is nothing joined, it flows, a river or a stream are the metaphors by which it is naturally described. In talking of it thereafter let us call it the stream of thought, of consciousness, or of subjective life.[11]

Our thoughts are in constant change. Awareness shifts from one aspect of the stimuli surrounding us to another, to a thought of the past, to a bodily sensation, to a plan, to a change in external stimulation, back and forth. The stream carves its own new path continuously. James would have agreed with the more recent and precise analysis that awareness is a simplification and a construction. He said:

> Looking back, then, over this review, we see that the mind is at every stage a theatre of simultaneous possibilities. Consciousness consists in the comparision of these with each other, the selection of some, and the suppression of others, of the rest by the re-inforcing and inhibiting agency of attention....The mind, in short, works on the data it received much as a sculptor works on his block of stone. In a sense, the statue stood there from eternity. But there were a thousand different ones beside it. The sculptor alone is to thank for having extricated this one from the rest....Other sculptors, other statues from the same stone! Other minds, other worlds, from the same monotonous and inexpressive chaos! My world is but one in a million, alike embedded and alike real to those who may abstract them. How different must be the world in the consciousness of ants, cuttlefish or crab![12]

A similar characterization of awareness is offered by the Indian yogi Vivekananda. He more negatively compares ordinary awareness to a "drunken monkey." He calls up images of awareness moving from one random thought to another—thinking about hunger, thinking about the past, glimpsing an aspect of the present, thinking of the future, planning an action—continuously bouncing around like a monkey from one thing to another.

The esoteric traditions in general have characterized conscious-ness in terms similar to those of modern psychology. Sufi teaching stories frequently focus on men who are too preoccupied to hear what is being said, or who misinterpret instructions because of their expectations, or who do not see what is in front of them, because of the limited nature of their constructs.[13] The Sufis emphasize the constantly changing biases that constitute our normal awareness. "What a piece of bread looks like depends on whether you are hungry," says a Sufi poet, Jallaudin Rumi. The Sufis quite explicitly consider the effects of our limited category system on awareness. Many of the Sufis' descriptions of awareness could have been a statement of Bruner's about category systems, e.g., "Offer a donkey a salad, and he will ask what kind of thistle it is." They emphasize that we can be aware of only that which we conceive to exist, and that which our senses will transmit to us.

The Sufi and other traditions contend that the selective and restricted nature of awareness is an obstacle to be overcome and that the process of meditation, among other exercises, is a way of turning down the restrictions that normally limit awareness. One specific aim in these traditions is the removal of the automaticity and selectivity of ordinary awareness. The Sufis characterize man's usual state as one of "deep sleep" or "blindness," as one of being concerned with the irrelevant dimensions of the world. Gurdjieff's image is that of man placing shock absorbers between himself and the world. "We must destroy our buffers, children have none, therefore we must become like little children."[14] In Indian thought, as we have seen, ordinary awareness is a "drunken monkey" living solely in his constructs—the world of "illusion." This same thought is the metaphorical meaning of the "fall" of man in the Christian tradition. All these metaphors, without their derogatory connotation, can be understood in terms of modern psychology as depicting our selective awareness, our model-building, our automaticity, our limited category systems.

An aim of meditation, and more generally of the disciplines involving meditation, is the removal of "blindness," or the illusion, and an "awakening" of "fresh" perception. Enlightenment or illumination are words often used for progress in these disciplines, for a breakthrough in the level of awareness—flooding a dark spot with light. The Indian tradition speaks of opening the third eye, seeing more, and from a new vantage point. *Satori*, the desired state in Zen, is considered an "awakening." The Sufis speak of growing a new organ of perception.

Reports of the experiences of practitioners of the disciplines of meditation indicate that a primary aftereffect of the concentrative meditation exercises is an "opening up" of awareness, a "deautomatization," as Deikman calls it.[15] Some speak of seeing things "freshly" or as if for the first time. To William Blake, "if the doors of perception were cleansed, everything would appear to man as it is, infinite." Others, like Gurdjieff, use a loose metaphor and compare their experiences to that of a child who presumably has not yet developed many automatic ways of tuning out the world. In Zen, one speaks similarly of seeing something the five-hundredth time in the same way one saw it the first time.

These characterizations of consciousness represent a point of encounter between the concepts of contemporary psychology and the metaphors of the esoteric disciplines. We speak of man as controlling his input, building models, responding "automatically" to the external environment. The esoteric traditions refer to this process as man's lacking awareness of his surroundings and consider this "blindness" the barrier to his development. The model-building process is specifically what is to be dismantled through the practice of meditation. In Zen, one is instructed to stop conceptualizing while remaining fully awake. In Yoga, the aim is to leave the "illusion"— to cease identifying the external world with our models.

The three major traditions that we've considered each speak of developing an awareness that allows every stimulus to enter into consciousness devoid of our normal selection process, devoid of normal tuning and normal input selection, model-building, and the normal category systems.

The same metaphor is used in many traditions to describe the desired state of awareness. The Sufi poet Omar Khayyám says: "I am a mirror and who looks at me, whatever good or bad he speaks, he speaks of himself." The contemporary Zen master Suzuki Roshi says: "The perfect man employs his mind as a mirror, it grasps nothing, it refuses nothing, it receives but does not keep." Christ said in prayer: "A mirror I am to thee that perceivest me." The metaphor of consciousness as a mirror fits well with some of the psychologists' own metaphors. A mirror allows every input to enter equally, reflects each equally, and cannot be tuned to receive a special kind of input. It does not add anything to the input and does not turn off repetitive stimuli; it does not focus on any particular aspect of input and retune back and forth, but continuously admits all inputs equally.

This metaphor leads to another consideration. Many of the traditions claim to allow men to experience the world *directly*. The Sufis speak of attaining an "objective consciousness," others of "cosmic consciousness," and the statement is often made that one can have *direct* perception of reality. Whether one can perceive "reality" directly is not yet a question for science, but some comment within the terms of psychology might be made. The ability to be a mirror, to be free of the normal restrictions, of the tuning, biasing, and filtering processes of awareness, may be part of what is indicated by "direct" perception. This state can perhaps be considered within psychology as a diminution of the interactive nature of awareness; a state in which we do not select, nor do we bet on the nature of the world, nor do we think of the past, nor do we compel awareness by random associations, nor do we think of the future, nor do we sort into restrictive categories, but a state in which all possible categories are held in awareness at once. It has been described also as living totally in the present; not thinking about the future or of the past; a state in which everything that is happening in the present moment enters into awareness.

In many ways the aims of the disciplines of meditation—total attention to the moment, "dishabituation," "extended" awareness—are the same ones we seek in many of our "ordinary" activities. We buy new products, new clothes, new records; we slightly change our surroundings to attempt to return them to awareness. Dangerous sports, for example, engage our awareness and bring us into the present moment in which we think of nothing else but the activity in which we are engaged. We arrange the conditions so that it is *absolutely necessary* for us to pay full attention to what is taking place at that moment. When we race a sports car or motorcycle, or ski or ride a toboggan down a slope, or sky-dive, anything less than complete awareness to the moment may lead to injury or to death. The necessity of opening up our awareness is perhaps one of the reasons people are willing to risk injury or even their lives in dangerous sports. Much of Western art is similarly an attempt to "cleanse" perception, to return our awareness to things that are seen automatically.

Although many of our endeavors are directed toward achieving a meditationlike state of awareness, these means are held to be inefficient by the esoteric traditions. If we actually do achieve states of total awareness to the moment by ordinary means, this achievement does not last for long, does not carry with it a permanence. Our success fades, our love ends, we must come down from the mountain.

It is interesting to note the similarities between the esoteric and the modern psychologies of consciousness. Both stress that our awareness of the environment is a process of selection and categorization, that our sensory systems serve the purpose of discarding much of the information that reaches us, and that we finally construct our awareness from this heavily filtered input.

The meditation exercises can be seen as attempts to alter the selective and limited nature of our awareness, to change the habitual way in which we respond to the external world. In physiological terms it might involve a reduction in the efferent modification of input and in the "models" that we usually make of the external world. In some of the traditions specific exercises are performed for the purpose of returning awareness to actions that usually occur "automatically," a practice analogous to "dishabituation."

The attempt in [this] chapter has been to begin the process of extracting the psychological aspects of these Eastern meditative disciplines. No attempt has been made to provide an airtight case sealed by relevant experiments at each point. But we may begin most usefully by the simple process of translating the metaphors of the esoteric traditions into those of contemporary psychology and physiology, and noting the overlap.

NOTES

1. Huxley (1954).
2. Pribram (1969).
3. Furst (1971).
4. For a development of this idea, see Sokolov (1960).
5. Bruner (1957).
6. See Mischel (1968).
7. Bruner (1957).
8. Spinelli and Pribram (1967).
9. Sperry (1951).
10. For current psychology's most sophisticated account of the "constructive nature of awareness," see Neisser (1967).
11. James (1950).
12. Ibid.
13. See Shah (1968).
14. Walker (1957).
15. Deikman (1963). Also Deikman (1966).

13

Meditation and the Unconscious: A New Perspective

John Welwood

Among other things the unconscious in any given individual is his body, along with the body's psychological expression in temperament. The great error of modern psychology has been to ignore this fact and to speak of the unconscious as though it were some kind of unknowable. ... But insofar as the unconscious is the body...the unconscious can be known and studied, both behavioristically and introspectively. And insofar as it is...timeless principle, the unconscious can be...finally realized in an act of unitive knowledge.

Aldous Huxley

We are unconscious of our minds. Our minds are not unconscious.

R. D. Laing

For Zen the main point is that the entire structure of being, including its unconscious aspect, must be radically broken through. The aim of Zen is not for the unconscious aspect of being—whether personal or collective—to come to consciousness. The aim of Zen is, rather, the breaking-up of the very dualistic structure of consciousness-and-unconsciousness.

Richard DeMartino

Meditation has not been perceived accurately by Western psychology in general. A major attempt to interpret meditation in light of a complete psychological theory was made by Jung, who analyzed it in terms of his notion of the collective unconscious. However, Jung's view is unsatisfactory to many meditation practitioners, who find the dualism inherent in his notion of conscious and unconscious inappropriate for describing their experience. This chapter explores a new way of looking at unconscious process that may be more useful in this regard.

It is important to note at the outset, however, that meditation can never be completely understood objectively, with the categories of thinking mind, precisely because its nature is to transcend these categories. Meditation is not so much a particular kind of experience, but is rather *a way of seeing through experience*, always eluding any attempt to pin it down conceptually. Therefore, no attempt to discuss meditation psychologically could ever be a substitute for the personal understanding of meditation derived from actually practicing it.

THE TRADITIONAL MODEL OF THE UNCONSCIOUS

The unconscious is perhaps the most powerful concept in all of modern psychology. The significance of a broad range of human behavior and experience that had been difficult to explain before Freud, such as dreams, neurotic symptoms, symbolic visions, selective forgetting, slips of the tongue, is now widely recognized, thanks to the explanatory power of the concept of the unconscious.

However, if we look closely at the notion of the unconscious, asking what it actually means, certain problems emerge:

1. There has been little specification of what the unconscious actually refers to in concrete experiential terms, or agreement as to how the word should be used. The unconscious has become a catch-all term that appears to explain phenomena for which there is no other explanation, without explaining very much at all insofar as its precise meaning remains obscure. Western psychologists have used the term in at least sixteen different senses![1] Thus it has become an "ungrounded" concept that enables us to think we understand things that we actually do not understand very well.

2. The unconscious has been understood as an aspect of mind "inside" the organism, inherently separate from the total world process. Freud tried to objectify and analyze mind as a separate system of events taking place inside the individual, as a "psychical

apparatus." Underlying this view is the outmoded Cartesian dualistic assumption that mind is "something distinct and apart, a place or realm that can be inhabited by such entities as ideas."[2] Thus depth psychologists speak of "unconscious contents," such as instincts, drives, wishes, repressed emotions, or archetypes as if they were "contained" inside the mind.

3. Not only are mind and world dualistically separated in this view, but furthermore, consciousness and the unconscious are seen as fundamentally separate principles. Freud saw unconscious impulses as essentially antagonistic to conscious purposes. Although Jung saw the conscious–unconscious duality as complementary rather than antagonistic, he still tended to ascribe an autonomous agency or power to the unconscious, as when he stated: "The unconscious perceives, has purposes and intuitions, feels and thinks as does the conscious mind."[3] Consequently, Jungians still talk as though the unconscious has a "mind of its own," with contents that are like those of consciousness, except that they remain below the threshold of awareness. This creates a dualism within a dualism.

4. In splitting off the unconscious from consciousness, depth psychology defines the unconscious half as unknowable. We may be driven by unconscious forces, but we can never see these parts of ourselves directly. Thus it might appear that the unconscious is an untamed "heart of darkness" inside us.

5. The inherent dualism in the conscious–unconscious dichotomy makes it difficult to understand meditation, transpersonal experiences, and spiritual insight properly. These latter phenomena radically transcend dualism insofar as they overcome splits and separations both within oneself and between self and world. Freud interpreted the mystical experience of overcoming boundaries as "regression," a return to more primitive modes of behavior. Although Jung recognized the validity of mystical/spiritual experience for integrating internal schisms, he nonetheless viewed meditation as a form of "introversion." However, if meditation is seen as an introverted probing of the hidden contents of the unconscious, it may appear to be a dangerous occupation or another form of "new narcissism." The traditional view of the unconscious, like the notions of classical physics, "works" within certain limits. It has been useful in explaining pathological symptoms, although even here its validity has been questioned by many critics.[4] It completely breaks down,

however, when it tries to account for meditation and nondualistic experiences (which are akin to the macro- and microscopic data that led to the development of relativity and quantum theory in physics).

It is important to understand how unconscious process is an important aspect of one's everyday experience which one can actually connect with. To do so, it is necessary to interpret the unconscious in a nondualistic way, which will also enable us to see how it is possible for meditation to put us in direct touch with "things as they are."

JUNG'S INTERPRETATION OF MEDITATION

Within the depth-psychology model, meditation has been conceptualized as a method, like dreams, for contacting the unconscious. For instance, Kretschmer says, "Dreams are similar to meditation, except meditation gains the reaction of the unconscious by a systematic technique which is faster than depending on dreams."[5] He sees meditation as a therapeutic technique that can be used as a "provocation of the unconscious" in order to "make its creative possibilities available in the healing process."[6] Jung referring to Buddhist meditation, sees it as a direct route into the unconscious:

> Meditation does not center upon anything. Not being centered, it would be rather like a dissolution of consciousness and hence a direct approach to the unconscious condition.... The meditation our text has in mind seems to be a sort of Royal Road to the unconscious.[7]

The questions these passages raise are: How does meditation "provoke" or "approach" the unconscious? Why is a meditation that does not center on anything equated with a dissolution of consciousness? If the unconscious, by definition, cannot be experienced, is meditation to be conceived as some kind of narrowed awareness, similar to dreams?

If the unconscious is conceived as an inner realm of the psyche, and meditation is a means of contacting it, then it might appear that meditation is a purely interior journey that would neglect one's relationship with the world. Maupin cites this danger:

> The deepest objections to meditation have been raised against its tendency to produce withdrawn, serene people who are not accessible to what is actually going on in their lives.... With

meditation it is easy to overvalue the internal at the expense of the external so that they remain split apart.[8]

This objection to meditation, which is shared by many Westerners today, is based on a misconception that is reinforced by the model of the unconscious as a realm of mind "within."

Jung, the first major psychologist to explore fully the relation between Buddhist meditation and the Western notion of the unconscious, made a valiant effort to connect them. However, the limitations of his model of the unconscious, and his apparent lack of direct experience with the practice of meditation hampered his investigations. Jung saw meditation as a onesided attempt to withdraw from the world, betraying what he called the "introverted prejudice" of the East. Introversion, the fixation with one's inner world, was by definition opposed to the extroverted stance of dealing with the objective world. He saw meditation leading primarily to an indefinite experience of oneness and timelessness. For him these characteristics were a hallmark of the collective unconscious, leading him to conclude that meditation was a kind of surrender to the unconscious—a dangerous indulgence that could work against relating realistically with the world's demands.

Eastern talk of egolessness also suggested an introverted prejudice, for Jung saw dissolution of the ego as leading back to a more primitive state of mind dominated by the unconscious, to the detriment of differentiated consciousness. Jung's assumption of the real existence of an unconscious mind led him to posit the real existence and necessity of the ego as well. The ego was what allowed consciousness to function, presenting the main line of defense against the possibility of being overwhelmed by unconscious dominants:

> To us, consciousness is inconceivable without an ego. If there is no ego, there is nobody to be conscious of anything. The ego is therefore indispensable to the conscious process. The Eastern mind, however, has no difficulty in conceiving of a consciousness without an ego. . . . Such an ego-less mental condition can only be unconscious to us, for the simple reason that there would be nobody to witness it. . . . I cannot imagine a conscious mental state that does not relate to an ego.[9]

These statements reveal certain philosophical assumptions of Western culture that have only recently begun to be questioned. The idea that conscious experience is only possible for a separate self-conscious subject (ego) has roots in Plato's separation of thinking mind (form) from the total natural process (matter). Jung admits this separation of mind from the world-process as a basic feature of Western thought:

> The development of Western philosophy during the last two centuries has succeeded in isolating the mind in its own sphere and in severing it from its primordial oneness with the universe.[10]

By contrast, such dualistic notions as the unconscious as a separate mental realm, or mind as independent of world are the root of *samsara* and confusion in the Buddhist perspective. According to Chōgyam Trungpa:

> Where there is...the concept of something that is separate from oneself, then we tend to think that because there is something outside, there must be something here as well. The external phenomenon sometimes becomes such an overwhelming thing and seems to have all sorts of seductive and aggressive qualities, so we erect a kind of defense mechanism against it, failing to see that that is a continuity of the external, and this creates a kind of gigantic bubble in us which consists of nothing but air and water, or, in this case, fear and the reflection of the external thing. So this huge bubble prevents any fresh air from coming in, and that is "I"—the ego. So in that sense there is the existence of ego, but it is in fact illusory.[11]

In other words, the notion of the unconscious as a real "other," "external" or alien to consciousness, would create, from a Buddhist perspective, both its "seductive and aggressive qualities" and the sense of a real ego that must be defended against these qualities. In fact, Jung advised Westerners against practicing meditation for this very reason: the seductiveness of ego-loss could lead to a dangerous uprush from the unconscious. But his concept of the unconscious was built on a conception of mind thoroughly rooted in the subject–object alienation to begin with, which for the East is the very root of ignorance, defensiveness, and suffering.

Thus Jung apparently did not conceive of enlightened mind as described in Eastern texts as a clear and precise way of being and living in the world. Instead, he saw it as referring to the inner realm of the unconscious:

Thus our concept of the "collective unconscious" would be the European equivalent of *buddhi*, the enlightened mind.[12]

The "seeing of the Mind" implies self-liberation. This means, psychologically, that the more weight we attach to unconscious process...the nearer we draw to the state of unconsciousness with its qualities of oneness, indefiniteness, and timelessness.[13]

Jung's interpretation of meditation as approaching the "state of unconsciousness" contrasts sharply with that of Buddhist teachers, who stress clear awareness of the world as it is:

Therefore the practice of meditation does not require an inward concentration.... There is no centralizing concept at all.... In fact without the external world, the world of apparent phenomena, meditation would be almost impossible to practice, for the individual and the external world are not separate, but merely co-exist together.[14]

But from the Buddhist point of view, the point of meditation is not to develop trance-like states; rather it is to sharpen perceptions, to see things as they are. Meditation at this level is relating with the conflicts of our life situations, like using a stone to sharpen a knife, the situation being the stone.[15]

The enlightened man...has cleared out his mind.... When you wake up fully, you see everything clearly. You are not distracted because you see everything as it is.[16]

When the texts say that enlightened mind cannot be described, Jung equates *indescribable* with *unknowable*, assuming that they must be referring to the unconscious. Trungpa's perception-sharpening stone becomes dulled into the vague philosopher's stone:

The statement that "the various names given to it (the Mind) are innumerable" proves that the Mind must be something as vague and indefinite as the philosopher's stone. A substance that can be described in "innumerable" ways must be expected to display as many qualities or facets. If these are really "innumerable," they cannot be counted, and it follows that the substance is well-nigh indescribable and unknowable. It can never be realized completely. This is certainly true of the unconscious, and a further proof that the Mind is the Eastern equivalent of our concept of the unconscious, more particularly of the collective unconscious.[17]

But the awareness developed in meditation must always encompass more than one could ever say about it, since any way of describing it, from one of the innumerable vantage points of focal articulation, must always be partial. It is like taking pictures of Mount Fuji from every possible angle, yet none of the pictures, nor even the whole series, truly expresses the presence of the mountain. Jung misinterprets such a fact to mean that Mount Fuji can never be seen or known clearly and directly, simply because it can be described from so many different perspectives.

TOWARD A NEW MODEL OF UNCONSCIOUS PROCESS

We need to understand unconscious process in a way that will enable us to approach unitive experience and the awake state of mind properly, rather than as "inner" states arising from an unconscious psyche.

Two basic assumptions, which should be amenable to Eastern psychologies and Western humanistic approaches, can help create a new picture of unconscious process:

1. The human being can be understood as an ongoing process that is always *in relation to* situations. These situations—environmental, social, personal, spiritual—are both inherited and, to some extent, created by the human organism itself. From this perspective, all organismic processes are ways of organizing relationships. Psychological events must be understood as forms of interaction, rather than as separate mental phenomena.

2. The word *organism* refers to the *whole* ongoing process that we are. This holistic model, in which no autonomous psychological functions pursue their own ends apart from the whole organismic process, is corroborated by many biologists.[18]

In light of these two premises, conscious and unconscious may be understood as two different ways in which the organism organizes interaction with the world, rather than as two separate parts of a psyche. What is unconscious are *holistic ways of patterning experience, modes of relationship* which work with multiple connections as a whole, without having to distinguish their separate parts. As background modes of relationship, they are usually overlooked by normal everyday attention, which may be characterized in two major ways:

1. Attention is normally highly focalized, fixating on separate objects one at a time. This kind of focal attention cannot perceive holistic patterning without breaking it into discrete elements.

However, there is also a "diffuse attention"[19] that perceives experiences all at once in their wholeness, without analysis into separate parts. (A simple example: hearing the many parts of a symphony orchestra all at once.) Diffuse attention, while usually playing a secondary role in everyday awareness, is primary in meditation and nondualistic awareness, where experience is attended to with a broader consciousness that does not fixate on subject-object boundaries.

2. Everyday focal attention is normally *passive* in relation to the wider background of the organism. This may be readily observed in the ways in which attention is continually being "hijacked," seemingly without rhyme or reason, by successive thoughts and feelings.

Meditation, by contrast, is the development of an *active* attention to one's experiencing, which may bring to light patterns of being-in-the-world previously overlooked. Thus *active diffuse attention* (to be referred to more simply here as "diffuse attention") seems to be an essential factor in the changes that meditation can effect.

Three features of the figure-ground relationship are particularly relevant for understanding unconscious process:

1. Figure and ground are constantly alternating in attention. Figures, once articulated, become incorporated into, and subsequently function as part of the background whole (hence unconsciously). For example, everything I know and have experienced about a particular person now functions as the global background against which I notice this new quality in him. This new quality stands out as figure for a while, and then also becomes part of the ground, allowing further qualities to stand out. Thus many focal bits may function holistically as ground, without my being conscious of them in a differentiated way. This is one sense in which the organism "knows," as we say, "unconsciously," more than focal attention can ever articulate serially. This accounts for how what was once conscious now functions unconsciously (as ground), and how from this ground, which functions in a prearticulate holistic way, a figure may suddenly become articulated as though it had been there all along in the "unconscious." It was not there as a discrete "content of

the unconscious," but was felt implicitly as part* of a wider experiential background. This is what William James points to when he says:

> In the pulse of inner life immediately present now in each of us is a little past, a little future, a little awareness of our own body, of each other's persons, of these sublimities we are trying to talk about, of the earth's geography and the direction of history, of truth and error, of good and bad, and of who knows how much more? Feeling, however dimly and subconsciously, all these things, your pulse of inner life is continuous with them, belongs to them and they to it. You can't identify it with either one of them rather than the others, for if you let it develop into no matter which of those directions, what it develops into will look back on it and say, "That was the original germ of me."[20]

Gendlin makes a similar point:

> What we go through is much more than we "have".... Any moment is a myriad richness, but rarely do we take time to "have" it. When we do, what we are focused on is usually only some specific. Going through a simple act involves an enormous number of familiarities, learnings, senses for the situation, understandings of life and people, as well as the many specifics of the given situation. All this goes into just saying "hello" in a fitting way to a not very close friend.... The feel of doing anything involves our sense of the whole situation at any moment, despite our not focally reflecting on it as such. This is the myriad multiplicity.[21]

2. The ground is implicit in the figure, in that the figure assumes and "needs" the ground to stand out as what it is. To use a cognitive example, if I differentiate the concept *dog* into collies, beagles, and boxers, then *dog* becomes the cognitive background that remains implicit in my examining of the collie category. In this sense the unconscious ground does not "have a mind of its own," or live separately from consciousness, but is *actually present* implicitly in whatever is going on at the moment.

3. The word *ground* as used here has a deliberate double

---

* The word *part* here is logically wrong, for it implies discreteness. It is difficult to express linguistically how "parts" function holistically. That an element is already implicit in a larger whole, but only becomes itself as a discrete element when consciously focused on—this can only be verified experientially.

meaning. It refers not only to background, but also to the ground that underlies and makes possible this present moment. Insofar as this ground is not solid, but a changing flux of meanings, it is also a "groundless ground."

This new approach to unconscious functioning is based on a notion of the organism as already relating to the world in global ways prior to the articulations of thinking mind. The sense of being encompassed by a wisdom greater than oneself, which may be ascribed to an "unconscious mind," comes from this dependence of focal intelligence on the wider organismic process that is always operating beyond its range. Since we cannot pinpoint focally this organismic totality, we tend to deny its reality, or treat it as "other," separate from ourselves. But conscious and unconscious are not necessarily opposing tendencies, as depth psychology contends; rather, focal attention and holistic ground are complementary modes of organism/environment relationship. The organismic ground, moreover, is not truly unknowable in that it may be directly contacted in wider states of awareness.

What follows is a description of four levels of the normally unconscious background of experience, or progressively wider, more global ways in which experience seems to be organized. The word *levels* here refers to "fields within fields" or "grounds within grounds." The wider fields, or levels of ground, shape what we are conscious of moment to moment in an encompassing, global way, and are difficult to experience directly, at least in our linear culture, without some kind of special direction or practice. At the same time, the more "frontal" fields express aspects of the wider grounds underlying them, just as the words of any given sentence one speaks express many underlying levels of experiential structuring all at once (e.g., conveying the content one intends, taking account of the situation in which it is said, imbuing the words with appropriate emphasis and feeling, adjusting the words to what one has already said before, expressing one's aliveness and energy of the moment, and so on). Accordingly, the unconscious ground of experience may be seen to have at least four levels: (1) the *situational ground* of felt meaning—the way in which we have an implicit felt sense of the immediate situations we live; (2) the *personal ground*—how patterns of personal meanings presently shape our consciousness, behavior, and world-view in a background way; (3) the *transpersonal ground*—

the ways in which the whole organism is attuned to the patterns and currents of the universe and the life process itself; and (4) the *basic open ground*—pure immediate presence to the world prior to any identification with the individual organism.

THE SITUATIONAL GROUND: FELT MEANING

The most readily experienceable ground of focal attention is what Gendlin has called "felt meaning," the way in which the organism carries with it an implicit felt sense of the situations it lives.[22] A felt sense is the prearticulate way in which the organism feels a network of relationships. A simple example: If you the reader stop and think for a moment of some person you know, you may notice that behind any specific thoughts, emotions, or images you may have about that person, there is a whole fuzzy "feel" which is quite different from the felt sense that you may have for any other person. Felt meaning normally functions as the immediate situational background against which focal attention articulates particular objects of interest. Felt meaning is what we refer to when we want to find out how we feel, or when we lose track of what we were saying. This relatively accessible background corresponds to, and is an experiential rendering of, the traditional concept of the preconscious.

During meditation, aspects of the situational ground emerge in the form of thoughts and feelings about one's immediate life-situation. Since attention has no delimited object to focus on, attention begins to diffuse, and aspects of the background begin to emerge. One may remember things that have been forgotten, or find oneself mulling over decisions, problems, situations in one's immediate life. One starts churning up feeling-and-thought textures related to immediate life situations. By not following up these thoughts and feelings, one finds that their compulsiveness may diminish if one sits in meditation long enough. Given enough time, one begins to get bored with, and move beyond, this "subconscious gossip," as Trungpa calls it. Then the next widest level of the organismic ground may emerge.

THE PERSONAL GROUND

The personal ground of consciousness is somewhat less accessible. It is the way in which personal meanings and associations, developed during the individual's life history, presently shape consciousness in a background way. Situations have a unique set of personal meanings for each individual, and together they determine to a large extent *what* an individual sees and how it is seen. In Merleau-Ponty's terms, there is a "sedimentation" of layers of meanings that make up one's habitual style of relating to the world. But instead of seeing them as contents stored in the unconscious, we can understand them as a presently functioning background whole that influences and shapes one's personal style of being-in-the-world. The use of specific methods that develop diffuse attention, such as hypnosis, psychotherapeutic introspective techniques, or drugs, make this ground accessible for further conscious elaboration.

Focal attention, by its very nature, screens out wholes in favor of differentiated parts. Personally identifying with fixed, habitual patterns (ego) sets up distortions that the organism tends to "correct" through behavioral and emotional manifestations (e.g., dreams, fantasy, neurotic symptoms). This phenomenon, basic to psychopathology, is what Jung personified as the *shadow*, the compensatory function of the unconscious. But the shadow function can be understood as an instance of the "holistic tendency" of the organism, rather than as the work of a separate unconscious principle. Overemphasizing any extreme at the expense of the balanced whole sets an opposite tendency in motion, as part of a larger equilibrium process. Ego tends to get out of alignment with the whole organism by selectively carving out and attending to only certain meanings from the organismic totality, thereby creating its mirror reversal in that part of the experiential field not taken account of. "Messages from the unconscious" may be reinterpreted as manifestations of the play of opposites inherent in all dynamic systems (e.g., in electricity, magnetism, kinetic laws, and weather patterns). Insofar as mind is part of the total natural process, it must also participate in these same cycles.

In meditation the personal ground (both in terms of habitual tendencies and the "shadow") emerges in the form of memories, fantasies, projections, desires, aversions, and by continually churning emotional upsurges. Normally we are too busy, and focal attention too limited, to take account of all that is happening in the whole experiential field, much of which is "swept under the rug" and ignored. In the absence of a project to occupy oneself with, one begins to see very clearly the character of one's personal world. One starts to understand one's personal neurotic style of identifying with and maintaining one's separate self-sense. By watching thoughts go by, one comes to understand one's own strategies, tendencies, and self-deceptions. Diffuse attention allows things swept under the rug to emerge and be acknowledged. There is something very powerful about this neutral observation of thoughts, without either indulging or suppressing them. At this level, meditation can lead to "therapeuticlike" insights, as this clear observing of personal patterns seems to have some alterative effect on them.

THE TRANSPERSONAL GROUND

The next widest ground seems to be a level where there is an identification with the whole organism as being embedded in the larger organism/environment field. As Ken Wilber puts it, this is "where man is not conscious of his identity with the All and yet neither is his identity confined to the boundaries of the individual organism."[23] This transpersonal ground comprises all the ways in which we function as human organism, as body-in-the-world, beneath the more differentiated types of self-consciousness.

In this approach, archetypes, instead of being seen as inborn psychic structures or contents of the collective unconscious, may be understood as universal patterns of body-in-the-world. The orientation of the organism, as a body-mind totality with a given genetic background, seems to be the transpersonal basis for the specific individual meanings that a person develops and actualizes during his lifetime. For instance, the meaning of up and down, the very notion of "higher" states of consciousness, derive from the transpersonal meaning of being an upright body rooted to the earth by the force of gravity. Thus being "high"—physically or psychologically—carries with it archetypal overtones that are exciting and/or frightening, in that we seem to be cut loose from our normal grounded position. A given individual's fear of heights (acrophobia), developed out of specific life-history experiences, is one way in which these archetypal meanings might be felt in a *personal* form. The universal associations of left and right, active and passive, yin and yang, which assume a personal form with every individual, also seem to be related to transpersonal patterns of bodily orientation to the world, possibly correlated with the differentiated functions of the right and left hemispheres of the brain.[24]

Another aspect of the transpersonal ground is the forward impetus of the organism in its developmental process, the natural wisdom of the organism (what Carl Rogers calls the "organismic valuing process"),[25] which continually functions as a background guide and inspiration for the individual's growth. The organism "transpersonalizes" situations by structuring individual problems in wider contexts of relationship, resulting in sudden insights, inventions, creative inspiration, dream visions, resolutions of personal problems. These phenomena seem to arise out of an incubation process during which the organism feels out and integrates whole textures and networks of relationships, in ways that are impossible for the serial method of focal attention. This "organismic resolution of problems" is an essential factor in therapy or healing.

The transpersonal ground may be experienced directly in many different ways. The ecstatic perception of oneness in mystical experience, where the organism is felt as totally embedded in the universe, is one instance. Nature mysticism seems to be this kind of experience, as in the words of Thomas Traherne:

> You never enjoy the world aright till the sea itself floweth in your veins, till you are clothed with the heavens and crowned with the stars.[26]

In meditation, at a very simple level, this organismic wholeness is often experienced as a state of well-being, simply sitting here, breathing and feeling alive. Although not particularly encouraged to do so, many people find their most creative ideas arising during these times.

The transpersonal ground as described here seems to correspond to what some schools of Buddhism refer to as the *alayavijnana*. The Yogacara school sees the *alayavijnana* as a transitional phase between totally open, unconditioned awareness and the separate self-sense,

> the first phase in the process of self-differentiation. . . . It is not the absolute consciousness since it already contains the seed of self-disruption. Consciousness has already started bifurcating. . . . The *alaya* is the first phenomenalization of the Absolute.[27]

The subtle identification with one's organism, while including a sense of wholeness and relationship, seems to provide the basis for the development of the individual self-sense.

> ...the *Alaya* is mind in its deepest and most comprehensive sense, while it manifests itself as individualized in our empirical consciousness and as subject to the momentary changes that are taking place in it.... Though it is pure and immaculate in its original nature, it allows itself to be affected by *Manas*, the principle of individuation. And thus affected, the dualism of subject and object is created in it, which issues in the appearance of a world of particular objects.[28]

The *alayavijnana*, as Suzuki describes it above, seems to correspond to the broad, undifferentiated transpersonal ground that normally we are aware of only as it is shaped into the more easily focalized forms of personal meanings ("*Manas*, the principle of individuation"), situational meanings ("subject to momentary changes taking place"), and focal meanings ("individualized in empirical consciousness").

In experiential terms, *alayavijnana*, or transpersonal ground, refers to the concrete felt presence of "being-here" as a process of relating—to life, to other people, to the varieties of awareness itself, to all things. This *interrelational presence* is the immediate sense of being that persists behind all the differentiated changes in objects of attention. As F. S. C. Northrop points out:

> This explains how it is possible for one to apprehend the blueness of the sky and the color of the rose and the moving beauty of the sunset with precisely the same immediacy with which the pain of one's local toothache is apprehended.... Thus, it is quite erroneous to conceive of a person, after the manner of the Lockean mental substance, as a completely local, independent thing having nothing in common with all other persons and things. There is an all-embracing indeterminate continuum of feeling common to all creatures in their aesthetic immediacy.... The ineffable, the emotionally moving, the aesthetically vivid...is the immediate, purely factual portion of human nature and the nature of all things. This is the portion of human knowledge that can be known without recourse to inference and speculative hypotheses and deductive logic.... This we have and are in ourselves before all speculation, with immediacy and hence with absolute certainty.[29]

This relational immediacy is so close and encompassing that it usually falls into the background of the experiential field, while the differentiated objects of attention—thoughts, emotions, perceptions —occupy the focus of attention. For instance, as I listen to a bird singing, my attention is normally on the differentiated sounds and tones of the song (focal meanings), the feelings the song arouse in me (situational felt meanings), or the associations and memories that may arise (personal meanings). Unless I am directed to it, I tend to ignore the sheer vividness of the being-here that underlies and surrounds this experience (transpersonal meaning). Thus, this normally unconscious aspect of experience can be seen as a feature of relationship usually overlooked, rather than as a structural component of the psyche. Further implications of this difference in perspective will be mentioned below.

THE BASIC OPEN GROUND

The transpersonal ground may be felt as a sense of oneness and relatedness between self and world. Nevertheless, a subtle sense of identification with one's organism still persists. It does not quite reach the sense of "zero-ness" which marks an even deeper relatedness which Chögyam Trungpa has called the "basic ground."

This widest ground of experience appears to be pure, immediate presence before it becomes differentiated into any form of subject-object duality. As Trungpa describes it:

> This basic ground does not depend on relative situations at all. It is natural being which just is. Energies appear out of this basic ground and those energies are the source of the development of relative situations.... Both liberation and confusion are that energy which happens constantly, which sparks out and then goes back to its basic nature, like clouds...emerging from and disappearing back into the sky.[30]

Split-second flashes of this open ground, which Buddhists have also called "primordial awareness," "original mind," "no-mind," are happening all the time, although one does not usually notice them. Buddha spoke about literally developing awareness in terms of fractions of a second, to awaken people to the fleeting glimpses of an open, precognitive spaciousness that keeps occurring before things get interpreted in a particular perspective.

> Our most fundamental state of mind...is such that there is basic openness, basic freedom, a spacious quality; and we have now and

have always had this openness. Take, for example, our everyday lives and thought patterns. When we see an object, in the first instant there is a sudden perception which has no logic or conceptualization to it at all; we just perceive the thing in the open ground. Then immediately we panic and begin to rush about trying to add something to it, either trying to find a name for it or trying to find pigeon-holes in which we could locate and categorize it. Gradually things develop from there.[31]

This fleeting sense of openness underlying all our thoughts and conceptualizations is not particularly esoteric, but is a part of ordinary experience that is normally overlooked. The psychologist Matte Blanco notes it as follows:

The findings of introspection suggest that there is, in fact, a very fleeting instant of *prise de conscience,* or "becoming aware," or "assumption of consciousness" when sensation is in consciousness in a naked state, not clothed in either explicit or implicit propositions, not even rudimentary ones. But an essential feature of this phenomenon is that it is fleeting. As soon as it arises in consciousness, sensation is caught by thoughts, wrapped by them.... So, sensation seems to be born in consciousness in a naked state, like a baby. But the baby can be left naked whereas sensation, in order to remain in consciousness, in order not to disappear immediately *from existence,* needs to be clothed in thoughts.[32]

It is this fact that leads Buddhists to say that we are constantly re-creating our versions of the world from moment to moment, as awareness emerges from the basic open ground and locks into particular interpretation schemes that are cloaked with personal meanings and associations. This "locking-in" is reinforced by the overlapping sequence of perceptions, thoughts, feelings which create a dense texture of mind that obscures the underlying ground of pure awareness. Nevertheless, it is possible, once sensitized and taught to do so, to notice the split-second holes in this fabric of mind. (First thing in the morning, lying in bed right after awakening, before one's thinking begins to take over, may be prime time for glimpsing such a space.)

In meditation, awareness of an open ground breaks through when one wears out the projects and distractions of thought and emotion. Then there is a sudden gap in the stream of thought, a flash of clarity and openness. It is neither particularly mystical or esoteric, nor any kind of introverted self-consciousness, but a direct participation in an egoless awareness.

Ignorance in this perspective is the lack of recognition of this nonpersonal awareness that surrounds the objects of thought and feeling, and the treating of the latter as solid, substantial realities. This ignoring seems to be an activity that is constantly re-created from moment to moment. When it relaxes somewhat, as in meditation, flashes of the underlying basic ground may come through. From a Buddhist perspective this pure awareness is our original nature, and meditation is the major way to let it emerge from its normally submerged background role. In Zen *satori*, the emergence of an open ground has a sudden and dramatic quality, which has been likened to the "bottom of the bucket breaking through" to the "thoroughly clear, ever-present awareness" in which the subject–object and conscious–unconscious dichotomies disappear, and things stand out simply as what they are. "The seer becomes the seeing and seeing becomes the seen."[33]

IMPLICATIONS

This chapter has presented a nondualistic interpretation of the conscious-unconscious polarity as two aspects of one whole process—the organism's interrelationship with the world. It has focused on the particular implications of this approach for making sense of meditation practice, which has been largely misunderstood by depth psychology.[34] The depth psychology model of the unconscious is inadequate for an understanding of meditation because it is dualistic in the following ways:

1. The mind is seen as a psychic system with given contents, as though it had a substantial existence that could be observed as an object separate from the knower and the process of knowing. This model misconstrues meditation by making it appear to be only an exploration of "regions of inner space," the various territories of an unconscious realm of the mind. This model has led some Jungians to interpret the awakened state of mind in terms of "an extraordinarily significant and numinous content [that] enters consciousness," resulting in a "new viewpoint."[35] But this language is not

experientially precise, for enlightenment is a radical doing away with
"viewpoints." Awakening is not additive, in the sense of unconscious
contents breaking through into consciousness, but if anything,
subtractive, in that it removes fixations with any particular contents.
In such awakening, as Guenther points out, "attention is on the field
rather than on its contents."[36]

2. The unconscious is typically seen as "other"—alien, unknowable, even threatening. In this perspective meditation is conceived as
potentially dangerous, in that it may subject the ego to "the
disintegrating powers of the unconscious."[37] Such possible confu-
sions led the Zen teacher Hisamatsu after a conversation with Jung,
to distinguish the open ground of awareness from the depth
psychology model of the unconscious:

> The "unconscious" of psychoanalysis is quite different from the
> "no-mind" of Zen. In the "unconscious"...are the *a posteriori*
> "personal unconscious" and the *a priori* "impersonal unconscious,"
> namely the "collective unconscious." They are both unknown to
> the ego. But the "no-mind" of Zen is, on the contrary, not only
> known, but it is most clearly known, as it is called..."always
> clearly aware." More exactly, it is clearly "self awakening to itself"
> without separation between the knower and the known. "No-
> mind" is a state of mind clearly aware.[38]

3. The inner demands of the unconscious and the outer demands
of the world are seen as two opposing worlds. This perspective views
meditation as an inward journey that is separate from the process of
relating with the world. The confusion here stems from the dualistic
interpretation of *inner* and *outer*. *Inner* is assumed to mean "inside
me," that which is psychical, immaterial. However, the new approach
presented here allows us to recast the inner–outer duality in a
different way. *Inner* truth, *inner* reality does not refer to a realm of
the psyche *inside the organism*, but rather to the living, dynamic,
holistic process that shapes and structures the *outer* reality of
constituent parts. In this sense everything in nature has an inner
reality (its holistic, formal, expressive side), which is not separate
from the inner reality of the human process. Zuckerkandl makes this
point in relation to music:

> The voice of music testifies against interpreting the "inner" of
> "inner world" as synonymous with "in me." The place of this
> "inner world" is just as much outside me as in me; the inner world

extends as far as the world itself, the world itself is divided into an "inner" and "outer." The boundary is not vertical, running between self and world, but horizontal running through both.[39]

The inner aspect of music makes something living out of its outer elements, such as "vibrating air" or "auditory frequency." In the same way, unconscious process can be seen as the inner reality of human mind, without necessarily being interpreted as a "region of inner space," inside the organism.

In this chapter the unconscious process has been reformulated to show that:

1. What is unconscious generally are patterns of organismic structuring and relating, which function holistically as the background of focal attention.

2. This background consists of wider and wider interpenetrating levels, which can be contacted experientially through differing intensities and ranges of diffuse attention. The paradigm here is one of "fields within fields." These fields are dynamic patterns of relationship, each of which allows for certain kinds of knowledge and experience to occur. They do not in themselves contain any "mental stuff," any psychic contents. They do not exist in the sense of being any kind of substantial entities. Rather, they are functional determinants of consciousness that actively shape how we relate to things from moment to moment. Awareness begins with openness, becomes humanized at the transpersonal level, individualized at the personal level, and particularized at the situational level. Awareness thus becomes more and more faceted, further and further shaped with each more differentiated level. Nonetheless, in the very midst of the most differentiated moment of awareness, there remains a totally open, unconditioned quality, although it is normally very much in the background.

3. The basic open ground of awareness, though beyond the span of focal attention (and in this sense "unconscious"), is not a mysterious psychic region, but is perfectly knowable, both in fleeting glimpses and in "sudden awakening."

This open ground reveals a level of total organism/environment interpenetration that is so far beyond conceptualization and thought that it becomes hidden beneath the overlay of focal thoughts, feelings, and perceptions with which we are normally so preoccupied. Meditation, by opening up this wider attunement, allows for a more direct, precise relationship with "what is." At this level of open awareness,

> The meditator develops new depths of insight through direct communication with the phenomenal world.... Conceptualized mind is not involved in the perception and so we are able to see with great precision, as though a veil had been removed from our eyes.[40]

The open ground is present all the time. At any moment, especially if one develops some sensitivity to the process of consciousness through meditation, one may glimpse this ineffable, nonspecifiable, omnipotential open awareness that underlies specific perceptions. The fundamental nature of awareness seems to have this open quality, this complete receptivity that becomes progressively faceted, shaped, articulated, elaborated, while remaining open and "empty." In Hui-neng's words, "from the very beginning, not a single thing is."

CLINICAL CONSIDERATION'S

If, as we have seen, what is most deeply unconscious in man is his nonpersonal relatedness to all things, this has important implications for the understanding of neurosis, defense mechanisms, repression, and psychopathology in general. What is most threatening to the ego in this view is not instinctual demands, but rather the groundless, open quality of our basic being-in-the-world. We find that we cannot establish our ego securely, our self-identity keeps slipping away, we are subject to little deaths from moment to moment, there is nothing to hold on to. Thus anxiety signals a threat, not so much from instinctual demands, but rather from the insubstantial nature of the basic ground of our existence. Guilt can be interpreted in this light as arising from a commitment to "small mind," as opposed to "big mind." We may feel guilty when we choose our small version of the world, at the expense of the larger, expansive vision that arises from the basic relatedness of self and world. Resistance, repression, and defenses can be recast here as ways of armoring ourselves against this relatedness that undercuts our notions of our separate self.

Letting go of habit and self-created identity is painful. There can
be a resistance to the openness that underlies us at the same time that
we are drawn to it, which is the root meaning of ambivalence.
Maslow recognized this fact in his description of the Jonah
syndrome:

> We fear our highest possibility.... We are generally afraid to
> become that which we can glimpse in our most perfect mo-
> ments.... We enjoy and even thrill to the godlike possibilities we
> see in ourselves in such peak moments. And yet we simultaneously
> shiver with weakness, awe, and fear before these same
> possibilities.[41]

Ernest Becker points to the same reality when he says that "normality
is neurosis," in that it constitutes a refusal and repression of our
groundlessness, our complete openness and vulnerability to the
world. Dominated by fear of both life and death, we fear living fully,
in touch with the supraindividual power and richness of our being:

> ...the child could not out of himself muster the stamina and the
> authority necessary to live in full expansiveness with limitless
> horizons of perceptions and experience.[42]

> ...these defenses...allow him to feel that he *controls* his life and
> his death, that he really does live and act as a willful and free
> individual, that he has a unique and self-fashioned identity, that he
> *is somebody*.[43]

This avoidance of the fullness of life on the supraindividual level is
also an avoidance of death; for at this level, one is constantly dying,
as there is nothing permanent and solid to cling to, to maintain
oneself with. In schizophrenia this fear of life and death becomes a
full-blown panic, where the potentially creative basic ground is felt as
an overwhelming threat to one's very existence. Wilson Van Dusen
discovered that blank spaces (what we might call embryonic glimpses
of the basic open ground) play a major role in all psychopathology:

> More and more it came to appear that these blank holes lay at the
> center of psychopathology. The blank holes came to be the key
> both to pathology and to psychotherapeutic change....[44]

In this light, therapies that tend to fill up space only play into the
schizophrenic's basic problem. A more direct therapeutic approach

would lie in the direction of helping the patient make friends with and accept the prepersonal open ground of his being, rather than colluding with him to fill it in and avoid it further. As Van Dusen points out: "The feared empty space is a fertile void. Exploring it is a turning point toward therapeutic change."[45]

CONCLUDING REMARKS

In conclusion, I would like to emphasize that the point of this paper has not been to "explain" meditation, but rather to provide Western psychology with a way of approaching it in light of a revised notion of unconscious process. Misconceptions of meditation as a spiritual practice are very common in the West. On the one hand, it is tempting to view meditation as another technique for self-improvement, for mastery over the world and other people. On the other hand, meditation may be seen as an avoidance or passive withdrawal from the world into a private inner realm. The approach developed here allows us to avoid both these pitfalls, grounded as it is in the understanding of the total interpenetration of organism and environment, self and world. Thus meditation can be understood as a process of self-discovery that is simultaneously a world-discovery, insofar as we are both continually re-creating our world, and, beyond that, we *are* world, we are not other than world. The way in is the way out. In this light, the following description of meditation from a Tibetan Text begins to make sense:

> One should realize that one does not meditate in order to go deeply into oneself and withdraw from the world.... There should be no feeling of striving to reach some exalted or higher state, since this simply produces something conditioned and artificial that will act as an obstruction to the free flow of the mind.... The everyday practice is simply to develop a complete awareness and openness to all situations and emotions, and to all people, experiencing everything totally without mental reservations and blockages, so that one never withdraws or centralizes onto oneself.... When performing the meditation practice, one should develop the feeling of opening oneself out completely to the whole universe with absolute simplicity and nakedness of mind.[46]

Notes

1. Miller (1942).
2. MacIntyre (1958), p. 45.
3. Jung (1933), p. 185.
4. Broad (1949); MacIntyre (1958); Boss (1963); Binswanger (1963); Gendlin (1964); Miles (1966); Matte Blanco (1975).
5. Kretschmer (1969), p. 224.
6. Ibid., p. 234.
7. Jung (1958), pp. 501, 508.
8. Maupin (1969), pp. 182–83.
9. Jung (1958), p. 484.
10. Ibid., p. 476.
11. Trungpa (1969), p. 55.
12. Jung (1958), p. 485.
13. Ibid., p. 496.
14. Trungpa (1969), p. 52.
15. Guenther & Trungpa (1975), p. 22.
16. Dhiravamsa (1974), p. 32.
17. Jung (1958), p. 502.
18. Goldstein (1939); Portmann (1954); Sinnott (1955); Szent-Gyoergyi (1974).
19. Ehrenzweig (1965).
20. James (1967), pp. 295–96.
21. Gendlin (1973), p. 370.
22. Gendlin (1962, 1978).
23. Wilber, chapter 1 of this volume, p. 18.
24. Ornstein (1972).
25. Rogers (1959).
26. quoted in Huxley (1944), p. 67.
27. Chaterjee (1971), pp. 18, 19, 22.
28. D. T. Suzuki (1930), p. 197.
29. Northrop (1946), pp. 461–62.
30. Trungpa (1976), p. 58.
31. Trungpa (1973), p. 122.
32. Matte Blanco (1975), p. 230.
33. Hora, chapter 6 of this volume, p. 73.
34. Elsewhere (Welwood, 1974) I have discussed how this nondualistic interpretation of unconscious process can illuminate the nature of creativity, artistic intuition, mystical experience, and transpersonal symbolism.
35. Kirsch (1960), p. 85.
36. Guenther & Trungpa (1975), p. 27.

37. Horsch (1961), p. 148.
38. Hisamatsu (1968), p. 31.
39. Zuckerkandl (1956), p. 370.
40. Trungpa (1973), pp. 223, 219.
41. Maslow (1967), p. 163.
42. Becker (1973), p. 62.
43. Becker (1973), p. 55.
44. Van Dusen, chapter 18 of this volume, p. 218.
45. Van Dusen, chapter 18 of this volume, p. 219.
46. Trungpa & Hookham (1974), p. 6

IV
Beyond Traditional
Psychotherapy

Introduction

Perhaps the most practical applications of the ideas and experiences discussed so far in this book to the field of Western psychology lie in the area of psychotherapy. With the decline of traditional religions in Western culture, and the concomitant loss of culturally and personally relevant spiritual practices, psychotherapy has functioned in a way that often appears similar to Eastern paths of liberation. Psychotherapy, insofar as it fosters greater awareness and acceptance of one's personal reality, increased warmth and openness toward other people, and more effective functioning in the world, has taken over many of the functions that religious practices have traditionally served within a culture. However, increasingly, many psychotherapists in this culture have begun to realize the limits of a psychotherapy in which ego strength (as discussed in chapter 9), is the major, and often final, goal. If as Maslow contended, self-transcendence is the ultimate human need, can psychotherapy speak to this need? Or is it merely an interim device that may serve as a stepping-stone to self-knowledge disciplines that *can* allow people to realize this ultimate condition?

Of course, the word *psychotherapy*, like the word *meditation*, means many different things to different people. There are as many different kinds of therapy as there are therapists, so that it is difficult to speak of it in sweeping generalizations. The thrust of this section of the book is to question traditional attitudes toward psychotherapy and to explore what new directions and approaches the Eastern psychologies suggest in this area.

The opening chapter, by the great Swiss psychotherapist Medard Boss, is the result of travels that he made to India in the 1950s. He went in search of a foundational understanding of human nature that would help him relate to the increasing number of patients coming to him for treatment for what seemed to be basically *spiritual* problems. As he described this situation:

> The Western psychotherapist can simply not keep up with the problems of the increasing number of patients who do not come to him because of clearly defined neurotic symptoms, but who are suffering "only" from the diffuse meaninglessness, vacuity, and ennui of their lives, or who are reduced to despair by the question: "Why is there being rather than nothingness?" . . . Our psychology never really tells us what human freedom is. Nor does it explain why we are here on earth at all. Nor does it make clear how our life here is to be justified. Hence all the basic concepts of our psychology paradoxically lack an authentic basis and so are not really tenable. The psychotherapist who depends solely on this science thus remains condemned to not knowing rightly what he is doing, how he is doing his work, and to what end.[1]

A number of illuminating points emerge from Boss's chapter. One is struck by the case of the Indian who studied Western psychology and returned to India much less able to accept the vicissitudes of life, as well as by the example of the Westerners who used Eastern "formulas of wisdom" to inflate their egos. Thus Boss clearly points to real dangers in the mixing of Western psychology and Eastern teachings. Twenty years later, during the current upsurge of interest in Eastern psychologies, we can detect the same dangers at large. It is all too easy to adopt Eastern ideas and techniques without having fully assimilated them. Many Westerners seem to assume that they understand Eastern ideas if they can use the correct jargon and key phrases, while underestimating the radical changes in one's life orientation that the Eastern paths are pointing to. These dangers have been pointed out both by Eastern teachers such as Chögyam Trungpa in his discussion of "spiritual materialism," as well as by such Western observers as Harvey Cox and Jacob Needleman. For example, Cox sees a danger in Eastern ideas falling prey to the

Western "consumer mentality" and greed for new experiences:

> Western psychology's present love affair with the Orient seems to
> me...unpromising and possibly even dangerous. The danger lies
> in the enormous power psychological ways of thinking now wield
> in our culture, a power so vast that the current psychologizing of
> Eastern contemplative disciplines—unless it is preceded by a
> thorough revolution in Western psychology itself—could rob these
> disciplines of their spiritual substance. It could pervert them into
> Western mental-health gimmicks and thereby prevent them from
> introducing the sharply alternative vision of life they are capable of
> bringing to us.[2]

Needleman warns against a "haste to promote and apply great ideas
not fully digested or understood"[3] as well as a tendency to espouse
"ideas emanating from the disciplines of the *path* without...follow-
ing these disciplines, thus turning the awakening force of great ideas
into fuel for the engines of egoism."[4]

Thus it is well to point out that there are important differences
between psychotherapy and Eastern disciplines and that there are
many pitfalls in prematurely and unwisely trying to mix the two
approaches. Perhaps the most important point that can be made in
seeking possible applications of Eastern teachings to Western
psychotherapy is that this wisdom must be personally realized to
some extent before it can be applied. Such a realization would be
evidenced by changes in the therapist in the direction of greater
openness and less ego territoriality as a result of his or her training in
these disciplines.

The danger of applying Eastern ideas and techniques in some
preconceived manner is also stressed by Chögyam Trungpa in his
dialogue with psychotherapists. He points out how the attitude of
trying to cure suffering and get rid of the patient's pain is
questionable, in that suffering may be one of the clearest pointers to
the basic character of one's existence. Normally, much of Western
psychotherapy is directed toward problem-solving or decision-
making. However, focusing too narrowly on the goal of getting rid of
problems may keep one from seeing how the problem points to and
expresses a whole way of living which is out of balance. Thus
problems may be valuable, almost precious opportunities that can
lead one to change one's life orientation in radical ways.

In the Tibetan Buddhist view, neurosis is actually seen as a path to enlightenment, in that liberation arises from a deepening awareness of the ways in which one imprisons oneself. Genuine awakening would not be facilitated by seeking merely to eliminate one's pain and imprisonment, but rather by fully facing it, accepting it, and directly working with it. Marvin Casper has worked closely with Chögyam Trungpa in developing a Buddhist approach to therapy with such an orientation, called Maitri (meaning "unlimited friendliness"). In his chapter he points out how neurosis may be understood as different styles of freezing space or fixating one's energy. The therapeutic approach he outlines has to do with making friends with one's neurotic tendencies, so that one no longer struggles against them as though they were an "Other," an "It." Then one may begin to glimpse one's basic sanity at the same time, as one relaxes the struggle of ego to *maintain* or *protect* a manufactured sanity that tries to exclude neurosis and pain from its territory.

Gary Deatherage presents an exploratory study of the use of mindfulness meditation as an adjunctive aid in short-term psychotherapy. An important result was to help his patients realize that their emotionally churning thoughts, which keep them locked in their grip, are *just thoughts*, rather than the way things actually are.

Finally, Wilson Van Dusen explores how the relation to empty spaces and gaps in a person's experience may play a critical role both in the generation of psychopathology and in its alleviation. He implies that it is the fear of groundlessness and open space that leads the schizophrenic to fill up and solidify his world. In fearing the groundless, open quality of experience, the schizophrenic tends to convert these empty spaces into a terrifying vortex that threatens to suck him down. However, in light of Eastern teachings, Van Dusen suggests that befriending these groundless spaces can lead to a turning point in the therapeutic process which releases new energy to the patient for working with his situation.

NOTES

1. Boss (1965), pp. 10–11.
2. Cox (1977), p. 75.
3. Needleman (1975b), p.14.
4. Needleman (1975a), p. 92.

14

Eastern Wisdom and Western Psychotherapy

Medard Boss

None of the leading scholars and great wise men of India I had the pleasure of meeting ever failed to point out with special emphasis one thing: all the Indian philosophical systems that matter have always been concerned with the same two problems. They dealt with the fact of the endless suffering that people had to endure and the equally undeniable fact of man's powerful longing for release from suffering and for happiness. Owing to the strict focusing of their thought on these two vital circumstances of our life, the Indian philosophers became veritable pioneers of the ways to salvation. At the same time, they never elevated the intellectual investigation of the truth as their ultimate aim, as did Western philosophers, but regarded it as merely one of the possible provisional means of producing a release from suffering.

If what I had heard from such authoritative spokesmen was the case, the Indian philosophies were nothing more than spiritual prescriptions against human suffering in all its forms. Then we should call them psychotherapies rather than philosophies, if the Indians had ever believed in the existence of a "psyche." Instead, Indian thought always understood man as an essentially luminating *atman*-being, belonging directly to *Brahman*,* the hidden matrix of all appearing,

Brahman in Hindu thought refers to the ultimate reality of things which goes beyond all forms of appearance or conceptualization (Ed.).

being, vanishing and nonbeing. Indian philosophy sees in this conception not only the truth about the basic nature of man but also the only effective therapeutics to ensure genuine cures and lasting salvation. Therefore—aside from the always despised materialists—it is the common aim of all Indian schools of philosophy to explore ways and means fully to elucidate this truth in terms of an experience that encompasses man as a whole. Thus it would be more appropriate to call the Indian philosophies "elucidation therapies." And yet this other name removes them only apparently from the methods of treatment called "psychotherapies" in the West. In reality, it brings the two therapies, Eastern and Western, so close to each other that their point of contact becomes visible at once. For had not *Freud* very early discovered that the criterion setting his psychoanalytical method apart from all other medical therapies is the simultaneous occurrence of illuminating insight into the hidden nature of a neurotic disturbance and of therapeutic liberation from this suffering? Could he not also sum up the principle behind his method of treatment in the words: where "id" was, let there be "ego"? And ever since Freud, have not all Western psychotherapies worthy of the name endeavored to make patients themselves see into their unveiled nature, to make them transparent to themselves? It does not matter how various in kind are all the secondary, theoretical superstructures erected above these therapies. But where could there ever be an elucidation (lux=light), a transparency, a shining-through, without light and a light-giving source?

However, no matter how closely Eastern philosophies and Western psychotherapies agree, the *degree* of illuminating power that the Western psychotherapies are as a rule capable of attaining struck me as so insufficient that I began to look for assistance in the Indian tradition. I had a unique experience at the very beginning of my Indian stay; it drove home the point that our psychotherapeutic methods needed urgent improvement of their capacity to illuminate. I had made friends with the family of an Indian philosophy professor, a very perceptive and learned man. He had felt a need to supplement his mastery of ancient Indian teachings with a knowledge of European psychology and psychotherapy. To employ his own words, he hoped that, thus equipped, he could render more individual assistance to patients than before. Therefore he had come to Europe for two years and had successfully completed a course of study at a psychotherapeutic institute. Nevertheless, since his return to India he himself had been complaining—and his family concurred—that he had been made much more unhappy by learning about Western psychotherapy. Whereas formerly he had accepted the vicissitudes of life, like illnesses in the family, with great calmness, now every trifle made him nervous, restless, and pessimistic. Now he always thought he had to do this or that at once, and he made everything worse with his haste. He had forgotten how to wait patiently, and had become harder and more loveless. Obviously, from his training in Western psychotherapy, he had learned to see himself as a "psyche," i.e., a balanced system of mental functions, libidinous dynamisms, and archetypical structures and forces within the psychic realm of a subject. Now he had to find his way through the bustle and tumult of an external world, based on nothing but a fundamentally unknowable, anonymous, id-like "unconscious." He had lost so much of his former Indian wisdom and poised calm that his confidence-inspiring realization of his participation in all-encompassing, sustaining "Brahman" had shrunk to a fragile dependence on individual authority figures and their psychological notions. I learned all this not only from his waking behavior but also from the troublesome dreams which had begun to torment him toward the end of his psychoanalytical training, and which still bothered him here in India. It does not matter which school of psychoanalysis this was. Any Western psychology would have involved this Indian philosopher in the same difficulties. Nevertheless, there is little doubt that the same psychotherapy would have been of the greatest use to many a hardened, ego-obsessed European or American. But my friend had previously been living in the vastness of Indian thinking and feeling, and Western psychotherapy seemed to him like a prison demoralizing him with its narrowness.

Still less encouraging were my first experiences with European and American people who had gone in wholeheartedly for Eastern wisdom. Even before my Indian trip I had met patients who had had to pay with a severe mental illness for their newly acquired acquaintance with the Indian tradition. Their attempts to sink into meditation in the Indian fashion and to yield themselves up to *Brahman* had unleashed in them a schizophrenic chaos. The first thing the doctor had to do was to divert their attention from all Indian ideas and to bring them back into their native world with the aid of occupational therapy.

In India itself I met altogether eight European and American people who had entered upon one of the Indian ways of salvation. They were living either in a retreat in the mountains or had joined the ashram of a holy man and donned the Indian monk's or nun's garb along with the corresponding ascetic discipline. With one exception, however, they had remained in the depths of their hearts self-willed, envious, and intolerant Occidentals. They had merely inflated their very limited egos with Indian formulas of wisdom instead of with large bank accounts or other means to power. Clear evidence of this was their ungenerous contempt for Western culture and for Christian beliefs. The human magnanimity of their Indian teachers did not appear to have left any traces on them as yet.

The misfortune that had befallen my Indian philosopher friend was a clear warning against trying to force a person at peace in an Eastern wisdom into the framework of a Western psychological theory. On the other hand, these experiences with Occidentals taught me to keep all Indian knowledge about the nature of man far removed from my future therapeutic work.

And yet there were the exalted figures of the sages and holy men themselves, each one of them a living example of the possibility of human growth and maturity and of the attainment of an imperturbable inner peace, a joyous freedom from guilt and a purified, selfless goodness and calmness. The means and aims of our Western psychotherapy struck me as quite inadequate in comparison with the teachings and the behavior of these masters. Of course, our psychologies furnish students with easily assimilable psychological formulas and concepts. Their obvious handiness nourishes our belief that they give us something really solid, something we can rely on. They make us forget that they are for the most part only intellectual reductions of the nature of man to unreal abstractions.

However, the aims behind a rightly understood training analysis, as required by every serious school of psychotherapy in the West, coincide in many respects with the instructions of the Indian sages. But compared with the degree of self-purification expected by the latter, even the best Western training analysis is not much more than an introductory course. Above all, Western psychotherapies had previously taught me never to expect more from my patients than the possibility that they might grow into a conscious appropriation of all their vital capacities and become able to live with their fellow men in a spirit of mature love. But there was no hope that a person would actually get rid of his "shadow" by means of psychotherapy. The therapist had to be satisfied if a patient under analysis became aware of his aggressive, destructive animal drives. For in that way he at least got control of them. They could no longer emerge from repression and with their false pretenses wreak their havoc in the shape of pathological symptoms, and treacherously disturb the natural goodness in man. Yet, at best, we all had to live out our lives consciously in the presence of the dark and evil forces of our natures.

Nevertheless, the Indian sages seem to have worked the miracle of truly freeing themselves from evil. I was forced to the conclusion that in them there is nothing at all evil, covetous, destructive, fearful, guilty, or dark, to be consciously controlled and unconsciously repressed. No matter how carefully I observed the waking lives of the holy men, no matter how ready they were to tell me about their dreams, I could not detect in the best of them a trace of a selfish action or any kind of repressed or consciously concealed shadow life. They seemed to me to consist of pure love, which had long since redeemed in them all hate and desire. Yet such a liberation and such unclouded bliss—they had always taught me—presupposed *vairagya*, the renunciation of all self-seeking attachment to things and to people. *Vairagya* did not need to have anything to do with a bodily withdrawal.

Whenever I listened to the Indian sages, I always asked myself whether I would not have to overhaul my whole psychotherapeutic knowledge or give it up entirely.

I was so perplexed by the contradictory experiences of my Indian journey that finally my tormenting doubts overcame me in the presence of my Kashmiri teacher. He could see my trouble in my face, broke off in the middle of a sentence, and went on: "Do not think you would have to apply in some way, in your profession, what you have learned in India, or derive from it a new psychotherapeutic technique. You had better not say anything at all to your patients about it. Don't make the slightest change in your psychological technique of free association and in your analysis of resistance. I told you, when you described for me the basic principles of Western psychoanalysis, that from time immemorial Indian teachers too imposed on their pupils a corresponding 'training-analysis,' a realization of their own desires and passions. Of course, what you call psychotherapy and psycho-analysis are only preliminary treatments. They may be doubly necessary, indispensable, and tedious for Occidentals. People in the West have for centuries been disciplined in their consciousness of a self-contained personality, in their overemphasis on rational, conceptual thinking, and in their divisive idea of the sinfulness of the bodily and instinctual side. And yet, at bottom, no person anywhere in the world will attain to truly profound and restorative knowledge unless he has freed himself from all false ideas about himself and from any attachment to immature, childish needs. How should one obtain the strength of spirit to overcome one's ego-attachment and the vision of the ordinary man—and grow into the much more encompassing state of consciousness called *samadhi*, complete enlightenment, unless one had conscious control of all one's vital capacities? If, however, a man attempts this before he has attained the necessary maturity and freedom, he will surely break down, fall into confusion, or become exalted.

"Tell all whom it may concern that the attainment of truth by meditation does not presuppose a weak, unprepared mind, but an especially mature frame of mind and a powerful consciousness capable of comprehending all human capacities. Meditation should never be misunderstood as a retreat or a regression to a pre-individual state. A person who truly meditates becomes not less but more than what you call a 'personality.' He develops a vision that transcends everything individual. He never gives up his so-called ego-consciousness in order to drift in a state of self-dissolution, but in order to attain the state of a much profounder and more comprehensive consciousness. That is no child's game. The wise men of India had always warned against all 'wild' meditation experiments and repeatedly stressed the necessity of a proper introduction and guidance by an experienced teacher. In this they are also in accord with you, since, as you tell me, you are familiar too with the necessity of a careful training in this field."

Thus, without being asked to do so, this man had largely resolved my confusion. I now understood the regrettable events that made Occidentals in contact with the Indian tradition either self-willed, sentimental fantasts or confused schizophrenics. Their mental structure was obviously too restricted, too hardened; and its basis was too narrow, weak, and fragile to enable them to integrate such insights. They would all have greatly needed psychoanalysis first, which the master had understood as a preliminary treatment.

However, had not the wise man at the same time explained the situation in a way that decidedly put me in my place? Had he not spoken out clearly enough against any attempt of a Western psychotherapist to overstep the bounds of just such a "preliminary treatment," when he advised me to keep silent about all my Indian experiences, and would not hear of any change in my previous psychotherapeutic methods?

To make sure, I asked again: "Then, my whole Indian journey can at best expand my own horizon a little, but cannot benefit my patients in any way? Is my relationship to them really to remain as it was before?"

"Externally, of course," was the reply of the master. "The outward aspects of your work will hardly change. For the best thing you can do as a conscientious doctor is quietly to assimilate your Indian experiences. If these have impinged deeply enough, everything else will follow of itself. Your patients will sense that your actions are becoming meaningful in and for themselves. Do you remember how I asked you to lie flat on the floor here one evening after we had first met? How tense you were, as if you could not trust these thick boards and the rock underneath to hold you up, as if even in lying you had to hold yourself together by an effort of sheer will in order not to perish! But how should a person who does not trust his own basis and does not dare to yield to it have the calmness and strength to give aid to others who need it?

"However, some people can experience in the last fibers of their being, by tireless concentration and contemplation of the true nature of all phenomena, their immediate participation in *Brahman*, the one ineffable but most real of all givens. With such people, every single action, no matter how slight or how close to all previous actions, every word takes on a new, fuller, and more beneficent significance. For an unshakable confidence is radiated by everything such a person does or leaves undone. It is the primordial trust in what is inconceivable by conceptual understanding, incalculable by all calculations, in which all things are rooted. Even though all this is still a deeply veiled mystery to you, it will one day dawn on your intellect as that great beginning which, though incalculable, is never just the contrary of a calculable order, merely chaos, but is always what sustains all chaos and order together.

"Many another precondition of a fruitful psychotherapy will be automatically established if you are prepared to make the effort of tireless, open, still, and concentrated listening to what goes on within, to the root-melody of all being—instead of a 'straining of the intellect,' to employ your own term. You would never again fall prey to a superficial fascination with any kind of psychotherapeutic techniques or psychological theories. Neither would you, of course, despise psychotherapeutic devices and think you are entitled to do without them and replace them by sentimentality. You would only use psychotherapeutic equipment like all other inventions of technology, in freedom, rejoice in its good effects and so be able to play with it, without taking it for something ultimate. At the same time, you would be immune to all the pathological cramps of an eternal compulsion, obligation, and will to determine everything yourself. You would know that true human progress occurs only when every will to progress has vanished and a relaxed waiting and ability-to-let-be has replaced it. When all the phenomena of the world and all their interrelationships become transparent in their deepest nature and hidden perfection to you as a truly aware person—no matter how tormenting and destructive they may appear to a rigid and constricted intellect—then you will be able to enjoy an unperturbed and liberating happiness. Only then would you never again feel yourself to be torn into an ego, into menacing anonymous drives and into a hostile conscience. You would, rather, be able to understand all your psychic possibilities as related articulations of one and the same comprehensive root-being.

"Out of the same understanding, a genuine healer also sees everything that happens in his patients as stemming from the same origin as his own life, constantly pervading it and actually constituting it. Therefore he is open to and capable of an acceptance of the Other that is unlimited because, from his viewpoint, there are no longer any barriers between an *I* and a *Thou* and the ultimate ground. But, then, these barriers have never been erected *in such a way* that there ever would be the danger of an entangling and merging of two small subjects, for example, a mutual mindless infatuation. Rather, the barriers are overcome in such a way that the true healer helps the other person to become increasingly aware of the essential native root-nature common to both of them, until, in its light, a time comes when all pathological distortions and constrictions vanish spontaneously."

Then the master was silent. Like my previous Indian teachers, he had also early requested me to look him straight in the eyes, as often and as long as possible. That helped understanding, promoted mutual access to the essential human core in each of us, and cut through the superficial cultural and social masks that we all wear. Here, too, I overcame my Western shyness, my fear of offending by such unabashed staring. In this intimate contact with the master I gained for a while the great peace that simply allows all things to come to pass. This simple thing was the certainty that what our psychotherapy needs above all is a change in the psychotherapists. If our science of mental health is to become more effective, psychotherapists will have to balance their knowledge of psychological concepts and techniques with a contemplative awareness. This will have to be an awareness that exercises itself day after day in quiet openness; it must address the inexpressible origin of all that is, of the healthy and the sick and also of all psychotherapeutic interventions. Then psychiatrists, in their own way, will be able to help people who are becoming increasingly alienated from their roots. They will then be able to restore to these people that sense of basic warmth that is more protective and sustaining than all the institutions and techniques that have ever been devised.

A Dialogue with Psychotherapists

Chögyam Trungpa

Chögyam Trungpa: We have a tendency in our lives to seek some kind of eternity, to confirm the seeming continuity of our past and future, so perhaps we could discuss the question of eternity and nowness. We want to stretch out the sense of a solid situation. This attempt to keep on top of the situation all the time makes us anxious, since we continually have to struggle to maintain our goal. In the practice of meditation we may discover that eternity does not exist as a long-term situation, we may discover a sense of presentness or nowness.

Q: Could you discuss the differences between meditation and psychotherapy?
A: The difference is in the individual's attitude toward undergoing the disciplines of meditation and psychotherapy. In the popular therapeutic style the individual's attitude is one of trying to recover from something. He looks for a technique to help him get rid of, or overcome, his complaint. The meditative attitude accepts, in some sense, that you are what you are. Your neurotic aspects have to be looked at rather than thrown away. Actually, in popular Buddhism, meditation is sometimes regarded as a cure, but that's myth, nobody knows what's going to be cured, what's going to happen. When you meditate properly, the notion of cure doesn't come into the picture. If it does, then meditation becomes psychotherapy.

Q: How do you relate that to the use of the term *neurotic*?

A: The neurotic aspect is the counterpart of wisdom, so you cannot have one without the other. In the ideal case, when enlightenment is attained, the neuroses are still there but they have become immense energy. Energy is the euphemism for neurosis from that point of view.

Q: In psychoanalysis and Reichian character analysis the practitioners claim to alter the fundamental character structure and eliminate the continuation of neuroses. You seem to be saying that the neuroses, even in an enlightened being, will continue. That seems to be distinctly different.

A: The basic idea is that mind cannot be altered or changed, only somewhat clarified. You have to come back to what you are, rather than reform yourself into something else. Reformation seems to be going against the current, from a Buddhist point of view.

Q: Do you think that if therapy was done with the idea of helping someone become more aware of themselves it would then be consistent with the Buddhist point of view?

A: Basically, yes, since there is a sense of self-dislike and not wanting to see oneself, so the idea is to project a sense of friendliness to oneself. The role of the teacher or therapist is to help someone make friends with himself. That's why our psychology program is called Maitri, which means friendliness.

Q: In the Maitri experience you talk about transmuting energies, taking neurotic qualities, solid qualities, things that make one anxious and transmuting them, making them finer, giving them clarity. It seems, in psychotherapy, when one is experiencing negative feelings, that one is encouraged to express them, and in the expression there is some type of release. I am wondering how you see that in relation to, say, just being in the Maitri postures, just being with the negativity and watching it. It seems to be two different ways to be with the energy.

A: The idea is to be able to actually see the texture, the quality, the rising and the falling of emotion. At first, we are not particularly concerned with what we are going to do with it. We just examine the whole thing. Before we do anything, we have to make a relationship with our emotional energy. Usually, when we are talking about expressing our energies we are more concerned with the expression than with the energy itself, which seems to be rushing too fast. We are afraid that it will overwhelm us. So we try to get rid of it by action.

Q: You're not saying to suppress our feelings, are you?
A: No, you don't keep them down. Suppressing them is also doing something with them. Suppression involves a separation between you and your emotions, and therefore you feel that you have to do something with them. When energy is related to properly, it rises, peaks, and then returns back to one's energy bank. A recharging process takes place.

Q: Is that the transmutation process?
A: Yes, transmutation is turning the lead into gold.

Q: In Reichian or primal therapy they encourage people to let out all their anger or hatred. Their theory is that the reintegration of the ego will come by the expression of these energies. From your point of view, by merely relating to the energies, not expressing or repressing them, by just being with them, that a certain kind of change ...
A: Once you have developed a harmonious relationship with your energy, then you can actually express it, but the style of expression becomes very sane, right to the point. The idea is that expressing energy properly is the final crescendo, the final power, it is at the level of tantra. So from the Buddhist point of view, skillful, accurate expression is the culmination of one's development. To do this you have to have a harmonious relationship to your energy, to be completely in your own energy. If you try to release your energy at an earlier point you are wasting a lot of valuable material.

Q: So in the meantime while we are trying to make the relationship, do we just sit with anger if it comes up?
A: Not necessarily. The question is whether the anger is part of you or something separate. You have to make a greater connection between the anger and yourself. So even just sitting with it is not enough. It could still be like a bad marriage where there is no relationship. Emotions are part of you, your limbs. If you don't have energy or emotion, there is no movement, no way to put things into effect. You have to regard emotions as part of you to begin with.

Q: How can I be graceful and totally aware all the time? It seems impossible.

A: Awareness does not mean beware, be careful, ward off danger, you might step into a puddle, so beware. That is not the kind of awareness we are talking about. We are talking about unconditional presence which is not expected to be there all the time. In fact, in order to be completely aware you have to disown the experience of awareness. It cannot be regarded as yours—it is just there and you do not try to hold it. Then, somehow, a general clarity takes place. So awareness is a glimpse rather than a continuous state. If you hold on to awareness, it becomes self-consciousness rather than awareness. Awareness has to be unmanufactured, it has to be a natural state.

Q: What is enlightenment?
A: The Buddhist method is to first find out what isn't enlightenment. You begin to peel off all the skins and then you probably find that in the absence of everything, some sort of essence exists. The basic idea of enlightenment is the Sanskrit word *bodhi*, which means wakeful. Ultimately, it is an unconditional state of wakefulness, which happens to us occasionally. Intelligence is present all the time, but it gets overcrowded. So one has to peel off the excess layers to allow it to shine through.

Q: The initial impact, other than Maitri, which is a whole development of the application of Buddhism on therapy, will simply be the effect of Buddhist practices on the therapist and then maybe something will slip through no matter what the context is. Whether you are a behavior modification therapist or you're a psychoanalyst it doesn't make any difference, it could have a really powerful effect.
A: I don't see any particular problems here. At this point we are talking about taking an attitude which is based on Buddhist experience. Out of that, any kind of style or technique will be used, as long as the presentation doesn't become too dogmatic. In any case, in therapeutic situations you can't always go by the books; you have to improvise a great deal when you are working with somebody else. So I think we are not so much talking about "should be doing this," or "should be doing that," cookery book style. We are talking about developing some kind of insight. I think an understanding of the ideas of impermanence and ego is a very important contribution. Then everything is an individual application. Problems could occur if there is no relationship between the patient and the doctor. If there is

no relationship, then all you can do is go along with the books, what the original prescriptions were. That seems like a second-rate therapy. If a real relationship takes place and everything becomes a part of one's journey, then I don't see any problems.

Q: Could I add another word to that? My hope when I think of what Buddhism can contribute is that it will soften or lessen the need that therapists I know seem to have, which is to have a changing effect on their patients or clients. I think that is the most important part of the message. It goes along with everything you've said: you were spelling it out and I was generalizing it in terms of the tremendous pressure that the client and the therapist bring to the situation, to have something to change. And that is absolutely not what is necessary.

I was first drawn to you when I read in one of your books, in which there was a voice saying just that: "Look at it, don't try to change it." It seems to me that Western therapy could go back to that. That's what I think Freud was standing for in the first place. Freud was basically an investigator, he was much less interested in curing than in finding out. If we could only encourage our colleagues to go back to that position in itself, that would be a tremendous change in a very subtle way.

A: Precisely.

16

Space Therapy and the Maitri Project

Marvin Casper

The Maitri Project is an application of Tibetan Buddhist psychology and meditation practice to the problem of neurosis and mental disorder. This chapter presents the general theory of space awareness used in the Maitri approach, and a vision of its application in a therapeutic community which Chögyam Trungpa has begun to establish.

Maitri is an attitude of openness, friendliness, humor, and loving appreciation toward ourselves, other people, and the world as a whole. It allows one to greet everything, beautiful or ugly, with simple appreciation, without resistance or rejection. It allows one to free oneself from imaginary ideals and strategies, thus leaving space for others to reveal themselves as they are.

The therapy involved in the Maitri approach occurs in a small, closely interacting residential community. The patients will be highly neurotic, but capable of at least marginal functioning in society. In addition to the discipline of communal living, the patients also practice a specific therapeutic discipline adopted from Buddhist meditation practice, termed "space therapy." This practice highlights one's states of mind and relationships to the world, inspiring an attitude of Maitri toward whatever comes up. There is room to explore one's pride, passion, paranoia, frustrations, and aggression, as well as one's gentleness, bravery, generosity, and intelligence.

In order to understand the dynamics of this space therapy, it is necessary to review the basic principles of Buddhist psychology upon which the therapy is based.

According to Buddhist psychology, the basis of neurosis is the tendency to solidify energy into a barrier that separates space into two entities, "I" and "Other," the space in here and the space out there. This process is technically termed "dualistic fixation." First there is the initial creation of the barrier, the sensing of Other, and then the inference of inner or I. This is the birth of ego. We identify with what is in here and struggle to relate to what is out there. The barrier causes an imbalance between inside and outside. The struggle to redress the imbalance further solidifies the wall. The irony of the barrier-creating process is that we lose track of the fact that we have created the barrier and, instead, act as if it was always there.

After the initial creation of I and Other, I feels the territory outside itself, determining if it is threatening, attractive, or uninteresting. Feeling the environment is followed by: impulsive action—passion, aggression, or ignoring—pulling in what is seductive, pushing away what is threatening or repelling, ignoring what is uninteresting or irritating. But feeling and impulsive action are crude ways of defending and enhancing ego. The next response is conceptual discrimination, fitting phenomena into categories, which makes the world much more manageable and intelligible. Finally, whole fantasy worlds are created to shield and entertain ego. Emotions are the highlights of the fantasies while discursive thoughts, images, and memories sustain the story line. A story of ego's hopes and fears, victories and defeats, virtues and vices is developed. In highly neurotic people elaborate subplots or "problems" then develop from the initial drama. The subplots become very complicated and compelling, often overshadowing the main drama. In psychotic people, the subplots completely overshadow the main drama. The different stages of ego development—the initial split of I and Other, feeling, impulse, conceptualization, and the various fantasy worlds are technically referred to as the five *skandhas*. From moment to moment the five *skandhas* are recreated in such a manner that it seems like the ego drama is continuous. Clinging to the apparent continuity and solidity of ego, ceaselessly trying to maintain I and Mine, is the root of neurosis. This effort clashes with the inevitability of change, with the ever-recurring death and birth of ego, and therefore causes suffering.

The degree of neurosis and suffering that a person experiences is related to the amount of inner space and clarity available to him. If a person feels that his inner resources for coping with and appreciating life are very limited, then the world outside seems highly alien, seductive, and threatening. He feels compelled to struggle to remove threats and draw in what is valuable. But the struggle is self-defeating. It intensifies the solidity of the barrier and results in feelings of inner poverty and restricted space. Thus, to a highly neurotic person, the outer world feels extremely claustrophobic and confusing. The level of psychosis is reached when the fear of outside is so great that we panic and become absorbed in a fantasy world that has little connection with our surroundings.

The goal of Maitri therapy is to give a patient a sense of more inner space, more strength and intelligence, more acceptance of himself and the world. The clarity and calm possible with such an inner space is the first step toward sanity. The relationship of inner and outer spaces is stabilized sufficiently so that the struggle with the world is relaxed. Further psychological development involves clearly seeing how the emotions and fantasies develop, and how they are used as entertainment and defense. But before we can fundamentally question the dramas in which we are involved, there must be some calmness and clarity, some spaciousness in our outer world. Only then, after the turbulent waters become gently flowing and clear, can the outline of the barrier itself be seen. So, in a sense, the goal of Maitri therapy is to have the patient become more familiar and comfortable with ego, to make friends with his neurotic ways. At this level we are not so much cutting through a person's drama as we are cutting through the subplots that obscure the main story line: thus, clearly seeing the transparency of the subplots, then the dramas, then the concepts and finally the barrier itself. One works with more and more refined levels of dualistic fixation.

The subplots and dramas are neurotic distortions of basic styles of relating to space. The therapeutic process is not to eliminate these styles of relationship but to cut through the ego game of territoriality associated with each style. The whole idea of Buddhist therapy or meditation is therefore to work with the core of neurosis, clinging to territory, rather than try to change a person's style of relating to the world. Individual differences in energy flow, and in cultural and historical circumstances are not problems. Released from the distortions caused by territorial clinging, the styles manifest as sane expressions of intelligence. Thus, we need not build up positive or sane qualities. If we part the clouds of confusion, the sun of sanity will shine through.

The basic styles of relating to space are classified in terms of the "Buddha families"—*vajra, ratna, padma, karma, buddha*. According to Tibetan Buddhist Tantra, the Buddha families are fundamental patterns of energy which manifest in all phenomenal experience. Thus landscapes, colors, sounds, foods, and climates, as well as personality types, can all be classified in terms of the Buddha families. In the following descriptions of the basic styles of relating to space, the neurotic aspect will be emphasized.

Vajra movement involves sweeping over and surveying the entire area facing you, clearly mirroring the field of vision. It is like clear water freely flowing over a surface. It fills all the space but the surface underneath it can be seen clearly. *Vajra* neurosis involves fear of being surprised, confused, or overwhelmed by outside, so one continually monitors the environment for threats. When a threat is detected, we respond by cold or hot anger—pushing the world away by creating a cold wall that holds phenomena at a distance or a hot front that repels them. *Vajra* is associated with abstract intellect, with mapping relationships so as to have a clear, comprehensive view of a situation. In the neurotic state, the abstracting process becomes compulsive and loses contact with phenomena. One becomes self-righteous, justifying everything in terms of one's "system" and filtering out inconvenient facts. It also leads to intellectual frivolousness, getting caught up in word games divorced from experience, or compulsively figuring out how things fit together and what rule of conduct applies to a situation. On a bodily level it involves excessive visual and head orientation, always trying to see around the corner or behind your back, watching every corner.

Ratna is associated with substance. It involves expanding to fill up and solidify every container. *Ratna* neurosis is connected with feelings of not being substantial or solid enough. The world in here is insufficient, poor. The richness, the substance is out there. So the tendency of the *ratna* neurosis is to expand its substance to incorporate the outside into its territory. There is a tendency to be overbearing, mothering, imperious—trying to be the center of one's world, the principal object of affection, attention, approval. One is always hungry and needs the food of more possessions, more psychological gratifications, more confirmations of one's richness. Intellectually, *ratna* neurosis manifests as indiscriminate collecting and spewing out of facts, words, ideas, contacts, an overstuffed mind. The emotion associated with *ratna* is pride. One is continually building monuments to oneself, reassuring oneself of importance and worth—you are heavy, significant, central in relation to your world. Physically *ratna* is very concerned about material comfort—ornate surroundings, much rich food, soft furniture. Life is a series of nourishing or unnourishing events.

In *padma* neurosis one tries to draw things into one's world, to seduce phenomena. There is a sense of incompleteness, a seeking of something to entertain or enrich ourselves. The basic quality of *padma* is relating to the immediate presence of "Other." While *karma* is associated with direct movement and *vajra* with clear seeing, *padma* is feeling presence. The more we panic about losing the presence of "Other," the more we struggle to hold on to Other so as to feel its presence. We want to draw "that" into "this" area and keep it here, possess it in order to feel it. Intellectually *padma* neurosis involves getting caught in a succession of unrelated details, scattering one's attention. One gets lost in the surfaces. A project is started with great enthusiasm but one quickly loses interest and goes on to the next thing. Emotionally *padma* neurosis involves passion, grasping desired objects, and the frustrations of rejection or loss. There is a tendency toward continuous friendliness, sugary sweet kindness and hypersensitivity to rejection or coldness, to any withdrawal of presence. Physically, one is preoccupied with pleasure and pain.

Karma is associated with thrusting movement, jumping from place to place, trying to control phenomena by direct manipulation. It is symbolized by a sword and the wind. It is like an army thrusting forward by achieving a long, narrow penetration of enemy lines, trying to destroy the enemies' headquarters. But since its thrust is narrow and long, it is vulnerable to attacks from the flank. At the head of the column, the general can only see ahead of him. He is afraid that the enemy will cut him off from his home base. Consequently the characteristic *karma* neurosis involves paranoia— fear of being attacked, fear of being inadequate, fear of being left out, fear of losing track. This leads to a preoccupation with controlling situations, with speedily busying oneself in organizing things, making things work efficiently. One must speed about to keep up with the continual changes that threaten disorder. The more preoccupied we are with order and control, the more disturbing and clearly defined chaos becomes and the more we must compulsively speed to re-create order. Intellectually *karma* neurosis thinks compulsively in terms of means and ends, sequences of doing this and that to achieve something. There is also excessive concern with details to check that nothing was missed, no possible action undone. Furthermore, points of reference or comparisons are needed to frequently reassure ourselves that our position is secure, our identity is solid, our world safe. So envy and jealousy are important aspects of the *karma* neurosis.

Buddha is associated with space and intelligence free of ego. It accommodates all phenomena, including the play of *ratna*, *padma*, *karma*, and *vajra* energies. *Buddha* neurosis involves the absence of spaciousness, the dulling of intelligence, and the freezing of the play of energies. The neurotic *buddha* world is like a small, thick, walled concrete box with no windows—a secure womb. Intellectually, *buddha* neurosis involves rigid habits of mind, fixed ideas, stubborn resistance to new information, a self-smug, self-righteous attitude. You just plod along oblivious to messages from the environment, following familiar habits. Intelligence and energy are ignored. Dirty dishes pile up, work is left undone, close personal relations are neglected, the same shirt is worn for a week. There is a tremendous fear of changes in rules, routines, views of right and wrong. Emotionally there is a dull neutrality, and unresponsiveness to stimulation.

How does one work with these neurotic styles of relating to space? The foundation of the Buddhist approach to unraveling neurosis is meditation. By sitting quietly and still for a lengthy period of time, one begins to see how the mind works. During that time "problems" are not confirmed or fed by the world around us. This allows an opportunity for gaps to occur in which we glimpse our struggle from the perspective of space, which contains fundamental intelligence. We step out of the I–Other drama for a moment. So the practice of sitting meditation involves neither feeding nor repressing thoughts but clearly seeing them without getting caught up in them. Usually, techniques that cut the chain of thoughts are used as aids— attention to a sound (*mantra*) or the breathing process is most common. Gradually our world becomes more spacious, our dramas less intense and all-consuming. The sitting meditation carries over into everyday life and we begin to see more clearly how we create our worlds.

Unfortunately the sitting meditation discipline is not effective with highly neurotic people. Their mental processes are too speedy and confused to allow much space to develop. So Trungpa has adopted some specialized meditation techniques to substitute for sitting meditation. These techniques constitute space therapy.

In this therapy a person maintains a posture within a specially designed room for a lengthy period of time, usually two forty-five minute sessions daily. Attention is focused on the space in the room. The rooms highlight the view of the world characteristic of each neurotic style and the postures highlight the neurotic response to that world. Of course, the inside and outside, "my response" and "the world's response to me" are intertwining parts of one process. To contract the space around you in response to what you perceive as claustrophobic surroundings intensifies their claustrophobic quality of the outside. To attack space in response to phenomena intensifies their resistance to your clutches, which intensifies your struggle to hold on to them. Likewise, *straining* to know panoramically narrows one's perspective, which in turn leads to greater strain.

In each case, struggle intensifies the solidity of the barrier, the imbalance of inside and outside, and the vulnerability and impoverishment of inside. From moment to moment one is faced with the alternative of letting go, of opening to a saner, more balanced relationship to the world, or panicking and intensifying the struggle to manipulate it.

The long period of holding the posture, the monotony of the surroundings and the task of attending to space, allow the possibility of being less caught up in habitual thought patterns. Furthermore, the postures are all somewhat uncomfortable and therefore demand attention to the body and ground as well. These conditions can break the chain of thoughts sufficiently so that a person glimpses his neurotic relationship to space. He may come to realize that the "external world" is always the same in these rooms and therefore his shifting perceptions of the room are his own creation. This insight may allow him to relax his struggle with space sufficiently to glimpse a sane way of relating to it.

In the *vajra* posture one lies belly down, hands extended to the sides, palms flat on the ground, and face to the side. In the *vajra* room the windows are small slits along the wall. Since a person with *vajra* neurosis is always scanning his surroundings, facing the ground and looking at windows that only tease him can be very frustrating. He doesn't know what is above him or outside the room. The positions and rooms thus force the practitioner to confront how he relates to his world by frustrating or exaggerating his ordinary style. The positive potential in the *vajra* posture is to discover that you don't have to literally see what is above or around you. There is the conviction that you already know what is happening; excessive confirmation is unnecessary.

In *ratna* posture the arms are perpendicular to the body, legs are spread wider than in *karma* posture, and the hands are flat down against the ground. The *ratna* room contains a large circular window on one wall. Its color is gold. From the posture one sees the outline of the window without being able to see out. This suggests the possibility of expanding beyond the room, of incorporating the richness outside, but one cannot. Extending the arms and legs as much as possible also suggests expansiveness. But since the richness is outside one's reach it is very frustrating and poverty-stricken. This exposes the *ratna* tendency to compensate for feelings of poverty and insubstantiality by expanding its territory to feed itself. In the positive case, one feels rich; the external world doesn't especially need to feed you.

Padma posture is lying on the side, one arm extended out fully and the other resting on the hip. The room is square with large windows on two walls. The room suggests something seductive outside it, and the posture suggests keeping your door open to seduce passers-by to come and visit. But nothing passes by, nothing entertaining happens, there is no new presence to feel, your seductive gestures are futile. The positive potential is that one discovers an already existent presence to which nothing needs to be added.

The *karma* position is lying flat on the back, hands close to the sides, the back of the hand flat on the ground, legs spread apart. In this posture, unlike the others, attention is directed to the arms and legs. The room has a 4′ × 4′ square window on top and is colored green. Attending to the limbs accentuates the *karma* tendency toward movement, and the window high above invites thrusting movement toward it. Thus, the karmic tendency to speedy movement is exaggerated. Furthermore, being forced to lie on the ground, motionless, frustrates the impulse to activity and heightens the *karma* fear of vulnerability. The space seems to be cutting through you. The positive potential in this posture is that one gives up the struggling to defend oneself by jumping about and realizes that space is not attacking one and one need not attack space.

Buddha posture is resting on one's knees and elbows, chin between the palms of the hands. The room is small, with no windows, a low ceiling and dim light, and is colored white. The posture suggests contraction, drawing inward, protecting by closing up. The room reflects the ignoring of environment, the creating of a closed, secure space to cope with an acute sense of claustrophobia. Positively, one discovers the possibility of being open even in such a potentially claustrophobic situation.

Dealing with the fundamentals of the mind needs to be supplemented with daily-life practice in which the historically unique blocks and deceptions of a person are worked through—his relation to work, parents, sex, identity, hopes and fears, etc. The key to an effective daily-life practice is the development of an environment of sanity. The basic premise is that if the staff can act sanely in relation to each other and patients, then the social milieu will be therapeutic. An environment of sanity breaks the reciprocal buildup of neurosis. The high percentage of staff in the community facilitates this process.

To realize a sane community, the staff must practice a very demanding discipline. In addition to participating in sitting meditation and space therapy, the staff must discipline themselves to work with their own neurosis as it arises in daily life. The staff discipline is not to get caught in the neurotic games that the patient is trying to play with them. This requires, on the part of the therapist, an acute sense of his own vulnerability to seduction or irritation. Much of the energy of staff, therefore, is directed to working with each other's neuroses. The usual ego props of therapists are stripped away. The staff are sensitive to any tendency to secure territory. On a social level, jobs are rotated and decisions are made democratically. More subtly, the tendencies toward status building and rationalization are guarded against.

Patients are included as part of the community, sharing work and decision making with the staff. The tone of the community is not that sick people are being helped by sane people, but rather that people with different kinds and degrees of neurosis and sanity are sharing their lives together. Maitri staff see elements of sanity in the patient's actions as well as elements of insanity in their own actions. Moreover, they are willing to open themselves to the patient's neurosis. They find that they take on the patients' neuroses collectively to some extent and cure themselves of it—thereby helping the patient. The Maitri staff consider themselves neurotic people working on their own neurosis by helping others. The idea that helping others is a vehicle for one's own development is deeply rooted in the Buddhist teaching of compassion. Traditionally the Buddhist practitioner takes a vow, the *bodhisattva* vow, that he will abandon preoccupation with his own development in order to help all sentient beings achieve sanity. He does not protect himself from being contaminated by his patient's neurosis nor try to build up a self-image of being superior.

Since patients develop complex, elaborate strategies to cope with what they perceive as a claustrophobic world, the life at Maitri is simplified to cut through the complexity. Manual work and simple social interaction centering around obviously necessary tasks reduce the potential for complicated thought games. Let's do this now! There is a general suspiciousness of too much analyzing and strategizing since analyzing problems or emoting about them usually feeds the fantasy worlds out of which the problems arise. The patients just do the postures and live in the community. The philosophy behind it is rarely discussed. Similarly, among staff there is a danger of using the Buddha families as simply an intellectual typology. This one-sided approach is strongly discouraged. The meditation practice of the staff and the space therapy participated in by staff and patients tunes one into *feeling* and *seeing* one's own and others' world-creating patterns. The ideal is an integration of intellect and intuition, a balancing between spontaneity and deliberate action, abstract ideas and gut feelings.

The staff further works through the patient's fantasy world by not feeding it. In this case the staff gives a patient space to explore his hopes, fears, and reactions without immediate censure. Neuroses are not repressed nor indulged—they are openly recognized but not necessarily acted out. The proper attitude toward them is to see and feel the emotion or fantasy arising and cut through its neurotic aspect. To just act it out and expect cathartic release is not enough, one must see the root of the neuroses, the heavy hand of ego. Whether the therapist exaggerates, mirrors, confronts, allows, or smooths over neurosis depends upon what he feels is appropriate in a situation. Such actions are spontaneous responses to the ongoing life situation rather than prearranged therapeutic strategies. Aside from the rooms and postures, no techniques are used. The danger of using too many gimmicks is that they become a substitute for living, an entertaining and often dramatic highlight in one's day. Following this emphasis on ordinary life, patients are encouraged to visit family and friends, to leave Maitri and live ordinary lives and then return at a later time. Staff are rotated frequently to keep them from developing an ingrown, therapeutic mentality.

Whether the therapist exposes the patient's games directly, or mirrors them by nonparticipation, or encourages in a sane direction, the key to his effectiveness is his willingness to work with his own vulnerability. Since, according to the Buddhist view, neurosis is multidimensional, that is, there are more and more subtle layers of neurosis, or conversely various degrees of relative sanity, any attempt to solidify or secure ego at some level of relative sanity is considered neurotic. So the therapist can never rest on his achievement of sanity. He assumes that he will be acting somewhat neurotically to his patients but goes ahead anyway. He works along with his patient, each on his own neurosis.

17

The Clinical Use of "Mindfulness" Meditation Techniques in Short-term Psychotherapy

Gary Deatherage

In recent years, modern Western psychotherapists have begun to discover the rich diversity of potential psychotherapeutic techniques, most originating many centuries ago, which are available to us in the Eastern "psychological literature." The purpose of the present report is to briefly discuss one such set of techniques and to demonstrate its use with short-term (two to twelve weeks) psychiatric patients in a clinical setting.

"MINDFULNESS" (SATIPATTHANA) MEDITATION

Specifically, the techniques to be described here are adopted from the Buddhist *satipatthana*, or "mindfulness meditation," described elsewhere by Soma,[1] Sayadaw,[2] and Thera.[3] Buddhism, far from being a "religion" concerned with higher beings external to the individual human, is more accurately an exquisitely introspective but highly systematic psychology and philosophy which obtains its data from the very bases of human experience, namely sensations, perceptions, emotions, thoughts, and consciousness itself, all of which taken together are frequently termed "mind." Buddhist psychology (*abhidharma*) makes each individual a scientist, carefully observing his own mental processes in order to be freed of the melodramas generated by those very processes. Particularly painful are the melodramas of the ego-oriented realities so prevalent in the population of persons seeking help from professional psychotherapists.

Thera renders the Pali term *satipatthana* as "mindfulness," stating that *sati* has the general meaning of "attention" or "awareness," and *patthana* as "keeping present." The *Satipatthana Sutra* is one of the oldest and most original teachings of the Southern or Theravada Buddhists, and outlines specific meditation techniques for cultivating mindfulness, or present awareness. This chapter is an attempt to acquaint the reader with the very striking effectiveness of the *satipatthana* techniques when used as primary or secondary psychotherapeutic techniques with a variety of psychiatric patients.

The mindfulness technique is a very "client-centered" approach to psychotherapy for at its heart is the assumption that only the individual has the ability to help himself. While the psychotherapist or other helping person can point the way for the client, only the client can carry out the psychotherapeutic process. Therefore, this technique is virtually a self-treatment regimen, and is thus highly efficient in terms of the therapist's time. As will be explained later, it is a technique which is compatible with either individual or group therapy and nicely complements most existing Western psychotherapies. It can serve as the primary mode of treatment with clients for whom it seems appropriate, or it can serve well as a supplementary form of treatment.

The doctrine of mindfulness is not in any way mysterious or mystical. It simply states three objectives: to come to know one's own mental processes, to thus begin to have the power to shape or control the mental processes, and finally to gain freedom from the condition where the mental processes are unknown and uncontrolled, with the individual at the mercy of his own unbridled mind. The goal, then, is to come to know and understand one's own mental processes.

Mindfulness is developed from what Thera chooses to call "bare attention," an accurate, nondiscursive registering of the events taking place without any reaction to those events through mental evaluation (good–bad), mental comment or naming (book, chair, dog), speech, or behavioral act. In fact, bare attention is the careful, deliberate observation of all mental and physical activity, the purpose of which is coming to know one's own mental processes as thoroughly as possible. The objects of observation in mindfulness training can be of four types: (1) body processes (natural events such as breathing, walking, pain, and discomfort), (2) emotions or feelings, (3) thoughts themselves (the present condition of consciousness), (4) mental contents (objects of consciousness).

Thera compares the mind's everyday activities to a dark and unkept room cluttered with refuse. Lack of vigilance and awareness of mental activities accumulates over a long period of time into a condition where a large proportion of mental activities take place in a kind of twilight state, a semi-conscious background from which unwholesome neurotic behavior easily arises. Just as dust settles ever so gradually in a room, resulting in heaps of dust over the years, ignorance and reduced awareness settle in the mind. This mental refuse reduces one's living space just as effectively as would the collection of refuse in a room of one's house. The *satipatthana* approach begins with inspecting, cataloguing, and coming to know intimately one's own mental refuse through the light of "bare attention."

PSYCHOTHERAPEUTIC APPLICATION

Mindfulness training with psychiatric patients has proven most effective by beginning with an obvious body process as the object of observation. Since many Westerners are overly self-assured that we know all there is to know about our minds, the first goal of mindfulness training is to begin to show the client the workings of his own mental processes. This is best done by instructing the client to sit quietly and comfortably in an upright chair for a period of several minutes and resolve to observe his own breathing without interruption. The patient simply "watches" as he breathes in and as he breathes out, and he also watches the gap before the next in-breath. As he attempts to concentrate on his own inhaling and exhaling, activities of mind become very apparent, for thought follows thought, and each thought constitutes a noticeable interruption in breath observation. This exercise, if carried out faithfully for several minutes, will serve to begin to make a patient aware of his own mental preoccupations, for some patients notice a predominance of thoughts about past events (memories) interrupting their breath observation, while others notice that they are most frequently interrupted in breath observation by thoughts pertaining to the future (fantasies, planning, or worrying). Each person who tries this beginning exercise will also find a diversity of momentary interruptions which stem from the "present." Noises, temperature changes, pains, and discomforts related to body postures all constitute interruptions in breath observation. If the patient is taught over time to note interruptions in breath observation and to label each interruption with neutral terms such as "remembering," "fantasizing," "hearing," thinking," or "touching," he will quickly discover a rather complicated, but comforting, situation where there is one aspect of his mental "self" which is calm and psychologically strong, and which can watch, label, and see the melodramas of the other "selves" which get so involved in painful memories of the past or beautiful and escapist fantasies of the future. Once the patient identifies for a time with the strong and neutral "watcher self" there begins to develop within him the strength, motivation, and ability to fully participate in, and benefit from, whatever other forms of psychotherapy are being provided to him.

Buddhist psychology, of course, takes the point of view that there is no real, permanent, or final "self" to discover or depend upon. All selves (collectively called the ego) are just a product of continuous brain processes. Thus, the "watcher self" mentioned above is only a tool to be used within the context of the present discussion, for it, too, is not permanent or real in any way. The actual purpose of establishing the "watcher self" is to ground the patient firmly in the present where there is a much higher probability of making significant progress in the psychotherapeutic process.

With continued work the "watcher self" becomes more mindful, first noting and labeling thought interruptions in the breath observation practice, then coming to see what causes thoughts to begin and pass away, and what causes the next thought in an endless thought chain. Later the observation process gives insights into emotions, which can also be labeled with terms such as "anger," "joy," and "fear." Emotions, like thoughts, when labeled and observed objectively, lose much of their power to cause discomfort and confusion, and are therefore good objects for contemplation. Still later the breath observation technique can reveal to the patient much about the causes of his own behavior, for one begins to notice that intentions precede any act of speech or behavior. By becoming aware of the intention process, one can then intercept and cancel unwanted words or deeds before they are manifested in behavior— something many patients find useful since it places control of their own behavior back at the conscious level. There are many other levels of insight available to those who work to develop mindfulness, but the present discussion will be limited to the few previously mentioned. Perhaps a few case studies of patients who have successfully used this mindfulness technique will illustrate its practical applications.

Case #1: Thought Contemplation. A 23-year-old newly divorced female patient complained that her thoughts about previous bizarre sexual demands made by her former husband were triggering bouts of depression and severe anxiety attacks. She was trained to carefully observe these thoughts of the past using *satipatthana* techniques, and to begin to label those bothersome thoughts as "remembering, remembering." Within a period of a few days she reported that while there was no significant decrease in the frequency of such thoughts about the past, there was a change in the way those thoughts affected her. The labeling process helped to break the causative relationship between the thoughts of the past and the depression and anxiety attacks, thus allowing the gradual disappearance of the anxiety and depression. What remained at that point were regret about the past, and considerable guilt, and these were worked on in a traditional group psychotherapy setting during the following weeks.

Case #2: Emotion Contemplation. During a group therapy session one member of the group, a 22-year-old married female who suffered from what had been diagnosed as an "endogenous depression," expressed despair at her inability to "feel anything anymore," relating a total lack of emotions of any sort. The only feeling which she could identify was one of gloom and depression. She was asked to begin to get in touch with her feelings, becoming more aware of, and carefully and accurately labeling any emotion which she experienced as she sat quietly watching her breathing or even during her normal daily activities. Over the next few weeks she increasingly found herself naming anger as her predominant emotion, and it became possible to identify the source of that anger in her marital relationship. She then began to become aware that she had been misinterpreting her emotions over a period of months, mistakenly believing that it was simply depression that she had been experiencing when there had been strong elements of anger, hostility, disappointment, and self-abasement as well. The realization that the feelings which she had been inaccurately labeling as depression freed her to begin to identify other feelings as well, and she was soon back in touch with the full spectrum of human emotions. Her depression disappeared, replaced by a renewed self-image and a greatly improved understanding of her feelings.

These examples demonstrate the use of selected mindfulness techniques applied to patients for whom the techniques were appropriate. Seldom is it appropriate or necessary to use the full range of mindfulness techniques with any individual patient. The following cases demonstrate the use of a somewhat wider range of techniques.

Case #3: Thought Contemplation, Concentration Training, "Watcher" Contemplation. A 27-year-old divorced female had been hospitalized for 2½ months for a condition which had been variously diagnosed as "manic-depressive psychosis," "depressive psychosis," and "schizophrenia." A period of several weeks of intensive group psychotherapy failed to produce relief of this young woman's symptoms, and she was soon readmitted to the hospital suffering from severe depression and thoughts of self-destruction. Her primary concerns were loss of concentration and racing thoughts, in addition to feelings of depression. The mindfulness technique used in this case was presented to the patient as a concentration exercise where she was asked to sit quietly and look at the second hand of an electric clock, trying very hard to attend fully to its movement. She was instructed to notice carefully when her concentration on the moving second hand was lost, then to identify what constituted the interruption, and to name that interrupting factor. She very quickly found that her concentration was constantly being broken by thoughts. Upon inspection, the nature of the thoughts which raced through her mind was always the same, being concerned with her past, her misfortunes with her ex-husband, and her regrets about that situation. She was instructed simply to label such thoughts as "remembering, remembering." The labeling process seemed to cause this young woman to withdraw some of her involvement in those depressing thoughts of the past and to give her the realization that there was more than just those thoughts present in her mind, for there was a "she" who could watch and name thoughts, too. She learned to identify herself as the objective watcher of her disturbing thoughts instead of the depressed thinker, and she began to feel relief from her psychiatric complaints. Upon reflection, this patient reported that as a result of this psychotherapeutic endeavor she came to see more clearly the nature of her former illness. What she subjectively perceived that had happened to her was that she had become totally immersed in thoughts and regrets about the past, thus becoming less involved in what was happening around her in the present. She subsequently had no involvement in her future as well. Her thoughts of the past caused discomfort and depression, even anxiety, so she used large amounts of energy to defend against and to try to make those thoughts go away. She felt that all of her energies during her illness had been consumed in thinking about the past and simultaneously fighting to stop such thoughts, leaving her no energy with which to run her own life. The mindfulness technique of labeling was effective with this woman because it allowed her to see that thoughts cannot be forcibly stopped or prevented, and it allowed her to stop expending the energy in fighting against remembering.

After only a few days of employing the "concentration exercise, this young woman reported a significant increase in the period of time she was able to concentrate. The increased concentration, which was accompanied by decreases in frequency and intensity of disturbing thoughts, allowed the woman to begin reading again, to carry on meaningful personal interchanges without the usual loss of what was happening, and to devote more time and energy to her personal appearance, which had been untidy during the period of her illness.

With the additional benefits deriving from the somewhat disguised *satipatthana* techniques being employed with this woman, it was decided to have her investigate the nature of the "watcher self" whom she had come to identify. This allowed her to get in contact with the calm and peaceful aspects of her own mind, her "center" as she identified it at the time, and served to reestablish some enjoyment and pleasure in her life—dimensions which had been missing for many months. This, too, contributed to further improvements in her interpersonal relationships. Within a few weeks of these observations, this woman was able to make the decision to terminate her therapy, after which she moved to another city where she had decided to try to begin a new life.

LIMITATIONS

Each of the cases cited above has primarily emphasized certain aspects of thought and emotion observation, followed by naming where those thoughts and emotions originate—in past, present, or future—thereby allowing the person direct and immediate insight into the workings of his own mental processes. As that insight builds, psychological discomfort stemming directly from previous lack of awareness about one's own mental processes (mind) is naturally alleviated. While this psychotherapeutic approach is extremely effective when employed with patients suffering from depression, anxiety, and a wide variety of neurotic symptoms, a caution should be issued regarding its use with patients experiencing actively psychotic symptoms such as hallucinations, delusions, thinking disorders, and severe withdrawal. To effectively carry out the *satipatthana* techniques for self-observation requires an intact and functional rational component of mind, as well as sufficient motivation on the part of the patient to cause him to put forth the effort required to do that observation. The absence of either of those factors in any given patient automatically eliminates the potential usefulness of the *satipatthana* techniques. In the experience of this author, it is necessary to postpone employing *satipatthana* techniques until the patient is able to use them effectively if maximal results are to be obtained.

A second caution is also in order concerning the employment of *satipatthana* techniques in psychotherapy with patients. The sincere psychotherapist who wishes to apply such techniques with his own patients will find that it is necessary to explore the techniques with himself first, thus coming to know experientially the meanings of the terms used, the steps through which one progresses as the techniques are applied, and the nature of the insights available using this approach. He will then be better prepared to facilitate the experience of patients using this approach.

It is hoped that this study which is much too brief to serve as a detailed guide for employing *satipatthana* techniques with patients, will instead serve as an example of a psychotherapeutic technique successfully adopted from Eastern (Buddhist) psychology, and will encourage other practicing psychotherapists to incorporate other appropriate techniques from sources other than traditional Western psychological theory.

NOTES

1. Soma (1949).
2. Sayadaw (1970).
3. Thera (1973).

18
Wu Wei, No-mind, and the Fertile Void in Psychotherapy

Wilson Van Dusen

From the first not a thing is.

Hui-neng

Though clay may be molded into a vase, the utility of the vase lies in what is not there.

Lao-tzu

At the very center of psychotherapeutic experiences there is an awesome hole. With Western modes of thought the hole tends to be seen as a deficiency which the therapist plugs by an interpretation of what it means. My point it quite simple. The hole is the very center and heart of therapeutic change. To my knowledge the only place its dynamics are adequately described is in ancient Oriental writings. From them one can learn to make practical use of this fertile void around which psychotherapy turns.

The void is not unknown in the psychoanalysis of the Western world. Freud discovered it in orality, regression, the going back to an infantile state. At a deeper level he once characterized it as Thanatos, the death instinct. Otto Rank put it in the womb. Pathology began by the trauma of leaving the womb. In Jung the void is not as clear, but in general it is found in the archetypes of mother, earth, and origin of things.

What will be treated here as the void is seen by Western

psychoanalysis as a going back, returning to the origin, as a destruction and loss of ego development. The going back can be totally destructive as in chronic schizophrenia, or it can be productive as in the so-called therapeutic regression in the service of the ego. The void is seen primarily biologically as a mouth or a womb.

Using the phenomenological method I discovered a world of tiny holes most of which were smaller than the orality of the Freudians. In the phenomenological approach one simply attempts to discover the world of the patient as it is for him without reducing it to any pseudoscientific categories (obsessional, anal, etc.). In a careful examination of the worlds of others I ran across many blank spaces. For a moment the patient couldn't concentrate, couldn't hear me, couldn't remember what he intended to say, or he felt nothing. At first it appeared these holes or great blank spaces were characteristic of schizophrenics only. But closer examination showed that these holes appear in all persons to a greater or lesser extent. More and more it came to appear that these blank holes lay at the center of psychopathology. The blank holes came to be the key both to pathology and to psychotherapeutic change. Though my knowledge of Taoism and Zen Buddhism is poor (grandmotherly, a Zen monk might say), it was these two that helped me understand the way in and out of the holes and their meaning.

First, what are the holes?—blankness, loss of memory, failure of concentration, or loss of meaning. They can be of very brief duration so that the person is hardly aware of a lack of continuity to his thoughts or feelings. Or they can last for years as in the chronic schizophrenic for whom decades can slip by without being noticed. A common mild example is to be unexpectedly caught by the gaze of another person and for a brief moment lose the sense of direction. Or, when in a group, one may lose the thread of conversation and several moments later realize one's fantasies have wandered from the group. In the hole one feels one has momentarily lost one's self. What one intended is forgotten. What would have been said is unremembered. One feels caught, drifting, out of control, and weak.

These holes and blank spaces are important in every psychopathology. In the obsessive-compulsive they represent the loss of order and control. In the depressive they are the black hole of time standing still. In the character disorders they represent an unbearable ambivalence. In schizophrenia they are the encroachment of meaninglessness or terror. In every case they represent the unknown, the unnamed threat, the source of anxiety, and the fear of disintegration. They are nothingness, nonbeing, death.

It is extremely important to know what people do when faced with encroaching blankness. Many talk to fill up space. Many must act to fill the empty space with themselves. In all cases it must be filled up or sealed off. I have yet to see a case of psychopathology where the blankness was comfortably tolerated. Even in very chronic and apathetic schizophrenics there is a filling up of the space. One examined a door hinge for an hour because not to fill his world with something was to die. This void is familiar to the Taoist or Zen Buddhist. The pathology appears to be in the reaction to the void. Normal and often very creative individuals can allow themselves to become blank and think of nothing with an expectation that they will come out of it with an idea for a painting or other work of art. Many have deliberately used the void to find creative solutions to problems. The neurotic and psychotic struggle against it.

In large part the culture of the Western world fosters this struggle. In the West the world is filled with objects. Empty space is wasted unless it is room to be filled with action. This contrasts markedly with Oriental painting, for instance, in which empty space is the creative center and lends weight to the rest of the painting. Subtly the culture of the West teaches one to fear and avoid blankness and emptiness and to fill space as much as possible with our action, with objects. Or we let the action of objects (cars, TV) fill our space. In the Orient emptiness may have a supreme value in and of itself. It can be trusted. It can be productive. The *Tao Te Ching* suggests that while thirty spokes make up a wheel, only in the emptiness of its hub is its usefulness. Walls and doors make up a house, but only in the emptiness between them is its livability.

Following the lead of the Orient I explored the empty spaces. If the patient obsessively plotted every move and worried everything into existence, he was encouraged to drift. If he anxiously filled space with words, we looked for a while at wordlessness. The person who feared going down in depression permitted himself to go down and explore the going down. The findings are always the same. *The feared empty space is a fertile void. Exploring it is a turning point toward therapeutic change.* A case will illustrate some of these points.

The patient is a thirty-year-old schizophrenic who has been

hospitalized nine years. He enters stiffly like a wooden puppet, sits awkwardly, and avoids my gaze. His eyes fix on my bookcase and he stares emptily. After several minutes I comment that he is at the bookcase and I ask him what it is like. In no way do I attempt to move him from the spot he has drifted to.

Slowly he says he is looking at the top books. They are decoration. That is, they have no meaning. This he says with no affect, punctuated by a sudden touching of the top of his head and repetitive movements with his fingers. I try not to disturb his state. A slow exploration indicates that really the whole world is like the meaningless book-decoration he sees before him.

He accepts this as a black, holelike world. In this black hole he can't think or remember, and this threatens him. I'm a strange doctor not to fill up the space with questions to occupy him. In the nothingness he is nothing. When he touches the top of his head or his nose, he exists for a moment, he feels himself there. Because I don't fill the void with questions, he tries to remember what other doctors asked so he can ask himself these questions, answer them, and thereby fill the void. A question should fill this empty space and move time on a bit. But he is dully threatened because he can't remember what he was trying to think of, even though he repeated it over and over. It too went out of existence. Again the dull concern: "I must concentrate, hold my mind from drifting, and find questions to fill my space."

I ask him if he will let himself drift. Because my request fills the void, he complies. We are silent. In a moment some feeling breaks forth. He reddens and laughs. He can't quite tell me what happened. Usually, in the past, these were feelings critical of me. I speak of drifting in the hole. When he drifts he seems to stumble on something new. Today he drifted and ran upon the fact that there was something in his left side. Explored further it turned out to be a flat black, oval mass. In subsequent sessions it changed and became a feeling of life in him. As the hour ended I asked whether he wanted to climb out of the hole. He said (with a trace more of affect) he would stay in it and see what else of interest might happen. I was pleased because he had discovered that of itself the void filled with new things. He didn't have to work so hard to fill it up.

The schizophrenic gives the purest example of the black void in human experience. Other disorders give examples of briefer and less empty voids. What I learned in these is quite simple. When we are threatened by the void and attempt to crawl out or fill it up by keeping our minds centered, the void grows and encroaches upon our will. When one allows oneself to drift, one stumbles upon surprising new things in the void.

The complete dynamism is relatively simple. Let me use an analogy with night and day. The two alternate naturally and spontaneously. We do not make the night or the day. If we try to stay awake indefinitely and thereby deny the night, we are dragged into fatigue and eventually sleep. (The schizophrenic by his constant plugging of holes is dragged into timelessness.) On the other hand, we cannot sleep indefinitely. We will be thrust into wakefulness. (The alcoholic who tries to drink away his responsibilities is dragged into the wakefulness of a hangover.) The day wears on to night when all things rest. Out of the timeless black night a new day emerges. This is the cycle of the Chinese yin and yang. In psychotherapy, all action is the day and all of the holes are the fertile void of night. The fertile void of night comes into psychotherapy so that we might dissolve a little and come out a little changed into a new day. I no longer fear the fertile void for either my patient or myself. The way to day is through the night. The night or the void is the no-mind of Zen. It is not nothing nor is it something. It is a fertile emptiness.

In Taoism and Zen there is a healthy understanding and respect for this night aspect of life. It is used in painting, in the tea ceremonies, in wrestling, in the building of houses; and in flower arrangement it is the space around a graceful branch. It is known and respected in its permeation of Oriental life.

The patient comes to one because he fears the void. If he didn't fear it, he would be a productive person and not need help. If the therapist also fears the void, he will be unable to help the patient. For each patient the void has different meanings. For the compulsive it may be disorder, for some it is age and death, for the young woman it may be the loss of self in sexual climax, for the early schizophrenic it is the force destroying the ego. The meaning of the void and how it appears in the transference relationship must be discovered anew in each case. A common way to try to fill the void is to find *the answers* as to what is wrong. Not only is there the major void in the presenting symptoms but the many little ones that appear in the immediate relationship with the patient. The way out is through the voids. The fears that keep one from entering them can be explored. As these are studied the void becomes less fearsome. Finally the voids can be entered. In each case one comes out a little changed, as in the case of the schizophrenic above who came out with more affect than he had known in a long time. Often the therapist cannot predict the direction of change. It is spontaneous and natural. It is change from within the patient and not a change in any way planted by the therapist. When fully recovered the patient not only no longer fears the void but knows and can use its productivity.

"From the first not a thing is." If a thing still is (i.e., there is action or talk or the patient is toying with *the* answer), one has not yet reached the first, which is the beginning. For literally at the first not a thing is. At this turning point one has no words, no actions, no answers. One may well not even remember. Even the problems besetting one may be unclear. The uncertainty can be painful. "Somewhere in all this there should be a solution if I could only think clearly enough to find it," is the feeling. It is a void, but it is certainly not empty. It is chaotic with possibilities. One feels helpless and waits. It is central that one's own will can no longer find the way out.

My apologies to the ancient teachers for a poor oversimplification of their work. But it must be done. Somewhere it is necessary to show not only that these teachings have practical value in psychotherapy, but that their relevance is ever present.

Conclusion

We are dealing with a new image of man. This is most important because from that everything else flows. All of man's work, all of man's institutions, which includes science...can be modified. The image of man is growing. There are more possibilities.

Abraham Maslow

At times increase of knowledge is organized about old conceptions, while these are expanded, elaborated, and refined, but not seriously revised, much less abandoned. At other times, the increase of knowledge demands qualitative rather than quantitative change; alteration, not addition. Men's minds grow cold to their former intellectual concerns; ideas that were burning fade; interests that were urgent seem remote.... Former problems may not have been solved, but they no longer press for solution. Men face in another direction.

John Dewey

It is necessary to think in a new way about science.... Modern man is searching for a new world view.... Even among scientists there are signs of a metaphysical rebellion.

Jacob Needleman

If our science of mental health is to become more effective, psychotherapists will have to balance their knowledge of psychological concepts with a contemplative awareness.

Medard Boss

In this brief concluding chapter I would like to suggest some implications that the Eastern traditions may have for modern Western psychology. Many of the chapters of this book point toward a new direction in psychology which is in the process of being born. It is an attempt to develop an integrative psychology that brings together insights and methods of both East and West in order to look more deeply into the nature of human experience and existence.

Modern psychology is like a patchwork quilt, made up of numerous different strands and influences. The major directions thus far have been experimental laboratory research and the development of theoretical systems to explain the origin and development of human personality and psychopathology. More recently, existential/ humanistic psychology emphasized another important strand—self-knowledge—the desire to know and understand one's experience more fully as it is lived and felt. However, as two of its founders, Abraham Maslow and Anthony Sutich, eventually concluded, the humanistic approach did not seem to dig deeply enough into the underlying nature of human existence. In Sutich's words:

> I felt that something was lacking in the orientation...and that it did not...give sufficient attention to the place of man in the universe or cosmos. A special problem was my growing realization that the concept of self-actualization was no longer comprehensive enough.... My long-standing interest in the psychological aspects of mystical experience continued to provoke disturbing questions about basic humanistic theory.[1]

Maslow and Sutich accordingly founded a new approach to study the wider relatedness between the human mind and universal life principles, which they called "transpersonal psychology." Since its inception, transpersonal psychology has been largely influenced by the Eastern traditions, which are concerned with a deeper kind of self-knowledge than has been pursued in Western psychology thus far.

Interest in the wider dimensions of human awareness is one of the new horizons in psychology today. Because transpersonal concerns are at the forward "cutting edge" of current knowledge, their aims and methods have not yet been fully clarified. I would like to close by suggesting four major features or directions that a new psychology might take. (Unfortunately, space permits me only to mention them briefly here without going into detail. However, they will be explored more fully in a later book.)

1. This new approach needs to be a *self-knowledge psychology*, based on an inner empiricism, an investigation of experience and its deeper nature. Such an approach would evolve as a *human science*,[2] rather than as a strictly natural science, with its own unique methods and areas of investigation. Its findings might be tested and verified by any individual who undertook to examine his or her own experience in an attentive, detailed, and disciplined way.

2. It would be a *psychology of relatedness*, rather than a psychology of separate individuals, thus laying a basis for social concerns in the "ecology of mind,"[3] which understands mind, not as

something inside the individual's head, but as the whole system of individual-plus-environment.

3. Its basic concern with the deep nature of human existence should also provide a framework for accommodating the *whole range* of human experience, from conditioned responses to unconditioned open awareness. To study meditative experience, say, apart from the whole context of ego functioning may be as distorting as it is to study ego apart from wider states of awareness.

4. It needs to be based on self-knowledge *disciplines* (such as the practice of meditation). Every body of knowledge is based on a certain discipline, an orderly and precise approach to observing, practicing, and learning. A self-knowledge discipline is one in which attention is trained to actively examine the nature of one's experience, to penetrate self-deception, and to develop some kind of contemplative awareness of the deep nature of existence. The development of this attention is analogous to the training one would have to undergo to perform scientific experiments. Such disciplines might provide an empirical basis that would distinguish this approach from the early schools of introspectionism, which relied on a more passive, almost random observation of the stream of consciousness, without ever calling into question the watcher or observer of experience.

In short, such a new approach in psychology, based on self-knowledge disciplines, would include the whole range of human consciousness in the study of human behavior: from the automatic responses that behaviorism has studied, to the unconscious patterns that psychoanalysis brought to light, to the farther reaches of human possibility that Maslow called self-transcendence. Such an encompassing approach might provide a meaningful context and framework for interpreting and guiding research in experimental and clinical psychology. It might also provide a secular framework in which people might begin to glimpse the possibility for a meaningful life beyond the confines of the isolated ego, and to realize a more ecological relationship with the world around them. This approach would not be a substitute for traditional spiritual paths, but might serve as a bridge to them, as well as a neutral meeting ground where practitioners of different self-knowledge disciplines could come together and work out common understandings of human development as a conscious process.

If the Eastern teachings seem to speak so directly to Western culture at this time, perhaps it is because their grounding in paths of personal discipline and realization continues to provide simple yet powerful practices which train the individual to see directly into the workings of his or her own mind in a new way. The radical shift in consciousness which seems to be required for a renewal of our culture cannot but be helped along by a more widespread involvement by psychologists and laypeople in self-knowledge disciplines. The great spiritual traditions of both East and West all agree that one becomes a fully open human being by realizing one's grounding in the universal principles of life. This transpersonal context, which one can realize directly, is finally what may provide complete self-knowledge, give strength and depth to one's life, and allow human beings to live in greater harmony with one another and with the natural environment. Insofar as modern psychology has a stake in such tasks, it needs to accommodate this larger kind of vision.

NOTES

1. Sutich (1976), p. 7.
2. Cf. Giorgi (1970).
3. Cf. Bateson (1972).

Notes on Contributors

MEDARD BOSS is Professor of Psychotherapy at the Faculty of Medicine at Zurich University. He is one of the leading figures in existential psychotherapy in Europe, having pioneered an approach based on the work of philosopher Martin Heidegger, called *Daseinsanalysis.* He is the author of many books, including *Psychoanalysis and Daseinsanalysis* and *A Psychiatrist Discovers India.*

MARVIN CASPER has served as Executive Director of Maitri, a Buddhist therapeutic community in Connecticut, and Director of Naropa Institute's psychology program in Boulder, Colorado. He is the author of several articles on Buddhist psychology and co-editor of *Cutting Through Spiritual Materialism* and *Myth of Freedom.* He is currently working on a book on Tibetan Buddhism in America, entitled *The Tantric Warrior.*

GARY DEATHERAGE has served as Assistant Professor of Psychology at the University of Lethbridge, Alberta, and clinical psychologist in the Department of Psychiatry at Lethbridge Municipal Hospital. He is presently a psychotherapist in private practice.

ARTHUR DEIKMAN is a psychiatrist in private practice and a clinical supervisor at the Langley Porter Neuropsychiatric Institute in San Francisco. He is the author of numerous articles on the psychology of meditation and consciousness, as well as the book *Personal Freedom.*

THOMAS HORA is an existential psychiatrist and the author of numerous articles on psychotherapy. He supervises the Postgraduate Institute of Psychotherapy in New York, and has won the Karen Horney Award.

CLAUDIO NARANJO is a practicing psychiatrist who was a major figure at Esalen Institute and later founded SAT, a nationwide group for personal growth. His works include *The One Quest, The Healing Journey, On the Psychology of Meditation* (co-author), and various papers on Gestalt therapy. He is on the faculty of the Nyingma Institute in Berkeley and the California Institute for Transpersonal Psychology.

ROBERT ORNSTEIN is a research psychologist at Langley Porter Neuropsychiatric Institute in San Francisco, and President of the Institute for the Study of Human Knowledge. He is author of *The Psychology of Consciousness, The Mind Field, On the Psychology of Meditation* (co-author), and editor of *The Nature of Human Consciousness.* He is also Director of the magazine *Human Nature.*

227

MICHAEL STARK is a clinical psychologist and Chairman of the Psychology Department of Indiana University at South Bend. His interests include personality theory, psychotherapy, and abnormal psychology.

TARTHANG TULKU is founder of the Nyingma Institute in Berkeley, and the author of numerous books, including *A Gesture of Balance*, *Kum-Nye Relaxation*, and *Time, Space, and Knowledge: A New Vision of Reality*. He is editor of *Reflections of Mind* and the *Crystal Mirror* series. He is a reincarnate lama and former head of Tarthang Monastery in Tibet. He has also served as Professor of Buddhist Philosophy at Sanskrit University, Benares, India.

CHÖGYAM TRUNGPA is the founder and President of Naropa Institute in Boulder, Colorado, and the author of *Born in Tibet*, *Meditation in Action*, *Cutting Through Spiritual Materialism*, *Myth of Freedom*, and *Glimpses of Abhidharma*. He is a scholar and meditation master trained in the Kagyu and Nyingma sects of Tibetan Buddhism, and he holds the degree of Khenpo, which is equivalent to a Western Ph.D. He has also founded a network of Buddhist meditation centers in the United States, Canada, and Europe.

WILSON VAN DUSEN is a practicing psychotherapist. He has been a clinical psychologist at the Talmadge State Hospital in Mendocino, California, and has taught at the University of California, Davis. He is author of numerous articles on psychotherapy, *The Natural Depth in Man*, and co-editor of *Gestalt Is*.

MICHAEL WASHBURN is Associate Professor of Philosophy at Indiana University at South Bend. His present interests include existentialism, meditation, and the theory of consciousness.

JOHN WELWOOD was trained as a clinical psychologist in the Rogerian and existential traditions. He has taught at the University of Chicago, the University of California, Santa Barbara, and Antioch University/West. He is an editor for the *Journal of Transpersonal Psychology* and *ReVision*, and is editor of an East/West psychology series for Center Publications. He has published articles on the interfaces of Eastern and Western psychology, and is author of a forthcoming book, *Full Circle Mind*.

KEN WILBER is the author of numerous articles on the psychology of consciousness as well as *The Spectrum of Consciousness*. He has also authored two forthcoming books which further develop his spectrum of consciousness framework into the areas of developmental psychology and anthropology. He is editor of *ReVision*.

Bibliography

Bateson, G. *Steps to an ecology of mind.* New York: Ballantine, 1972.

Becker, E. *The denial of death.* New York: Free Press, 1973.

Benoit. H. *The supreme doctrine.* New York: Viking, 1955.

Bertalanffy, L. *Problems of life.* New York: Wiley, 1952.

Binswanger, L. *Being-in-the-world: Selected papers of....* Edited and translated by J. Needleman. New York: Basic Books, 1963.

Bohr, N. *Atomic physics and human knowledge.* New York: Wiley, 1958.

Boss, M. *Psychoanalysis and daseinsanalysis.* New York: Basic Books, 1963.

Boss, M. *A psychiatrist discovers India.* Translated by H. Frey. London: Oswald Wolff, 1965.

Brandt, L. Process or structure? *Psychoanalytic Review*, 1966, *53*, 374–78.

Broad, C. D. *Mind and its place in nature.* London: Routledge & Kegan Paul, 1949.

Brown, G. S. *Laws of form.* New York: Julian Press, 1972.

Brown, N. O. *Life against death: The psychoanalytic meaning of history.* Middletown, Conn.: Wesleyan Univ. Press, 1959.

Bruner, J. On perceptual readiness. *Psychological Review*, 1957, *64*, 123–52.

Capra, F. *The Tao of physics.* Berkeley: Shambhala, 1975.

Chaterjee, A. *Readings on Yogacara Buddhism.* Benares: Hindu Univ. Press, 1971.

Coomaraswamy, A. *Hinduism and Buddhism.* New York: Philosophical Library, 1943.

Cox, H. *Turning East: The promise and peril of the new Orientalism.* New York: Simon and Schuster, 1977.

Deikman, A. Experimental meditation. *Journal of Nervous and Mental Disease*, 1963, *136*, 329–43. Reprinted in C. Tart (Ed .), *Altered states of consciousness.* New York: Doubleday Anchor, 1972.

Deikman, A. Implications of experimentally produced contemplative meditation. *Journal of Nervous and Mental Disease*, 1966, *142*, 101–16.

Deutsch, E. *Advaita Vedanta.* Honolulu: East-West Center Press, 1969.

Dhiravamsa. *The middle path of life.* Surrey, England: Unwin, 1974.

Ehrenzweig, A. *The psychoanalysis of artistic vision and hearing.* New York: George Braziller, 1965.

Eliade, M. *Images and symbols.* New York: Sheed & Ward, 1969.

Erikson, E. *Childhood and society.* New York: Norton, 1950.

Fenichel, O. *The psychoanalytic theory of neurosis.* New York: Norton, 1972.

Freud, S. *The problems of lay-analyses.* Translated by J. Strachey. New York: Brentano's, 1927.

Freud, S. *New introductory lectures on psychoanalysis.* Translated by W.J.H. Sprott. New York: Norton, 1933.

Freud, S. *Collected papers.* Vol. 4. Translated by J. Riviere. New York: Basic Books, 1959.

Freud, S. *The ego and the id.* Translated by J. Strachey. New York: Norton, 1961.

Fromm, E., Suzuki, D. T., & Martino, R. *Zen Buddhism and psychoanalysis.* New York: Grove Press, 1963.

Furst, C. Automatizing of visual perception. *Perception and Psychophysics,* 1971, *10,* 65–69.

Gendlin, E. T. *Experiencing and the creation of meaning.* New York: Free Press, 1962.

Gendlin, E. T. A theory of personality change. In P. Worchel & D. Byrne (Eds.), *Personality change.* New York: Wiley, 1964.

Gendlin, E. T. A phenomenology of emotions: Anger. In D. Carr & E. Casey (Eds.), *Explorations in phenomenology.* The Hague: Martinus Nijhoff, 1973.

Gendlin, E. T. *Focusing.* New York: Everest House, 1978.

Giorgi, A. *Psychology as a human science.* New York: Harper & Row, 1970.

Goldstein, K. *The organism.* New York: American Books, 1939.

Goleman, D. Meditation as meta-therapy. *Journal of Transpersonal Psychology,* 1971, *3,* 1–26.

Govinda, Lama A., *The psychological attitude of early Buddhist philosophy.* New York: Samuel Weiser, 1974.

Greenson, R. R. *The technique and practice of psychoanalysis.* Vol. 1. New York: International Universities Press, 1967.

Guenther, H. The concept of mind in Buddhist Tantrism. *Journal of Oriental Studies,* 1956, *3,* 261–77.

Guenther, H. The philosophical background of Buddhist Tantrism. *Journal of Oriental Studies,* 1959, *5,* 45–64.

Guenther, H. (Translator). The natural freedom of mind. *Crystal Mirror,* 1975, *4,* 113–46.

Guenther, H., & Trungpa, C. *The dawn of Tantra.* Berkeley: Shambhala, 1975.

Hanna, T. Three elements of somatology. *Main Currents,* 1974, *31.*

Hisamatsu, S. Additional note to: On the unconscious, the self, and therapy. *Psychologia,* 1968, *11,* 25–32.

Hora, T. Existential psychiatry and group psychotherapy. *American Journal of Psychoanalysis,* 1961, *21,* 58–73.

Horsch, J. The self in analytical psychology. *Psychologia,* 1961, *4,* 147–55.

Huxley, A. *The perennial philosophy.* New York: Harper & Row, 1944.

l

Huxley, A. *The doors of perception* and *Heaven and Hell*. New York: Harper & Row, 1954.

James, W. *The principles of psychology*. New York: Dover Publications, 1950.

James, W. *The writings of . . .* Edited by J. McDermott. New York: Random House, 1967.

James, W. *Essays in radical empiricism*. Cambridge, Mass.: Harvard Univ. Press, 1976.

Jung, C. G. *Modern man in search of a soul*. Translated by W. S. Dell and C. F. Baynes. New York: Harcourt, Brace and Co., 1933.

Jung, C. G. *Psychology and religion: West and East*. Translated by R. F. C. Hull. *Collected works*. Vol. 11. New York: Pantheon, 1958.

Jung, C. G. *The structure and dynamics of the psyche*. Translated by R. F. C. Hull. *Collected works*. Vol. 8. New York: Pantheon, 1960.

Jung, C. G. *Analytical psychology: Its theory and practice*. New York: Vintage, 1968.

Kirsch, J. Affinities between Zen and analytical psychology. *Psychologia*, 1960, *3*, 85–91.

Kretschmer, W. Meditative techniques in psychotherapy. *Psychologia*, 1962, *5*, 76–83. Reprinted in C. Tart (Ed.), *Altered States of Consciousness*. New York: Doubleday Anchor, 1972.

Laing, R. D. *The politics of experience*. New York: Pantheon, 1967.

Lowen, A. *The betrayal of the body*. New York: Macmillan, 1967.

MacIntyre, A. *The unconscious: A conceptual analysis*. London: Routledge & Kegan Paul, 1958.

Maslow, A. Neurosis as a failure of personal growth. *Humanitas*, 1967, *3*, 153–69.

Maslow, A. Theory Z. *Journal of Transpersonal Psychology*, 1969, *1*, 31–48.

Maslow, A. *The farther reaches of human nature*. New York: Viking, 1971.

Maslow, A., et al. The plateau experience. Edited by S. Krippner. *Journal of Transpersonal Psychology*, 1972, *4*, 107–120.

Matte Blanco, I. *The unconscious as infinite sets*. London: Duckworth, 1975.

Maupin, E. On meditation. In C. Tart (Ed.), *Altered states of consciousness*. New York: Doubleday Anchor, 1972.

May, R. Contributions of existential psychotherapy. In R. May, E. Angel, & H. F. Ellenberger (Eds.), *Existence: A new dimension in psychiatry and psychology*. New York: Basic Books, 1958.

May, R. *Love and will*. New York: Norton, 1969.

Mead, G. H. *George Herbert Mead on social psychology*. Edited by A. Strauss. Chicago: Univ. of Chicago Press, 1964.

Miles, T. *Eliminating the unconscious*. London: Pergamon Press, 1966.

Miller, J. *Unconsciousness*. New York: Wiley, 1942.

Mischel, W. *Personality and assessment*. New York: Wiley, 1968.

Murphy, G. The boundaries between the person and the world. *British Journal of Psychology*, 1956, *47*, 88–94.

Needleman, J. *A sense of the cosmos: The encounter of modern science and ancient truth*. New York: Doubleday, 1975a.

Needleman, J. The used religions. In J. Needleman & D. Lewis (Eds.), *Sacred tradition and present need*. New York: Viking, 1975b.

Neisser, U. *Cognitive psychology*. New York: Appleton-Century-Crofts, 1967.

Northrop, F. S. C. *The meeting of East and West*. New York: Macmillan, 1946.

Northrop, F. S. C. *The logic of the sciences and the humanities*. New York: Meridian Books, 1959.

Ornstein, R. *The psychology of consciousness*. San Francisco: W. H. Freeman, 1972.

Ornstein, R. (ed.). *The nature of human consciousness*. San Francisco: W. H. Freeman, 1973.

Perls, F. *Gestalt therapy verbatim*. Lafayette, Ca.: Real People Press, 1969.

Perls, F., Hefferline, R., & Goodman, P. *Gestalt therapy*. New York: Delta, 1951.

Piaget, J. *The construction of reality in the child*. New York: Basic Books, 1954.

Polanyi, M. *Personal knowledge: Towards a post-critical philosophy*. Chicago: Univ. of Chicago Press, 1958.

Portmann, A. Biology and the phenomenon of the spiritual. In *Spirit and nature*. Vol. 1. *Papers from the Eranos yearbooks*. New York: Pantheon, 1954.

Pribram, K. The neurophysiology of remembering. *Scientific American*, 1969, 73–86.

Putney, S., & Putney, G. *The adjusted American*. New York: Harper & Row, 1966.

Roberts, T. Beyond self-actualization. *ReVision*, 1978, *1*, 42–46.

Rogers, C. R. A theory of therapy, personality, and interpersonal relationships. In S. Koch (Ed.), *Psychology: A study of a science*. Vol. 3. New York: McGraw-Hill, 1959.

Sayadaw, M. *The satipatthana vipassana meditation*. San Francisco: Unity Press, 1971.

Schroedinger, E. *My view of the world*. London: Cambridge Univ. Press, 1964.

Sinnott, E. W. Biology of the spirit. New York: Viking, 1955.

Sokolov, Y. N. *Perception and the conditioned reflex*. New York: Macmillan, 1963.

Soma, Bhikku. *The way of mindfulness*. Colombo, Ceylon: Lake House Bookshop, 1949.

Sperry, R. Neurology and the mind-brain problem. *American Scientist*, 1951, *40*, 291–312.

Spinelli, D., & Pribram, K. Changes in visual recovery functions and unit activity produced by frontal and temporal cortex stimulation. *Electroencephalography and Clinical Neurophysiology*, 1967, *22*, 143–49.

Spitz, R. *A genetic field theory of ego formation*. New York: International Universities Press, 1959.

Suzuki, D. T. *Studies in the Lankavatara Sutra*. London: Routledge & Kegan Paul, 1930.

Suzuki, S. *Zen mind, beginner's mind*. New York: Walker, Weatherhill, 1970.

Szent-Gyoergyi, A. Drive in living matter to perfect itself. *Synthesis*, 1974, *1*, 12–24.

Tarthang Tulku. On thoughts. *Crystal Mirror*, 1974, *3*, 7–20.

Tarthang Tulku. Watching the watcher. *Crystal Mirror*, 1975, *4*, 157–61.

Teilhard de Chardin, P. *The phenomenon of man*. New York: Harper & Row, 1959.

Thera, N. *The heart of Buddhist meditation*. New York: Samuel Weiser, 1973.

Toulmin, S. Neuroscience and human understanding. In Quarton, G. C., Melnechuck, T., & Schmitt, F. O. (Eds.), *The Neurosciences*. New York: Rockefeller Univ. Press, 1967.

Trungpa, C. *Meditation in action*. Berkeley: Shambhala, 1969.

Trungpa, C. *Cutting through spiritual materialism*. Berkeley: Shambhala, 1973.

Trungpa, C. The basic ground and the eight consciousnesses. *Garuda*, 1976, *4*, 57–64.

Trungpa, C., & Hookham, M. (Trans.). Maha Ati. *Vajra*, 1974, *1*, 6–8.

Walker, K. *A study of Gurdjieff's teachings*. London: Jonathan Cape, 1957.

Walsh, R., & Shapiro, D. *Beyond health and normality: An exploration of extreme psychological wellbeing*. New York: Van Nostrand, 1979.

Washburn, M. Observations relevant to a unified theory of meditation. *Journal of Transpersonal Psychology*, 1978, *10*, 45–66.

Welwood, J. A theoretical reinterpretation of the unconscious from a humanistic and phenomenological perspective. Doctoral dissertation, University of Chicago, 1974.

Welwood, J. On psychological space. *Journal of Transpersonal Psychology*, 1977, *9*, 97–118.

Whorf, B. *Language, thought, and reality*. Cambridge, Mass.: M.I.T. Press, 1956.

Wilber, K. *The spectrum of consciousness*. Wheaton, Ill.: Quest, 1977.

Zuckerkandl, V. *Sound and symbol*. Translated by W. R. Trask. New York: Pantheon, 1956.

Index